CU00734402

Marching to a Different Beat

Sarah Ziegel

First Published in Great Britain in 2022

Copyright © 2022 Sarah Ziegel

The author has asserted their right under the Copyright, Designs and Patent Act 1988 to be identified as the author of this work.

All rights reserved. No part of this publication may be reproduced or transmitted in any form or by any means, electronic or mechanical, including photocopy, recording, or any information storage and retrieval system, without permission in writing from the publisher.

A CIP catalogue record for this book is available from the British Library

ISBN: 978-1-7396380-0-9 (print paperback)

ISBN: 978-1-7396380-1-6 (ebook)

Cover Design by Creative Covers
Typesetting by Book Polishers

For Jonathan

whose four living children grace the pages of this book

'Well of course…they are both autistic. It's a bit like vegetable soup. If we all had a bowl of vegetable soup, some of us would have more carrots in it than others,' he said casually.

Vegetable soup? This qualified consultant paediatrician was comparing my boys to a bowl of soup!

We had gone along for a routine hearing assessment. My twin boys, Thomas and Benjamin were both happy, lively boys who had no speech due to glue ear. They were nearly three years old and as unalike from each other as twins could be. Thomas was never far from me, needing my constant support. Benjamin was a much more independent little boy. He didn't seem to need me at all sometimes.

I wasn't worried at all about the tests that day. They were routine to us by now. I usually took them to most appointments on my own but for hearing tests, each boy needed to be tested alone in silence, sitting on my knee. Serendipity meant that today of all days, I had no one else to help me so Jonathan had taken a precious day off work. Benjamin had recently had grommets inserted in an attempt to relieve the pressure of the 'glue' on his eardrum which would hopefully improve his hearing. We were just expecting the usual tests and hopefully some better results.

We were shocked into silence and disbelief hearing the word autism. I couldn't think of a single thing to say and neither could Jonathan.

I called in our health visitor who happened to be just outside. I knew her well and trusted her. The doctor repeated his words of wisdom in front of her, with no empathy or seeming realisation of the effect his words were having on us. He said that there was nothing much that we could do about it and that he would see us again in six months for the next hearing test. And that was that. No formal assessment, no second opinion, no advice. A lifetime's diagnosis of autism delivered to us with no thought and no compassion, during a routine appointment for something entirely different.

Thank goodness Jonathan was there too to hear those words which we knew would change our lives forever. Neither of us said anything to the doctor. We were too stunned by his nonchalant manner. He had stated it as an accepted fact which gave us no invitation to question it. I didn't burst into tears; I just felt numb.

We had gone in with two little boys with hearing problems and had come out with two autistic boys.

We went home in shock. Autism? We thought glue ear was why they couldn't talk. I knew nothing about autism; I had never met a child with autism. What did it mean for our sons? All Jonathan knew was that he had known a young adult with severe autism, literally rocking in a corner. He now had an image of how our boys might become. Was that to be their future?

I don't think we actually believed it that day. We didn't want to believe it. They were happy, they smiled, they didn't 'rock' or hide in a corner. But, they couldn't talk or understand anything we said so it must be true, mustn't it?

Chapter One

Professional male, 34, interested in travel, walking, theatre and the arts hoping to meet like minded female 25 – 34.

That's how it all began, with an advert in the lonely hearts' column of the Guardian newspaper in September 1996.

I had developed a habit of trawling through the ads on Saturday evenings. It was painless; I called and chose which recorded messages to listen to. Mostly, I listened to men who were either trying to sound way too cool or those who were so boring that I cut them off mid sentence. This was quite satisfying in its own way, and all from the comfort of my sofa. But, after a few months of listening to these voices, I had yet to leave a message in return.

I wasn't that bothered by the romantic idea of finding a life partner at this stage. I had recently been 'burnt' by my last relationship, falling for a man who had turned out to be a charming manipulator and not the person he pretended to be.

Jonathan's profile ticked some of the boxes of the kind of person I was hoping to meet eventually although my expectations of meeting the love of my life through an advert were pretty low. He sounded normal. He wasn't too full of himself or too dull. Normal could be good.

So I left a message for him.

He rang and we chatted. I asked about the walking club he belonged to and we (or mostly I) arranged to meet at their monthly get together in Central London that week. The day before, he cancelled. No problem, I had the details. So off I went alone and signed up to go on a walking weekend in a few weeks time.

Being polite, I called Jonathan to tell him that I would be going to the walking club weekend trip to Derbyshire. Hearing that, he then decided that perhaps we should meet before then. I can still remember what I wore to that first date: some jeans and a favourite black fluffy jumper. I didn't want to overdress for an evening in Pizza Express.

We managed to find each other at the back of the restaurant without it looking too obvious that we were on a blind date. This was before the existence of mobile phones or even a computer to email a photo from. A brief description over the phone, me 5' 8", straight, dark brown hair; Jonathan, similar height, fair hair, was about all we had to go on.

Our first date was a success. We talked about travelling mostly, the countries we had backpacked across, no awkward pauses. We parted, agreeing to meet for a walk.

I drove home, smiling to myself all the way. I wasn't worried about where it would go. For now, I was happy to have met someone who I could talk to. We met for walks, an evening at a classical concert and then the walking club weekend in the Peak district at which he rather laid claim to me. I have a photo of us sitting together in evening dress with his arm around me even though we weren't actually in a relationship yet. For a few weeks, we were quite shy together. Well, he was shy. I don't really do shy in relation to men! I thought that perhaps he didn't fancy me but if friendship was all he wanted, I would settle for that. In fact, he hadn't had many previous relationships, unlike me. He was finding his feet. I wasn't going to spoil things and push him.

Eventually I nudged him a little and cooked him dinner. I don't like cooking so it was a big effort for me. Garlic king prawns rolled in breadcrumbs, fiddly and probably not the best choice for a romantic dinner but the gamble paid off.

A few weeks later, Jonathan went to Ethiopia with his brother for three weeks. I think we both realised while he was away that the relationship was developing into something more than just a walking friendship.

Although initially shy, Jonathan had a lot of female friends and is one of the most liberal and accepting people I have met who works outside of the caring professions. He worked as a lawyer within a large government department, mostly advising on employment issues. He was also working voluntarily for Citizens Advice and had volunteered as a student in a Saturday club run by Mencap. His acceptance of people in all their guises was to prove a very valuable trait for what was to follow.

By the spring, we were spending most of our free time together and commuting to and from each other's houses. Jonathan suggested we move in together. In May, me and my two cats moved into Jonathan's flat, renting out my little house where I had lived for five years alone. Five days later we left for our first real holiday together, driving across France to Italy on a road trip. Nothing was booked, we chose on impulse where we stayed. We spent a fabulous week in San Gimignano, driving out of town during the day to visit Florence and Sienna, returning at night for romantic dinners in lovely settings. At one stage, Jonathan lost his appetite and seemed preoccupied and a bit anxious. I asked him if he was worried about work.

Our last few nights were spent in Avigliana by a lake in an almost deserted hotel. Jonathan was still not quite himself. He succeeded in reversing his car off the edge of the hotel's car park leaving the rear end suspended in mid air.

On our final evening, we went for pizza. Returning to our room, we wandered out onto the balcony to admire the very picturesque view of the lake. He hadn't been able to eat his pizza. It wasn't like him at all,

'Are you feeling alright?' I asked.

'Would you like to marry me?' he replied.

I was silent for a moment. That was not what I was expecting. 'Can you say that again, please?'

My answer was an immediate yes. I hadn't been anticipating a proposal but I didn't have to consider it. Jonathan is not the most overly romantic of men but he had managed to pick the perfect spot and the perfect time.

Our living together trial had only lasted a few days. We drove back to London in a daze, making wedding plans as we drove.

The next few months were very busy. We wanted to get married as soon as we could as we both wanted children and at my age, 36, there was no time to lose. Almost a year from when we first met, we were married on a hot, sunny day in October in our family church. All went to plan, except that I had chosen a hymn sung to the tune of the German national anthem as Jonathan's parents had both come to England from Germany as teenagers around the time of WW2. The organist played the wrong hymn. After a few moments of hesitation, we all continued singing the right words to the wrong tune skipping the last two lines of each verse! The rest of the day passed in a whirl of speeches and dinner and dancing and flowers.

We honeymooned in Belize eating lobster nearly every night in small local shacks. On wedding anniversaries we always try to have lobster or crab, but none have quite matched those butter drizzled lobsters eaten as the sun set.

We spent a few nights in Devon for New Year and returned home to the shocking news that my mother Rosalie, had died suddenly, without any reason, on New Year's Day at the age of just 60. She had suffered with mental illness for most of my teenage years onwards, often spending months in bed or sometimes in hospitals on a voluntary basis. She also suffered from alcoholism and was in a miserable, abusive, second marriage. My only comfort was that the last day she had been anywhere out of the house was our wedding day and that she had made a huge effort to be there for us.

We had a family ceremony a few months later and buried her ashes under an oak sapling in Osterley Park where she had spent so many hours walking her dogs. Our childhoods had been spent living next to the park. It was where she would have wanted to be.

No cause for her death was ever found, despite an inquest six months later. I wonder if she couldn't bear life any longer and 'chose' to leave in some sort of unconscious way. By the time she died, she had seen all four of her children happily married. She had grandchildren too who she loved dearly. Perhaps she felt she had done her job in bringing us all up and that we no longer needed her, so she could let go of life. She was certainly very unhappy.

We started trying for a baby. Each month that I didn't conceive upset me perhaps more than it should have done. I would cry and hug Holly, my blue Persian cat. Had I had left it too late to have children?

Meanwhile, we started house hunting.

I refused to look at many houses despite persuasive estate agents and went with my gut instinct. We both walked into 'our' house and while still in the living room, before we had seen the rest of it, I said:

'I think we should buy it.'

'Yes, we should.' Jonathan replied without hesitation.

Jonathan operates in a similar way to me, trusting his intuition, so we can make decisions easily between us with no regrets. We would never have survived together if we had to stop and query every decision. Thankfully, instinct has never yet let us down.

The house was Edwardian and hadn't been touched for over forty years so it certainly needed a bit more than TLC. Our plan was to restore it to its former beauty and turn it into our family home. We were full of hope for our future together. Four bedrooms was a bit big for a couple on their own, but I was going on my intuition and years later, we did end up needing all those bedrooms and more.

I found out I was pregnant two days before moving in, surrounded by packing boxes.

'New house, new baby' as the saying goes.

We had both travelled extensively in our twenties. I had spent four years away, living in Sydney for a few years. We had a choice now between travelling together or having a baby. Due to my age, babies won.

Within a few weeks, the builder started knocking through downstairs to enlarge the kitchen. We escaped the dust for a couple of weeks, to Venice and Lake Garda in Italy, just over a year since our last holiday when Jonathan had proposed.

A week after we returned, I had the 12 week scan. Jonathan cycled from work to meet me at the antenatal clinic. My bladder was at bursting point when they called me in a few minutes early before Jonathan had arrived. I couldn't wait and miss my slot so I went in alone.

'Date of birth?' the man tapping away at the computer in the corner asked,

'Any history of twins in the family?'

I was staring at the ceiling, answering questions and hadn't yet looked at the screen.

'There are two live babies today,' the sonographer was expressionless as she carried on pushing the ultrasound nozzle over my stomach.

'Baby One... blah blah blah.' I have absolutely no idea what she said. I looked across at the screen and there were two babies! Just then, Jonathan came bursting in, sweaty from his cycle ride.

'Do you want the good news or the good news?' I asked him. 'We are having twins!'

The next twenty minutes were a blur. I do remember the sonographer saying quite firmly to make sure that we booked a double appointment the next time as she had run over time. I walked out beaming.

I was delighted; absolutely thrilled to hear we were having twins. One of my worries about my age was that we might only manage to have one child. Being one of four, I couldn't imagine having an only child. I scrutinised the piece of paper trying to work out whether they were identical or not. They weren't. Bizarrely, their due dates were three days apart. Twins explained why I had felt so sick as I had a double dose of hormones.

I felt so lucky to be having twins. There was no history of them in our family so it was totally unexpected and felt like a gift. I got used to feeling sick most of the time but continued to go to work, climb up ladders to hang wallpaper, supervise the builders and mostly carry on as usual.

I had scans every four weeks but I didn't want to know whether we were having two of the same sex or one of each although I twirled my wedding ring on a piece of cotton thread over my bump trying to guess. We had names ready: two boys' and two girls' names.

I was admitted to hospital at 34 weeks, looking like a beached whale in an enormous tartan nightie and no slippers as my feet were too swollen. My legs were like a Michelin Man from the fluid retention caused by pre eclampsia. I was as wide at the ankles as at the thighs. I spent the long days knitting a beautiful pink baby cardigan. By then, I was convinced I was having a boy and a girl (I still have it hidden away in a cupboard). There was no TV as I was in a delivery room and no mobile phone or computer to occupy me, just evening visits from Jonathan after he finished work. Knitting was my only distraction from the screams around me of women in labour, making me dread what was to come.

Finally, before 36 weeks, I was unwell enough to be induced. It took an excruciatingly long time, from Friday night until early Monday morning before I finally delivered my babies. When people asked me if I had the twins naturally, I usually responded with:

'Well, I didn't have a C-section but there was nothing 'natural' about their birth.'

There were drips and an epidural in case the second, breech twin got stuck. By midnight on the Sunday night, I was beyond speech and could only watch from afar as people did things to me. I thought it would never end. For the last hour or so I was in a theatre surrounded by so many people and bright lights. I just wanted my babies safely out by this stage and didn't care how that happened.

Thomas, whose name means 'twin' arrived first, pulled out by a device suctioned onto his head. Benjamin, whose name means 'the younger brother' did not appear until more than half an hour later, a footling breech, which meant his feet came out first. He was finally dragged out with forceps. He was blue and unresponsive; a frightening thing to witness. I didn't react; I was barely conscious by then. They managed to get him breathing and he turned yellow, being very jaundiced.

Words are inadequate for what I experienced next, but at the moment that he breathed, I felt that my job was done. I didn't need to stay in this world any longer. My babies were alive. I was drifting away from my life. I couldn't talk or move. I was watching the scene from afar. I wasn't frightened of dying; I think I was too far removed from it all to feel anything by then. Within a short period of time, perhaps only minutes, I 'came to' and could talk again. That was the nearest to death I have ever felt. I was back in the world. Our family had doubled in size.

Although both babies were a safe weight they were skinny and looked tiny, but they were perfect and beautiful. From the first moment, they looked totally unalike and have always done so. You would hardly pick them out as brothers, let alone twins. Thomas had some light brown hair and was very sweet looking, a pretty baby who people often mistook for a girl. Benjamin had wisps of strawberry blonde hair, a much rounder face and a big grin, much as he has now. For a while, a friend of the family nicknamed them 'Big Ben' and 'Tiny Tom' so she could remember who was who. They are often asked who is the oldest. Technically, Thomas is half an hour older, but his age was younger at 35 weeks plus a few days because he was due three days earlier than Benjamin who was exactly thirty six weeks when he was born. It's confusing for people to understand but it pleases the boys that neither of them is the oldest. These days they compete to be the tallest and there's barely an inch between them, but that inch really matters.

I gave them nicknames in the first few days. Thomas was a 'squally monster' as he never stopped crying. Benjamin was a 'little goat' as he made a noise which sounded a bit like a goat might sound if it laughed. Don't ask me how I know what a laughing goat sounds like! Between them, there was no sleep for me. They were starving all the time and hardly slept. My legs were still enormous and I struggled to get in and out of bed to feed and change them. It was not really the happy start to motherhood I had looked forward to.

A few days later, my blood pressure went sky high and I became a medical emergency for a few hours. On the plus side, I was given medication which meant I rapidly lost nearly four stone of fluid. I could walk again.

We were allowed home when the boys were five days old. Jonathan was a hands-on father from the start. We had two babies, one each and never had to worry about whose turn it was to hold the baby. We were so proud of our perfect boys, despite being hugely sleep deprived.

The babies were unsettled from birth. They didn't really sleep except when being pushed in the buggy, so I survived on two hours sleep at night for the first few months. I would walk with the boys for hours in Richmond Park. It was the only way they would sleep at all. In the evenings, we would sit on the sofa with a baby each snuggled up on our chests. That was the best part of the day before the long nights of feeding.

At three weeks, I had a post-partum haemorrhage. I asked Jonathan to call an ambulance. He knew this meant it was serious; being an ex-nurse I was usually so blasé about medical matters. I was calm, giving instructions in case I collapsed. After an emergency operation, I was home the next day, anaemic and exhausted. Jonathan had fed the babies overnight with bottles. It didn't mean sleep for me as I spent the night expressing copious volumes of milk from an ancient beast of a machine.

By six weeks, they reached newborn size. It was a precious time, to have tiny babies for a bit longer than most people had. I used to look at them in wonder. I had two perfect babies. I think it took me a while to fall in love with them as their arrival had been so harsh. I had been too ill to bond instantly. At their moment of birth, I just felt overwhelming relief that they were safe, rather than instant love.

We didn't have much family support so I was mostly on my own looking after them. I was truly sad that my mother never got to meet the boys, as she loved babies. Jonathan's mother, Liesel, was daunted by the thought of two babies at once and only wanted to observe rather than to do. I have the knack of appearing very capable so I don't think she felt she was needed. My sister had four children of her own and no time to spare. To be honest, in many ways, having twins suited me. I might have been a bit bored with only one baby to look after!

I was so proud of my beautiful boys. They were often admired in the street and people stopped to tell me their tales of twins in their own families. I still couldn't believe how lucky we were to have two healthy babies. We were in blissful ignorance of what the future held for them.

'Were you surprised when you found out you were having twins?' People asked.

I soon learned that this was their polite way of asking whether the twins were IVF or naturally conceived. But yes, I was taken by surprise at that twelve week scan. It was a lovely surprise though.

When they were five weeks old, we all went to Wales for a wedding. The babies were still newborn size and could fit together in one Moses basket. They needed feeding every few hours but we got to dance for a few moments while other women queued up eagerly to cuddle them. A friend managed to despatch a double mountain buggy over from New Zealand as they weren't available at that time in the UK so we could continue our active lifestyle. Walking on the coastal path in Cornwall when the boys were twelve weeks old was quite a challenge though, as at times the buggy was too wide for the narrow paths. I had never been aware before of how many stiles there are but we soon found a method; taking the boys out of the buggy, placing them on the ground, passing the buggy over the stile, strapping them back in and then pushing them until the next stile appeared, often just as they had fallen asleep again.

At six months old, we drove them to the middle of a not very exciting part of nowhere in France. To say it was not the most successful holiday ever would be an understatement. It was chilly, not the anticipated sunshine we had hoped for and all we could do was walk. On the few occasions we attempted to have lunch outside in a village, we had to take it in turns to eat while the other pushed the boys round and round. If the buggy was still, they screamed. They needed perpetual motion. We didn't understand why, just knew there wasn't much we could do about it.

The babies were terribly unsettled for the entire two weeks, especially Thomas. He refused to breastfeed or take a bottle and screamed and screamed most of the time. He wasn't unwell, just very obviously unhappy in different surroundings. As soon as we arrived home, he was absolutely fine again. Occasionally we tried a dummy, which calmed him, but Benjamin delighted in pulling it out of his mouth and chucking it across the room, so we gave up.

Thomas didn't have any 'saving reflexes' at his routine six month check which meant he didn't put his arms out to save himself if he toppled over. He also had gross motor delays. He couldn't sit until he was nearly a year old and if he wasn't in the buggy he spent much of his time lying on his back, flattening the back of his head. He would shift himself backwards across the floor while lying prone like a starfish, a form of upside down crawling. None of this seemed to be of great importance, though.

By a year he was crawling on his hands and knees and able to sit. No further mention was made of any of his delays.

Benjamin hit his milestones within the usual timeframes. That's when it got seriously tiring, two babies crawling at the same time in different directions. Benjamin 'commando' crawled with his tummy flat on the floor like a soldier crawling under wire. We had to use our only savings to buy a new hall carpet as the swirly red one that we acquired with the house had rips in it and bits of threads and fluff that the boys would grab in their little fists and attempt to swallow.

Both boys were big smilers and there were no obvious signs of any communication problems at this stage; well, not to us.

They were happy babies. We had lots of fun together, the boys and me. I went out every day with them. We went walking in Richmond Park, to playgroups, twins meet ups and mother and toddler groups. I still got very little sleep, so being busy kept me going through the perpetual tiredness.

By our second wedding anniversary I was pregnant again and delighted to be so. I wanted a big family. I used to write medical factsheets while the boys slept after lunch to earn a bit of money. One day while writing, I realised that although I was eight weeks pregnant, I wasn't feeling at all sick or tired unlike when I was pregnant with the twins.

'It's because you don't know how it feels to be pregnant with one' I was told but finally it was agreed that I could have a reassurance scan. I went alone to the scan, which was not at all reassuring, while Jonathan looked after the boys. I wished he were with me as they told me I must have my dates wrong, the baby was only six weeks and did not yet have a heartbeat. He came to the next scan, a week later. There was still no heartbeat. I had been ten weeks pregnant but the baby was not alive. It was a missed miscarriage and I needed an operation the next day to remove it; such a miserable end to our hope for a brother or sister for our boys.

It was Christmas and we managed our grief by hugging our beautiful boys. I didn't come home to an empty house, but I still felt empty with the loss. There was very little support for us following the miscarriage. It was almost as though people felt we had two babies under a year old and perhaps it was a good thing that we weren't having another just yet. 'You can try again', the platitude that we would grow used to hearing but which never gave us comfort.

The days were mostly long with just me and two babies. I really looked forward to Jonathan coming home for some adult conversation. The boys and I would wait on the sofa looking out of the window for him, while I sang nursery songs and did the actions. The boys would try to do some of the actions too. They were always so excited when they saw him approaching on his bicycle.

The boys turned one on the first of March and we had a tea party for them. How much they had changed in a year, as all infants do, from being tiny, rather scrawny babies into healthy happy toddlers. We had no inkling that there was anything different about them in any way. I had professional photos taken with them sitting on my lap, the boys in contrasting little checked shirts with Peter Pan collars looking adorable; their usual day wear at that time being mostly striped cotton tops which took the brunt of crawling around in the dirt and dust.

And then in March, I was pregnant, thank goodness. But it happened again. I had another miscarriage a few weeks later, a spontaneous one this time. I was shocked and so sad, but I didn't have time to grieve properly. The boys kept me busy and I hugged them even more tightly to me.

Barely, two months later and I was pregnant again. It had to be third time lucky this time. I had to believe that. I was so hopeful. A few months later though, I miscarried that baby too.

I'd had three miscarriages in less than a year. It was traumatic, a roller coaster of emotions, the joy and excitement seeing that magic blue line appearing... then the anxiety of waiting to see how the pregnancy progressed. It was constantly on my mind all day, every day. Time seemed to pass so slowly and of course each time, I had projected into the future.

'This time next year we will have two small children and a new baby.' We kept telling ourselves we were blessed to have two boys. Of course we knew that, but it didn't make the pain go away for the babies we had lost.

What was going wrong each time? We needed to find out. I couldn't bear to live like this with the constant hope and then the crushing sadness which followed it.

Months of testing and referrals ended finally at a recurrent miscarriage clinic who could find nothing wrong. We were told to keep trying. There wasn't anything they could do to help us. Recurrent miscarriage (three or more miscarriages in a row) is relatively rare and affects less than one percent of women. I would keep trying.

Chapter Two

'Two children were quite enough for me and your father, so why do you want more?' – Jonathan's mother, Liesel.

Life with two one year olds was full on. I learned the art of feeding two babies, side by side in high chairs, with one bowl and one spoon, alternate spoonfuls each. As they grew older, I had to let them try to feed themselves. It was obvious that Benjamin was left handed and Thomas was right handed as those were the hands they used instinctively to hold a spoon in. They, and I, learned that yogurt can go a long way when you throw it and make a lot of mess. They thought it was very funny. They wore bibs for years, graduating from the tie on ones to large all encompassing ones with long sleeves. Luckily, their high chairs were wipeable although the straps to keep them sitting in them weren't. I can still see those navy blue fabric straps with encrusted food on the buckles. They needed to be harnessed in or they would have climbed out of the chairs and fallen head first onto the floor.

They would only eat their food pureed. If there were any lumps they would gag and spit it out. I thought it was because of their enormous tonsils and, by now, recurrent tonsillitis that they couldn't swallow anything but puree. That was how it was until they were nearly three, even when they no longer had obvious tonsillitis. I remember batch cooking shepherd's pie and chicken livers with carrots and mashed potato, it doesn't sound tasty and it didn't smell good but they loved it. We took them on a trip to Jersey when they had just turned one with a pile of puree filled Tupperware boxes to put in the hotel fridge. Not eating lumps was a sensory issue but we didn't know that back then. Benjamin also suffered badly from gastric reflux. He had severe colic as a little baby and as a small child would regurgitate milk effortlessly as he toddled along. He developed car sickness which lasted until he was in his teens. He would never give any indication of feeling sick, not a sound, and the first noise you would hear was his instantaneous vomiting. He wasn't distressed by it, only by the mopping up and change of clothes it entailed.

I was permanently exhausted as they never stopped for a moment. 'That's just boys,' I thought as I pushed them round the park in their buggy, desperate for them to fall asleep.

They each had a push along walker before they could walk independently, a traditional one with coloured wooden bricks and the other was plastic with annoying buttons on the front that played tunes when you pressed them. Needless to say, they liked to play those electronic noises over and over. They would rush from one end of the lounge room, which was two rooms knocked through, pushing them to the other end and then get stuck as they could only go straight. It was a workout for me, running from one to the other, turning them round to face the opposite direction. We bought them cheap flimsy dolls buggies once they were steadier on their feet. They would fling the dolls out by their hair and race around with the empty buggies.

They were up and running by sixteen months. It didn't matter anymore that Thomas had been late with some of his milestones; he had caught up now. I attempted to put walking reins on them one day to walk safely around the block. They both just sat on the pavement in protest refusing to budge. I was back to gripping one each by the hand as we walked.

I loved their double mountain buggy. We could go anywhere. I have so many photos of the boys in the buggy, which document how quickly they grew. From tiny babies nestled in with plenty of space above their heads to two strapping toddlers filling the entire canvas sling seat. I had to strap them firmly in while out in the street. They had no sense of danger at all and would just run in opposite directions. They wouldn't stop if I shouted 'stop' or 'wait'. Other people were able to teach their children to stop at kerbs and not to cross roads. There was no chance of that with our boys; they didn't seem to understand what I said at all. They never looked back to check where I was either. I learned later that this was a sign of a lack of joint attention (the ability to focus and share something with another person), one of the diagnostic indicators of autism.

I was blissfully ignorant in those days and just presumed I had wilful, adventurous toddlers. I'm not sure why I didn't compare them more closely to other people's children or if I did, it didn't seem to matter much to me that my boys didn't behave as theirs did. In some ways, I am grateful that I had no idea that there was anything different about the boys until after their second birthday. I could enjoy them for who they were, two lively, happy little boys. I like to think I am not a competitive mother. I knew that physical milestones are mostly genetic. The age at which a child walks is not indicative of a 'clever' mother or a 'clever' baby, but just nature. I didn't worry about them being a bit delayed in some ways; they were twins after all.

We got a climbing frame and slide for the garden. They were fearless about climbing, in the same way that they were fearless about most things. I didn't know that children shouldn't be. They were boys and never having been a boy myself, I had no expectations of how they should behave. I would always stay close by though, ready to catch them if necessary.

On warm days we filled a paddling pool, one of their favourite things, but I couldn't turn my back on them for a moment. They absolutely loved water; bath water, swimming pools, the sea. They would pour water and watch it flow, over and over again, fixated by the repetitive stream of water. For years, they would systematically bail bathwater over the side of the bath and onto the bathroom floor. We replaced the vinyl tiles twice before I finally realised that we needed flooring which was cemented down and couldn't be damaged by water. If we filled the paddling pool, it would be emptied within hours.

Benjamin's happiest moments were when he could flood the garden with water and dig holes in the resulting mud. Our small garden looked like a bog some days before I eventually found a removable head for the outside tap. He also had a compulsion to 'bury' things in the mud that he had created. For years after, we would dig up little plastic toy people he had buried; a toys' graveyard in our flower beds.

Both boys had the same impulse with sand, to pour it from a bucket over and over again watching it flow. If there was no bucket, they would happily grab handfuls and let the sand fall through their fingers while staring intently at it. Now I know more about autism, I can pick out autistic children in playgrounds, staring at the flow of sand as they pour it continuously, seemingly not becoming bored of watching it and to the exclusion of everything else around them. That was my boys.

One thing I refused to have was a sandpit in the garden. I was busy enough looking after them both without having to sweep up sand on top of everything else. Besides, my rationale was they were more delighted when they went to a play group or playground that had a sandpit.

Some things were so much harder than they should have been. The boys screamed and screamed when we needed to cut their hair. We tried everything from giving them chocolate to eat to strapping them in the high chair in front of their favourite video. They still screamed. It was a dangerous activity wielding a pair of scissors. I knew a local nanny who had also been a hairdresser. Between us, we would attempt haircuts, one trying to hold them still while the other attempted to snip, accompanied by yelling and fierce wriggling. There was no way we could ever have taken them to a hairdressers. It didn't dawn on me that this was unusual.

The other thing they both vehemently hated was new shoes, something that was a necessity as their feet grew quickly. They would scream and fight if anyone tried to put new shoes on them, which made buying them quite tricky. Our strategy was to drive past the local shoe shop until it was empty of customers and we could seize the opportunity to go in. Jonathan would sit outside in the car while I took one boy in at a time. I would then swap him a screaming child for a quiet one who would soon start screaming too, once we were in the shop. The boys then had meltdowns every time the new shoes came out. After about 20 minutes, they would finally give up screaming and let me put them on. Within a week, the new shoes would no longer be a problem. Their feet were consistently half a size different from each other. In the winter, they wore stout little boots for walking. Benjamin's wellies were red, it was already his preferred colour and Thomas' were navy blue. In the summer they wore fully encasing leather shoes with T bar straps which were sturdy enough for all the climbing and walking and prevented their toes being stubbed unlike strappy sandals which we used only for the beach.

I didn't think very much about it, except that I really didn't like it and neither did the boys. I was mostly acceptant that it was just how things were. I didn't use a computer in those days to Google anything like 'screams at wearing new shoes'. Now, I would search online for whatever I think is unusual. I had never met an autistic child and I knew nothing about autism. So of course, it would not have occurred to me to suspect my boys might be autistic. Screaming about haircuts and new shoes were just what my boys did. I was totally in the dark, trying to find solutions myself and adjust to circumstances as I went along. I didn't think too deeply about it all. I hoped the next time we did something, it would be easier. Often it was worse.

Benjamin would not keep his seatbelt on. He would wriggle his shoulders out of the straps and climb out of his car seat. I would have to pull over and stop the car, over and over, to refasten him back in again. In desperation I would tie his harness straps together with a muslin square. I couldn't always pull over instantly and it was too dangerous for him to be clambering all over the car. What else could I do to keep him safe? I figured that in an accident, rescuers could easily cut through the thin cotton. It was an awful thing to have to contemplate. I was on constant alert watching him through the rear view mirror while driving. Some journeys took forever with the combination of him escaping and often being sick too. Poor Benjamin. He must have dreaded car journeys more than I did.

Benjamin didn't mind being told off at all. I never understood how other people's children could be 'told off' and made to sit for time out on the stairs. My boys would just carry on happily doing what they were doing and didn't care at all if I was cross with them. When they started to grow out of lunchtime naps, I would spend ages and get quite cross trying to settle them. It was my only free hour in the day and I desperately needed it. Years later when Thomas could finally speak and wanted to express his anger, he came out with:

'You go lie down' in a cross voice. To him 'lie down' was what he remembered me saying from the only times I was angry and therefore must be what you said to show your annoyance. He hadn't understood a word of what I said but had picked up on my tone of voice. Thank goodness I never swore in front of the boys! 'Lie down' was pretty innocuous.

In the autumn, when the boys were 18 months old, I was pregnant again. That magical blue line no longer meant joy... it meant waiting anxiously day by day to know if I would miscarry or not. Finally, at eight weeks, I had an early scan and there was the miraculous heartbeat in a tiny embryo. I was pregnant and we were really going to have another baby. We felt safe telling people our good news, as confirmation of a heartbeat means a 95% chance of a normal pregnancy. But by Christmas I was anxious again. I no longer felt sick. I didn't want to spoil Christmas, so I didn't have another scan until a few days afterwards by which time I was 12 weeks pregnant.

Jonathan and the boys came with me. A very kind doctor did the scans. She paused and kept looking and kept looking. Her silence was too long. The baby was no longer alive. I sobbed as she gently told me that I could try again. How many times had I heard that before? The misery we felt at that 12 week scan was in such sharp contrast to the happiness we had felt at the 12 week scan when we first saw our twins. I can't forget the irony of the nurse saying 'sweet dreams' as I fell asleep under the anaesthetic for the operation that would remove our dead baby. I cried most days for weeks afterwards. Jonathan carried on stoically at work.

We tried not to spend our time together being miserable but some days it overwhelmed us. The moments in particular when someone happily announced they were pregnant were so painful to hear. It was impossible not to feel jealous. I would paste on a smile and congratulate them while wanting to scream 'It's not fair!'

How could I have managed to carry twins yet now I couldn't keep a single baby? I had really believed this time was our 'turn'. That had been our fourth miscarriage in a row. The baby had Trisomy 15, a genetic defect which wasn't compatible with birth. The miscarriage consultant had phoned me himself to give me the results and announced without warning that the baby had been 'female'. I'm not sure I wanted to know that detail, but once known it couldn't be taken back.

On my 40th birthday in April, I was still grieving. I didn't feel able to celebrate, so we didn't.

I had to hide most of how I really felt from Jonathan. I pretended that I could handle my grief in order to be 'allowed' to keep trying to have another baby. He couldn't bear to see me so upset and would rather give up than watch me go through it again. We were usually very honest with each other, but in this case, I hid my true feelings.

Jonathan's mother, Liesel said to us:

'Two children were quite enough for me and your father, so why do you want more?' I am sure she voiced what others felt but didn't say aloud.

I wasn't giving up. I believe that if things are meant to work out they will. Fate, if you like. A few months later, I was pregnant for the fifth time in a row. I had problems carrying a baby but I didn't have any problems conceiving. Being pregnant consumed my thoughts every day, all day. We couldn't bear to tell anyone this time. After weeks of watching for every little sign that things were ok, numerous hospital appointments and some early scans, it was thrilling to finally see our baby sucking its thumb on a scan at 12 weeks.

By this time, the boys had turned two. Double trouble indeed! I started collecting wooden Brio trains and track, giving them a large piece like a station or bridge for each Birthday and Christmas for many years. We had a party at home for them, inviting mostly other sets of twins. Sixteen toddlers sat on miniature chairs eating jelly and then we did a singing session as that was what they most enjoyed doing at the playgroups. They looked so cute in their little corduroy dungarees. It was fun dressing them as twins in similar outfits but in different colours. Shopping for them was much more satisfying than buying clothes for myself. Thomas usually wore blue and Benjamin wore green. They still looked as different from each other as two brothers could. Thomas was fair haired and Benjamin had strawberry blonde ringlets and that almost translucent skin colouring which goes with red hair, but they both had matching vividly blue eyes.

They were happy, so we were happy too and oblivious that they were developmentally delayed. They were great walkers by now when away from traffic. We could take them for long walks with the double buggy at hand for them to rest in if they needed to. They loved jumping into puddles in their wellies. The only thing they didn't like was getting rained on. Thomas vehemently disliked the sensation of fine rain on his skin. He would dive under my jumper if it started to drizzle. I would have to walk along with his head hidden in a parody of a three legged race, a one headed, four legged one. It was a sensory issue we were to learn later on, but at the time we didn't understand why such light rain upset him more than heavy rain did.

They were partners in crime. I have a glorious photo of the day they decided to help each other empty the pasta drawer all over the kitchen floor. They look triumphant surrounded by a sea of spaghetti, pasta and rice and I had only left them alone for moments. They also managed to work in tandem in their shared bedroom, standing up in their cots, joyfully ripping bits of the wallpaper off that I had painstakingly hung when 28 weeks pregnant, and by then had the same size bump with twins as a full term single pregnancy would be. Once they outgrew their cots, we put them into basic pine beds. I so often found them asleep cuddled up together in one bed that we pushed their beds together.

There was so much fun in those days. We felt very blessed.

When I took them to playgroups, Benjamin was interested in other children and would scuttle over to join them. Thomas in contrast would cling to me and sit on my lap; he didn't want to investigate at all. But I persevered with the groups as Benjamin enjoyed them. They needed to mix with other children and not rely solely on each other. Their favourite part was the group singing at the end with actions. It was a balancing act to hold both of them and perform the actions with my hands all at the same time. They didn't join in the singing but sometimes they copied the actions to the songs and would follow the other children playing at 'sleeping bunnies' and then hopping up when everyone else did.

The boys appeared not to hear when we spoke or called their names. They never followed a spoken instruction like 'get your shoes, we're going out'. If I showed them their shoes and coats, they knew that meant we were going out and would be excited. But just saying the words was meaningless to them.

They weren't talking at all by two, not a single word, but still we weren't concerned. We should have been.

Off we went for the first of many hearing tests. The audiologist patiently taught them to respond to sounds by putting little wooden men into a boat. I can see that painted boat now, firmly imprinted in my memories. She pronounced that they could only hear muffled sounds because they both had glue ear. Ah, that made sense, no wonder they couldn't talk. It was nothing serious. Glue ear was quite common and totally curable.

Aged two and a half, we took Benjamin to hospital to have grommets inserted, a minor operation where tiny straws were put into his eardrum allowing all the fluid behind to drain out. We were able to take him home the same day. One of Thomas' ears had cleared by then, so they cancelled his op. A few weeks later, as I was singing ' the wheels on the bus' to them both, Benjamin spontaneously joined in and sang 'all day long' at the end.

Thank goodness! His first ever words. Now he could hear, he would soon start to talk, wouldn't he?

He didn't speak again for a year.

Thomas started to try and say the odd word here and there like 'dis, dis' for biscuit. There was still no real concern from anyone about either of them. We, in our oblivion believed the old wives tale which people often said to us, 'it's because they are twins' that they were slow to speak. We were also told that they couldn't hear before, but now they can, they will catch up. But they didn't. They didn't show any signs of catching up.

The red herring that was glue ear had caught us out. They should still have been trying to communicate with us in some way even if they couldn't hear, but they didn't. They never pointed to things or attempted to get our attention, they didn't shake their heads for no. The diagnosis of glue ear delayed us from realising that there was much more to their not talking or understanding language than temporary deafness.

That summer we just enjoyed having them running about

and were happy knowing that I was finally, successfully pregnant again and we would have a new baby just after Christmas. I was scanned for pre eclampsia and was deemed to be high risk but I never developed it, thank goodness. I did get a mild form of leaky kidneys which meant I wasn't allowed anything sweet because sugar went straight to the baby so that was the end of my chocolate cravings. I didn't care about that or the nausea or even a very painful few weeks of sciatica. It was all temporary. I was having a baby and that was all that mattered.

By the autumn, we finally started to wonder about the boys' lack of speech. It was still 'wonder' and not 'worry' at this stage. They were intrinsically happy little boys, they smiled, they laughed and we loved them. Was there really anything to be concerned about?

The boys had no fear. I was in Richmond Park with a friend Anne and her twin girls one afternoon. While I was balancing Thomas on a branch up in a tree, I turned around and saw Benjamin climb swiftly up onto a wooden picnic table. He ran along the top and kept running, straight off the end, falling onto the concrete below without stopping to look. I put Thomas down and ran to Benjamin. I somehow managed to get there in time and just catch his head in my hands before it hit the ground. He had no idea of danger at all.

They had no awareness of the danger of water. I often had to sprint to catch them before they ran straight into a pond as they couldn't yet swim. It terrified me. If we were knowingly walking near water, I used to harness them back in the buggy for their own safety and my sanity.

There was no need for me to do any other exercise with my two boys to run after! They needed to be watched every waking moment. I often kept them tightly strapped in the buggy because I couldn't run after two of them at the same time, particularly when they veered off in different directions. It would only take a split second for one of them to run out into the road and into the path of a car. I wasn't being over protective at all. Open spaces like parks or our garden were the only relatively safe areas where we could let them happily run around. They got frustrated when they tried to climb out of the buggy and I wouldn't let them. They wanted to be out and free. I tried to only take them shopping in that dead hour at the end of the day when they and I were tired and we were just counting down the minutes until bath and bed time.

I was expecting another baby. I had no childcare and no one to help me look after the boys. Fortunately, we had been on a waiting list for ages and the boys had two morning sessions a week booked at a local nursery starting in September. I would need those mornings once the baby arrived.

They only lasted there a week. We were asked to leave. The boys wouldn't follow any instructions and Thomas insisted on clutching a wooden twig all the time. When he went down the slide still holding it, it was the last straw. The nursery said it was a safety issue and he had to put the stick down. He wouldn't. We had to leave. They offered us no help, but said they would refund the term's fees if I removed the boys. I was clueless. I didn't know what I was supposed to do. I agreed to leave. Then, they refused to refund the fees and said I had chosen to leave. A few days later, I bumped into a fellow twin mother who told me she was delighted to have just been offered two spaces, two days a week at the same nursery.

They had filled the spaces immediately and of course, she was paying for those spaces but still they refused to refund us. It was our first taste of disability discrimination but we didn't yet know how to deal with it. We didn't even know that the boys were disabled at that time, only that they were increasingly different from other children and challenging to look after. Did the nursery suspect or recognise the signs of autism? In the end, after a few terse phone calls, we abandoned the idea of trying to reclaim the fees. It would have cost more to fight than to let it go. My immediate concern was more about how I was going to manage the twins and a new baby with no help. I appealed to my lovely health visitor who spoke to the community paediatrician about us.

He found us a nursery place locally for two sessions a week. It was for families with social problems and having no support meant we fitted into that category. An added bonus was that it was very close by. At the time he said

'There is a specialist autistic nursery in the borough but of course, your boys don't need to go there.'

Months later, that sentence was to haunt me when he decided emphatically that they did indeed need that specialist nursery.

By now the twins were much harder to look after than a newborn baby would be. Three under threes was going to be more than a full time job for me on my own. I would really need those few hours a week when I would have just one baby to look after.

There was a high ratio of staff to children, so each of them had a support worker and they were brilliant with the boys. One did a CHAT test for us, a questionnaire designed to identify the possibility of autism. It didn't flag up anything. Phew, we thought, we don't need to worry too much about their delayed speech. They told me years later, that Benjamin used to hide things behind the toy crates when he thought no one was watching, so he knew he shouldn't, but he thought it was funny. It was the first indication of his sense of humour emerging. They both learned to pedal a tricycle at the nursery which had an outdoor space. Their steering wasn't great but they got the hang of the pedalling. Benjamin liked to play with toys and they had lots of different ones there. Thomas preferred to do crafts like painting or water play.

I went into labour two weeks early on a Saturday night. Our young neighbours across the road were having a Christmas party. Our car in the driveway was blocked in by a car parked right across it. It didn't belong to anyone at the party but some young guys cheerfully came out and carried the offending car out of the way, gallantly helping a damsel in distress.

At the hospital, after a quick session on a monitor, I was whisked straight to theatre for a caesarean section. We knew the baby was a footling breech, feet first, then bottom, then head.

To be honest, I had willed the baby not to turn around but to stay breech as I knew that would mean a C-section. By then, I had begun to think that the twins' delays might have been caused by their traumatic delivery. I had been pleased to be told that I couldn't have a natural birth. It would be safer for the baby.

Hector arrived to the sounds of the 'Messiah' playing on a CD which we had packed into my hospital bag. His birth was such a contrast to the endless two days it had taken for the twins to be born. No panic, no trauma, no pain even though I was having regular contractions. His was a perfect, quiet and calm birth. Jonathan had found his name, Hector, meaning 'the strong one' or 'he who stands firm' a few days before. We wanted a name to signify the strength of this baby born finally after four miscarriages. He was beautiful, wisps of blonde hair and blue eyes, a perfect baby.

Hector was my early Christmas present. I looked at him and thought instantly, I could do this all over again. It was a strange thought, to desire another baby immediately after giving birth. That was how wonderful it all was. The misery of the miscarriages was forgotten for now.

I had a problem with the epidural after the delivery, a spinal leak which caused the most excruciatingly painful headache I have ever had. I could not sit up vertically and returned home in sunglasses to lie recumbent on the sofa for weeks. It was all worth it. I was so delighted to have my new baby that nothing else mattered.

Christmas was perfect that year with our three wise men.

Chapter Three

'Staff report that he is inclined to slide under the table at mealtimes, stretch across tables to grab what he wants, and roll, kneel and crawl on the floor inappropriately, like a younger child. He is unable to accept verbal direction.' (from the Educational Psychologist report on Benjamin).

The New Year began with me looking after all three boys on my own as Jonathan needed to go back to work. Someone had to bring in the money to provide for us all. I was sleep deprived and recovering from surgery, but we had no real help. I don't think our washing machine has ever stopped since, to be factually correct, machines plural, as their lives were short lived in our house. I abandoned the cloth nappies I had been washing for the twins for nearly three years, having three children all in reusable nappies was just too much work so I switched reluctantly to disposables. I wasn't going to even consider potty training with Thomas and Benjamin while they couldn't talk.

I had nearly secured a contract to write a book on twins, but it had fallen through six weeks before Hector was born. What was I thinking of? When would I ever have found the time to write it! I had a few hours with only Hector while Thomas and Benjamin were in the nursery for two sessions a week. A few hours with one baby didn't give me any time off but it gave me precious time to bond with him.

Due to having had a C section, I wasn't able to drive for another month so I needed a solution to get all of us out of the house. I found a second hand push chair which just about did the job. With Hector lying down at the front, Benjamin directly behind him, well strapped in to stop him escaping and Thomas behind him standing on a buggy board with my elbows tightly in against him to stop him jumping off and running away, I could just contain them all safely. It was narrow enough to get through doorways but long and cumbersome and almost totally unwieldy to get up the kerbs or to turn corners due to its weight. I abandoned it after a few months and thanked it kindly for its service. From then onwards, Hector in a sling and the twins in the buggy was the only way to get round the shops. The twins still had no awareness of traffic and I couldn't take them on a bus because I could never let go of them for even a second to fold up the buggy to get on, let alone hang onto them on a swaying, crowded bus. Without being able to drive, my life with the boys would have been severely limited.

One day I arrived home from the local shops to find Thomas clutching a packet of plasters that he had 'shoplifted', the downside of a wide buggy in a narrow shopping aisle. There was no online shopping twenty years ago, so we had to go out for supplies. Anyway, I would have been miserable being isolated at home all day, so it was a good reason to get out, among people. It almost felt like a bit of a break when they were in the buggy, not to be chasing around after them.

Hector was an easy, happy, smiley baby. It seemed like a miracle when he started sleeping through most of the night at just a few months old in comparison to the endless, sleepless nights with the twins when they were babies. He was a good feeder too and I didn't suffer from the exquisitely painful recurrent mastitis that Thomas had caused me on a regular basis as a baby. He was a very different baby to them. It didn't bear thinking about how I would have coped if he had been like they were.

I was worried that Thomas might be jealous of the attention I gave his baby brother but from the start he was so caring with him. He would bring me a cushion when I needed to feed Hector and stroke his head gently. Benjamin didn't seem to have any awareness that Hector was real and not a toy. I very soon realised that I could never leave Hector alone, in case Benjamin accidentally hurt him; not deliberately, but because he treated him like an object. Benjamin picked him up one day and sat him on the sofa, where he instantly fell off. It wasn't Benjamin's fault but mine for not foreseeing the danger. For the next 18 months, I carried Hector from room to room around the house with me.

Trying to keep all three boys safe was a real and constant worry, both in and out of the house.

It was hard having a new baby and no doting grandparents to help. I had friends whose mothers helped with their grandchildren and I admit, I was envious of them. I missed my mother, she had loved babies. She had been a huge support to my sister when she had her children and I know she would have loved mine. Jonathan and I had to be each other's support. It was a big demand on both of us, to fulfil so many roles; husband, wife, parents, carers, best friends.

So many marriages don't survive having special needs children, not that we knew in the early years that they had special needs. We always put the children's needs above our own. There was no other way. It left almost no time for us as a couple to enjoy each other's company. We had to become an impenetrable wall of strength for our boys and ourselves. We were older parents. Did it help that we weren't frustrated by the things we could no longer do, like travelling? While pregnant with the twins, we had discussed taking them to New Zealand, a country which I loved and which Jonathan had never visited. Now, it was a struggle some days just to leave the house. Travelling was not on the agenda.

Videos were my alternative babysitter while I fed Hector. I used to hunt down old Pingu videos at charity shops as they would entertain the twins for a short while. I still have them all tucked away at the back of a cupboard. A favourite episode of mine was the one where Pingu has to look after twin babies. I didn't know if the boys had a favourite episode; they couldn't tell me. I would put on videos with very clear spoken language like 'Rosie and Jim', two puppets who lived on a canal boat and could talk when the humans weren't around and 'Maisie', a white mouse who also featured in some board books we had, teaching basic single words. I hoped that they would absorb some language from them. At the very least, they gave me a few minutes of respite.

Looking back, there must have been tell-tale signs of autism. At a twins' club picnic when the boys were about 18 months old I spent the whole time chasing after one or other or both of my boys who just ran away from me, never looking back. Every time I sat us all down, they got up and ran away again. None of the other twins strayed far from their mothers' sight. It was a pattern that repeated itself wherever we went, my boys running off in different directions without a care in the world. We couldn't attend social occasions outdoors because we would spend the whole time chasing the boys and couldn't chat to people so there wasn't much point in going. We hadn't realised there was any special significance to this.

When they were about two years old, I started to worry about them not understanding a word I said. I would tell them where we were heading in the buggy, sometimes to Anne's house with her twin girls the same age, who they loved to see. They didn't react at all when I told them where we were going. When we got nearer to their house however, they would become animated and kick their little legs in excitement. They recognised places but not the words associated with them. If I said chocolate, they didn't react. If I showed them a piece of chocolate, they grinned and grabbed at it. That was how I knew they didn't understand a word I said, but never for a moment did I think they were autistic. At that time, I didn't even know what autism was.

Thomas and Benjamin were nearly three when that routine hearing appointment changed all our lives forever with those few words.

'Of course... they both have autism and there isn't much you can do about it.'

Autism? Our boys had autism?

Twenty years ago, an autism diagnosis meant something very different to what it might mean now. There were two very separate diagnoses back then, autism or Asperger's syndrome. Autism was the label given to the type of classic autism first identified by Leo Kanner in the 1940s. It meant our boys might never talk or understand language. It meant they might never read or write. It meant that they would in all likelihood need carers for the rest of their lives, perhaps in a residential setting. It was a disability which meant that they would in all probability never live independent lives. It was a very scary word to hear at that time, autism.

Children who were diagnosed with Asperger's had language within accepted parameters and average or above average levels of intelligence. Children with classic autism, like my boys, were mostly non verbal, had no understanding of language and additionally many had a learning disability. There were other differences, but many areas of crossover such as sensory issues, anxiety and difficulties with social interaction.

The two diagnoses of autism and Asperger's are now combined under one umbrella term, autism, which spans a wide range of abilities. The term no longer has the negative impact it had for us. For our boys, twenty years ago, it was a diagnosis of a severe lifelong disability. So when I write about autism, you need to remember that it meant something different two decades ago and I am writing about the type of autism my boys were diagnosed with at that time.

The paediatrician who had compared autism to vegetable soup said he would see us in six months time for the next hearing test. Telling us they were autistic was just an aside and seemingly of no major significance. Maybe it wasn't to him, but it was to us.

My denial stage about the boys had been fairly short lived. It was more ignorance than denial. How could I have suspected the boys had autism when I didn't know what it really was? I had never met a child with autism. I knew nothing about it. I thought they were just delayed for some reason, their traumatic birth, perhaps? The twins factor hadn't helped either; any delay was put down to them being twins. They both had glue ear, too. We had valid reasons for their lack of speech, but we could no longer sit around waiting and expect them to start talking spontaneously. Their autism meant they might never talk.

My only true denial stage was between seeing that community paediatrician and the appointment with a private paediatrician for a second opinion to confirm the diagnosis. The community paediatrician's attitude had been so blasé that we needed to see a doctor who we could trust. I still secretly hoped that he was wrong. He wasn't wrong as it turned out; he just had a terrible bedside manner. We had been put on a one year waiting list to see the community psychiatrist who would give us a definitive diagnosis as we had nothing in writing, just a throwaway comment from the community paediatrician and no mention of it on his audiology follow up report. Our options were to wait that year or to pay for a private consultation and diagnosis as soon as possible. It was a big expense but one that we were able to find the money for, and we were very grateful that we were able to do that. A year's wait would have been intolerable and most significantly would have meant a year's less therapy at an important developmental stage. I hurriedly found an expert developmental paediatrician who fortunately was able to see us within three weeks.

The diagnosis was pretty straightforward. It took one long appointment at a private clinic. No tests were needed; observation and questions were sufficient as it was a pretty clear cut diagnosis for him to make. The boys totally ignored us all, playing on the floor. The specialist health visitor took a crying two month old

Hector out of the room in his car seat so we could concentrate on answering his questions. This time we accepted the diagnosis as valid, as he explained his reasons for it. It didn't come as a shock, more as confirmation.

Once we had a definitive diagnosis there was no stopping me. I was going to find out what I could do to help my boys' development and as soon as possible.

I went into action mode, what I typically do when under stress, possibly to avoid thinking too much or reflecting too much. Action is an easier state as a coping mechanism and being busy is what I do best. We had already had a few sessions of speech therapy with a junior speech therapist when we thought they couldn't hear because of the glue ear. She was surprised when I told her they had autism. I needed better help than someone who didn't recognise the signs of autism.

What could we do for the boys? I didn't spend months researching therapies or interventions but I did decide to go with my gut instinct which was that we needed to do a home based intensive teaching therapy for our boys which focused on improving behaviours in areas such as social skills and communication, breaking learning down into incremental steps.

In real terms for us, this would hopefully mean giving our sons a form of communication they could use to lessen the frustration they experienced when they weren't able to express their needs, which was often. It would also teach them vital life skills.

Between the first appointment with the paediatrician who properly diagnosed the boys and the follow-up with him two weeks later, I was already in the process of setting up a home based early intervention programme. The doctor hadn't expected us to do anything but let the diagnosis sink in during the gap between appointments and was surprised by how quickly we had acted.

It was all pretty daunting to begin with. The programme was intensive and would cost us upwards of £40 000 to run for a year for both boys. That figure alone was enough to make us think very hard about doing it.

We learned that the education system did not fund early intervention programmes anywhere in the UK without a big, expensive fight by the parents at a special educational needs tribunal on behalf of each child. It felt very short sighted. Investment at a young age could save a huge amount of money over a life time in cutting care costs.

The only way we might, a very cautious might, get funding eventually would be to take our own local authority to tribunal. This would add a huge financial bill to our overall costs. We would have to fund the programme ourselves during the six month process of getting the boys a statement of special educational needs. We knew they would refuse to fund independent education in the statement and we would have to appeal against it. We would then have to fund the programme for a minimum of a further six months while waiting for a tribunal date. We therefore needed enough money to fund the programme for a minimum of a year plus the tribunal costs.

How on earth were we going to raise the finances needed? I hadn't worked since the twins were born except to earn some occasional freelance money proof reading and writing. I couldn't do that anymore because of how increasingly difficult it had become to look after the boys. But, if we didn't do any early intervention, what else was on offer for our boys? 'The system' had put us on a one year waiting list for diagnosis and offered only the bare minimum of speech therapy. If that was the speed at which the boys would get help, it didn't give us much confidence that they would get any proper therapy before they started school in eighteen months time.

There was no time to waste. The boys needed to start learning now. They were already falling behind other children their age in so many different areas, their lack of speech being the most obvious one.

It would save us money if we managed our own programme

instead of using an agency although this meant finding all the staff ourselves. But, that still left us needing a huge amount of money. How were we going to find it? We already had a lodger living in our house to cover our household expenses as I wasn't working. We went begging to the bank and managed to increase our mortgage but it still wasn't going to be enough. We approached Jonathan's parents and my father who thankfully offered to help make up the shortfall, so we had enough to fund the programmes for about a year.

'What if you lose at tribunal?' We were asked 'and you run out of money?' 'Will you have to sell your house?'

We could only think about now, our immediate future, certainly no further ahead than the coming year. We didn't know if the therapy would even help the boys. Actually, I couldn't bear to think at all about the future and what it might mean for them. My only hesitation was that we would have to take the boys out of the nursery and we would have to manage their therapy ourselves in our own home.

Within a few weeks we found a supervisor who would visit every two weeks to monitor progress, train the tutors and run team meetings. We found an independent programme consultant (the most expensive person on the team and the most qualified) who would spend a full day every two months overseeing the entire programme and all the tutors. The hardest part was the sole responsibility of recruiting tutors to work one to one with each boy for three hours every weekday morning and afternoon; a total of twenty sessions to fill. I decided from the start to keep our weekends sacrosanct as family time. No tutors on Saturdays or Sundays. I remained true to that throughout the years we ran the programmes.

There was no agency or website to recruit staff from. Mostly it was word of mouth in those days and very few mouths to hear it from. Finding and keeping tutors was to become one of the major causes of stress in my life.

Would I have started home based intervention if I had known how hard it would be for me at times? I look back and wonder how on earth I managed the programmes for over sixteen years. Finding, training and keeping good tutors was the responsibility of the person managing the programme, which was me, not the consultant or the supervisor. If we had used a provider, they might have sent us tutors but this way I could choose who I wanted to work with the boys, who I thought fitted with their personalities and most importantly, who I liked. They had to be in our house for hours at a time and we needed to all work as a team. Therapy was not something that could be done just in those hours alone but a methodology that we needed to stick to for all the hours they weren't with us, albeit in a different way.

I can say with absolutely no hesitation, the intensive therapy transformed the boys' lives but I didn't know then that the stress would be worth the outcome. It was all a big unknown gamble in many ways. Would it really improve the boys' lives? Would it be worth all the money? Would we regret the burden of the additional mortgage we couldn't really afford?

As well as being an educational therapy, it covered every aspect of daily living. It wasn't just about teaching our boys to talk or to read. They needed education but they also needed social and living skills. We would combine the two.

But before we could start, the boys needed some psychological tests. They were 37 months old. As part of the statement process the local authority sent a psychologist to their nursery to assess them. I didn't think it had been a good idea for them to be assessed by a stranger without me being present but, it did us a favour in some ways, as her report basically wrote them off as being incapable of even placing a brick on top of another. When we finally got to tribunal, we were able to show a 'marked' improvement from her baseline assessment.

Reading those reports now is still as distressing as it was then. They paint a clear picture of two little boys alone in their own worlds with no real form of communication.

'Benjamin accepted physical encouragement to take a turn but soon lost interest, stared into space and sucked his fingers for a while before leaving the group to fiddle with various objects' – the psychologist wrote.

'Staff report that he is inclined to slide under the table at mealtimes, stretch across tables to grab what he wants, and roll, kneel and crawl on the floor inappropriately, like a younger child. He is unable to accept verbal direction' – the nursery staff describing Benjamin.

'Thomas does not like changes in routine at nursery, or to be interrupted at play. He finds it difficult to join in with adult led activities, needing to be physically lifted to be directed to a group. He may then resist, cry or moan, run off and be disruptive.'

'Thomas has a low attention span and poor concentration skills. His play tends to be solitary, repetitive and lacking in purpose e.g. pouring sand. I observed him doing this repetitive activity for 10 to 15 minutes at a time.'

She attempted to assess Thomas' cognitive skills but she concluded that:

'He did not have the maturity, understanding or attention control to attempt such tasks.'

We also paid privately for some cognitive tests to establish some baseline levels in order to provide evidence later on of the progress we hoped they would make. They both scored zero on language tests, which was not a surprise to us. The assessor noted that Thomas had about 20 words he could use occasionally. Benjamin had no words at all.

They both got extremely low scores on all of the developmental tests. On daily living scores Benjamin scored 0.1 percentile and Thomas 1st percentile. It meant they were at the very lowest end of ability of 100 children of the same age.

They did a little better on gross motor skills like walking, hopping and climbing stairs and on some of the cognitive tests, for example completing puzzles, which required no verbal skills at all.

The results were stark and quite shocking. They showed just how severely developmentally delayed the boys were. In some ways it was a relief to have it declared by experts. It wasn't all in my imagination and I wasn't a bad mother. They weren't 'naughty' children. Finally we had a diagnosis and proof of their disabilities. I was, in essence, looking after three babies, two very large ones and one small one. I had been struggling to look after them. Perhaps now we would get the support and help we needed. I was also desperately in need of some emotional support. I was seen by many as too capable, I could always cope. People presumed I didn't need their help, but I did.

They were both severely autistic and no one could predict how they would develop. I really couldn't bear to think too hard about the future. Would Benjamin ever learn to speak? Would they be able to learn to read and write? What sort of lives would they lead? Would they ever be capable of living independently? I would put my trust, faith and hope in our newly formed team. Hope is a strong motivator. I needed all the hope I could muster to tackle the road ahead for us all, whatever that was going to be.

Most importantly, I needed to cope with the stress of not only looking after the boys but running their programmes too. I vowed never to turn to alcohol at the end of a hard day. There were too many hard days. Growing up with an alcoholic parent had taught me that drinking does not solve problems but rather, creates more.

At that time, we woke every morning to a smiling baby at the foot of our bed. Hector's joyful smiles meant that we started our days smiling too. I had suffered the utter misery of four miscarriages before finally giving birth to him. He and we were strong. We would rely on that strength now for his brothers.

In the midst of all this activity, we decided it was time to have Hector christened. All the focus seemed now to be on Thomas and Benjamin and none on our new baby. We needed to celebrate Hector's birth. He was christened in the same church as his brothers, where we had been married. We caught Benjamin red - handed swigging from a bottle of champagne. That set the tone for the afternoon. We switched off worrying about the future for that day and enjoyed the party. Our current lodger, who we had invited along, also swigged champagne and made a nasty remark about the boys to one of our friends. A few days later we asked her to move out. We replaced her swiftly and fortunately the next lodger stayed with us for over six years and was often away, leaving us in peace.

A couple of months later, it was Jonathan's 40th birthday. What felt like years before, in the pre diagnosis days, we had booked a house in France for a birthday celebration to include Jonathan's Uncle Ulli who was over from Australia, his parents and his brother, Nicholas. We had already paid the deposit and it might be the last holiday we could afford for a while, so we decided to honour the booking even though it meant paying our new tutors holiday pay after only working with us for a few short weeks.

'A change is as good as a rest.'

It wasn't. For us, change meant a great deal more work. The boys were away from their familiar environment and we had to be extra vigilant about their safety. We didn't get any kind of break or rest. Trying to be positive though, each time we took the boys somewhere different, it would improve their ability to adapt. We were laying down the benefits for future holidays.

Whenever we went away, they had a habit of emptying and destroying any room they slept in, like a couple of miniature burglars on a ransacking mission. The first day they emptied the chest of drawers of their clothes and strew them on the floor. Then, they pulled the drawers out and threw them on top of the clothes. They tried their best to pull the reading lamps off the walls but we had already pre empted them and removed the shades and bulbs, before we put them to bed. Fortunately the light switches were out of their short legged reach. Finally, they stripped the beds of sheets and quilts too, all within minutes while I was feeding Hector.

A few nights later, their room was empty of anything which we could remove and we presumed it was safe. We heard a crash. Running in, we saw they had managed to push the window up, take the window box from outside and throw it, fortunately unbroken, scattering earth and flowers everywhere inside the room. They were gleefully jumping up and down on the beds, too, in great excitement. By then, we were unperturbed by such behaviour but I think my parents in law were pretty shocked at how 'naughty' our boys were. We were so unbothered that we had a hard time controlling our laughter as we cleared up and hastily re planted the flowers. We didn't tell the boys off. They were just having fun in their own way.

Hector was six months old. I was pregnant again.

Why did I still want more children? My justification this time was that the twins had each other and he would need a playmate. Their autism diagnosis didn't put me off. If anything, I thought that the older boys being autistic might mean that Hector would feel isolated. I had conceived Hector with the help of a half dose of clomid (a drug to aid ovulation). I truly believed it was the magic cure we had been seeking to prevent miscarriage. I was pregnant again and I was convinced that it would all be fine. We would have a fourth child, a friend for Hector. My dream was just that, a wretched dream, as yet again. I miscarried early. Memories of all the previous miscarriages overwhelmed me. It was more grief to deal with on top of everything else.

A week later it was Jonathan's actual 40th birthday and we had a small party at home. I had to behave as though nothing had happened. All I wanted to do was curl up and hide but I had to put my usual brave face on and carry on. We hadn't told anyone that I was pregnant. I feared people's reactions if I told them how devastated I was to have had another miscarriage. I didn't want to be told:

'You have enough to do looking after three boys; you couldn't cope with another child.'

I would have coped. I had really, really wanted that baby.

Because we had been given money from our parents towards financing the boys' programme, we felt we couldn't spend any money on ourselves. The holiday in France was the last time we could spend money on anything not deemed a necessity. All that mattered now was helping the twins to develop and progress in whatever way we could.

Stress was a constant companion and I had to learn to live alongside it while appreciating the happiness in our home. Thomas and Benjamin were happy. They didn't know that they were different from other children. Hector was happy. But it was really hard for me to stay positive at times. Life was hard enough without me feeling negative about myself and my body, so I made a determined effort to lose all my baby weight and more. This meant barely eating which was not great self care. My weight loss was also about control, as eating often is. There was so much around me that I couldn't control. This was one thing I could and so I did.

I needed to stay in control. If I lost control, we would all go under.

Chapter Four

'Like his brother, Thomas has made progress in all areas of his development.' - from a developmental paediatrician's report.

Reluctantly, the boys had to leave the nursery where they had been happy. I don't know if they missed it, they couldn't tell us. Our house soon turned into a school. Thomas and Benjamin had individualised sessions away from each other in different rooms. They could be with their tutors anywhere in the house, so nowhere was sacred except the toilet. It felt so invasive at times to have my home taken over. I had become a boss overnight; recruiting tutors, paying them, managing them. The tutors did morning and afternoon sessions, a total of six hours a day, Monday to Friday. Trying to find enough tutors to fill 20 sessions a week was a constant struggle and I barely ever managed a full week's cover in over sixteen years of running programmes.

We soon needed new shelving for all the paperwork and various toys and games the boys needed. We had a play area off the kitchen, cluttered with brightly coloured boxes filled with equally brightly coloured toys. Inevitably, it was me who sorted all the toys out at the end of the day's sessions.

It was also my job to track down resources like specific toys depending on what they were working on. To teach attributes such as wet/dry or soft/hard needed some ingenuity. This might mean two blue balls of equal size but one was hard and the other was soft. Teaching 'ball' or 'blue' was a challenge but trying to teach a concept such as 'hard' could take a very long time, often months. Then of course, you couldn't use those same balls you had used to teach red and blue as that would be too confusing. The blue ball was blue. How could it be called hard when it was called blue? It was a minefield ensuring that we didn't teach the wrong word because unlearning it would be harder than learning it was.

When teaching wet and dry for example, we used two matching flannels so that the only difference between them was whether they were wet or dry. It took years to teach some of these concepts which other children acquired naturally with no additional help. The list was endless: hot/cold, long/short were basic labels. Eventually, we would have to teach prickly, furry, slimy and so many others.

Thomas would throw himself on the floor and scream if asked to do something he didn't want to do, such as putting his shoes on. All requests we made needed to be meaningful for the boys, not just for us. If we were going out, we needed Thomas to put on his shoes without screaming, so that might be one of his targets. When he put his shoes on, he would be taken out to play, something he really enjoyed. He learned to associate putting on his shoes with a positive reward. The ability to put on his shoes when asked to, without screaming, sounds like an easy task. It wasn't.

Every activity had to be broken down into tiny manageable pieces so that new skills could be taught. We might show photos of each step, as that was far easier than using language which the boys had yet to understand; a photo of Thomas' shoes, then another photo of Thomas putting on his shoes and then finally a photo of Thomas in the playground so he knew what he needed to do.

Our first consultant workshop didn't go too well. The consultant, who had never met the boys before, and three of the tutors decided that we needed to teach Benjamin sign language. At that time he made no attempts at speech, his only sound was a monotonous humming noise which he made while engrossed in play. I was his mother and I instinctively felt that he was on the verge of speech. I didn't want to start teaching him sign language. But who was I to say? I had no experience. It was made very obvious that I should listen to the experts. One of the tutors said quite angrily that if I wouldn't let them teach him sign language, then what were they going to do for six weeks until the next workshop? I decided that I was paying for all this and if I wanted to 'waste' my money, then that was my choice wasn't it? Of course I wouldn't leave him with no form of communication indefinitely but I just wanted six weeks to see what was possible. After the meeting, the fourth of my new tutors who I had engaged to be one of Thomas' tutors came to me and said:

'Give me Benjamin to work with. I'll get him to talk.'

He did. He used Benjamin's fascination with water to get him to speak. He spent hours out in the garden with his thumb over the end of the hosepipe teaching Benjamin that if he made any sort of 'request' for water in any verbal way, then he got some water. To begin with this was just a 'w'. He learned then, that everything has a label and if you ask, you get. It was a Eureka moment for him. Six weeks later, the consultant returned for the next workshop and no mention of sign language was ever made again. He didn't need it.

So, in six short weeks, Benjamin had grasped the meaning of language. This was a huge breakthrough for all of us. Our boys would learn to speak. We didn't know whether they would ever gain useable speech or be able to have a conversation, but for now, they could learn single words to get what they wanted. How amazing must that have been for them? I can't begin to imagine how frustrating life had been for them until now. Needing a drink or wanting a particular toy and having absolutely no way of getting it. No wonder they screamed when we couldn't guess what they wanted.

I tried not to project too far ahead. I couldn't bear to. It was too terrifying. It was better to stay in the moment and be grateful that Benjamin was learning to say words. We knew statistically that many children with severe autism might never talk, but it appeared that our boys hopefully would.

It was a high moment amid the recent low ones.

The therapy was already working and making a difference. We could justify its terrifying cost. We didn't have money for anything but paying our team. No expensive holidays, no nights out or new clothes. But what was the point of having those things in comparison to our boys learning to speak? Speech was priceless.

Some people thought we had expensive childcare. The tutors were not childcare. They didn't feed the boys or do housework, but they did teach them vital skills so much quicker than we would have managed to do, if we ever managed to at all. If the boys were easier to look after, our lives would be easier, too, but it was going to take a long time. We were in for the long haul and needed to get used to our altered lives.

I did have odd hours where I could go out and spend time just with Hector. I wanted to enjoy doing what other mothers did, going to playgroups and the swings. Hector wore mostly hand me downs from his brothers, me cherry-picking the nicest of each set. Sometimes it felt like I was leading a double life. When out with Hector, I pretended that my life was just like everyone else's, but I knew it wasn't. The strain of being the mother of two boys affected severely by their autism was already having an effect on me. I was permanently tired, with no let up in sight. I was stressed from running the programme in my own home. I felt guilty that I was neglecting Hector. I was too busy looking after his older brothers and doing endless paperwork and assessments to get their statements.

We also had to prepare to go to tribunal. We had been warned that it would be a really stressful year and the warnings were sadly, correct. It really was way too much for me to manage on my own. We couldn't afford for Jonathan not to work so most of it fell on my shoulders. Jonathan understood the tribunal process better than I did though and could sort through the paperwork once I had got it together. His knowledge of the legal system and documentation proved very useful, even if he didn't have experience of special educational needs law.

The boys were taught single words, one word at a time; a laborious process. We needed the boys to want to speak. This meant finding either objects they really desired or things they really wanted to do which would be strong enough motivators to get them to ask for them. In Benjamin's case, this was often a train. He absolutely loved all things Thomas the Tank engine and by now, we had a huge box of trains and wooden track. Thomas already had a few words. We needed to teach him to use those words and to learn lots of new ones. For him, learning to say 'push' for a push on a swing was highly motivating. Like the instructions they needed to follow, any words taught had to be useful for the boys. We offered choices to get the boys to name the thing they wanted. This meant the really desired object was offered alongside one we knew they wouldn't want. If Benjamin was offered the choice of a train or a cleaning cloth for example and encouraged to say train or any approximation of train, he got the train. With language, some words were even taught syllable by syllable, then as complete words. Finally two words were added together such as 'want train', 'want juice' and so on until they could use short sentences like 'I want juice'. That was to take years though. There was no short cut to teaching the boys to speak.

One very common word which we avoided like the plague was 'more', a word often taught to children with little or no language so they could ask for more of whatever they wanted. It was supposed to encourage interaction, which it did, but at the cost of other meaningful language. Our boys were taught to ask for each item by name. If we opened a packet of crisps and gave them a few, we encouraged them to ask for 'crisps' in whatever way they could to get another handful. The boys often used the nearest adult's hand as an object to get what they desired, never making eye contact, another classic sign of autism. They would take us by the hand and make that hand open a cupboard or turn on a tap. How much easier it would be for them once they could just ask for what they needed. That was our goal.

Fairly soon after starting the programme, we realised that they could learn new tasks that did not require language quite easily. Their autism meant they both had a severe language disorder but it was hard to gauge whether they also had additional learning disabilities alongside the autism. A high percentage of children with classic autism have learning disabilities. When they were first diagnosed we didn't know if they did or not but the likelihood was high. The fact that they could learn new skills when taught in a different way that didn't require language indicated that they probably didn't have a learning disability. But we would really have to wait and see, it was too early to predict anything.

It's hard to explain how language is learned so differently in a child with autism. If we were to point to a hot cup of tea and say 'hot' to stop the boys from burning their fingers, they might then think the word 'hot' actually applied to the cup itself. Days later, they might suddenly say 'hot' 'hot'. We might guess that they were feeling hot when actually they wanted a cup with a drink in it. We had to be so mindful of how we taught every single word. Then there was also the matter of generalising to consider. Pointing out a black and white cat and calling it a 'cat' is perfectly logical but we had a black and white cat and we called it 'Thumper'. How could we explain that not every black and white cat was a 'Thumper' but was actually a 'cat'? How then to explain that yes, a tabby cat was also called a cat. It is utterly confusing when you think about it to that extent. We had to be so careful not to confuse the boys who, once taught a label, stuck with it rigidly.

The programme wasn't just about teaching them to speak. There is so much more to communication than spoken words. The boys had never pointed; a fundamental form of communication. It's one of the leading questions asked before diagnosis and a known indicator of autism.

'At what age did they start to point?'

Neither of the boys had ever pointed spontaneously to show us or request things. I had never noticed that my boys didn't do this until I was asked at their autism assessment. Mums at coffee mornings or play groups were forever discussing their children's development, the age at which they reached developmental milestones like rolling over, crawling, walking and then first words. I had some awareness of what the boys were supposed to be doing at certain ages, but I don't remember anyone talking about their child pointing.

As soon as we were alerted to it, we started showing the boys physically how to actually point with their index fingers and then we adults pointed at anything and everything for a few weeks, naming the things we pointed at as we did so. We might offer them two items to choose from, one they really wanted and one that they didn't; pointing at the desired object meant they got it instantly. It didn't take very long for them to learn this new trick. Pointing was a very useful tool once they knew how to use it.

There are endless skills which we all take for granted; turning when someone says your name, waving goodbye, looking at or touching someone to gain their attention. The boys had acquired none of these in their first three years. Each skill had to be broken down and taught step by step. The tutors had to be very patient at times, but also fun and engaging. The boys needed to enjoy their sessions and want to learn. If they used words or did tasks correctly, the boys needed huge reinforcement in the form of being given something they really wanted as a reward, perhaps a favourite toy or something intrinsic like being thrown in the air or being tickled.

We made it through the first six months, losing just one tutor. We adjusted to all these new people coming and going in our house. Some of them we became close to and some we didn't. Most of the tutors really cared about the boys and the work that they did with them. Inevitably, some cared more than others.

Over the years, a pattern of tutors leaving and new tutors having to be found and trained became the norm. Sometimes it was due to personality clashes with me or even with the boys. One tutor declared she couldn't work with Thomas as she couldn't bear his meltdowns and took them personally. Talking to Thomas very recently, he has been able to explain now that he didn't like the tone of her voice, a high pitched American accent. He took an instant dislike to another tutor a few years later with a similar accent. Her voice distressed him. I wish he had been able to tell us at the time instead of trying to express his feelings by yelling at her.

Tutors often left to start different careers. Early intervention therapy was unregulated and no qualifications were needed. Anyone could do it or so they believed. For some, it was a stop gap job. For others, it was the beginning of a dedicated career. The trouble was, until someone was trained, you never really knew which option you were getting. It all added to the expense as training meant doubling up tutors. We were out of pocket, not the tutors, if they left. We couldn't afford any childcare but that meant that we as parents were one hundred percent consistent alongside the tutors in how we treated the boys. This was ideal for the programme to succeed but not so easy for me looking after three small boys alone most of the time.

The programme worked. It really worked. It was worth all the effort and expense and it would be worth fighting for it at tribunal. While we had to remain realistic, we did have so much more hope now for their futures. Progress was hard won at times but there was continued, real progress. A developmental paediatrician from the local health authority assessed the boys five months after starting the programme.

From Benjamin's report:

'Benjamin has made good progress in all areas of his development. Several words were heard including ball, tea and chair, used appropriately. He also made some incomprehensible sounds.' 'Benjamin knows some colours and was able to name several objects in a picture.'

From Thomas' report:

'Thomas now requests for things that he wants by name. Thomas' behaviour may be challenging but he reacts better to change. Like his brother, Thomas has made progress in all areas of his development when compared to previous assessments.'

Family wise it was a sad situation for everyone. I don't think any of the boys' grandparents ever really understood autism and how it affected Thomas and Benjamin. Perhaps they thought they would grow out of it? They never criticised our parenting openly but were often bewildered by how we managed the twins and particularly their behaviour. They couldn't cope with two boys who didn't really talk, who shrieked a lot and were very active. The boys didn't behave like they thought they should. They couldn't take on the role as grandparents that they expected to have. The previous generation's attitude to severe disability, particularly any condition seen as a 'mental' disorder was hard for them to dismiss. Children like ours had been sent away in the past to residential settings at a very early age. They were mystified by our belief that we could somehow manage our boys ourselves at home. There was little interaction between them and their grandchildren.

In September, I was pregnant again. Hector was nine months old, a bright little boy, always smiling. He had cherubic blonde ringlets and people often remarked on his beauty. He was already 'cruising' the furniture and was walking independently by ten months old. He hadn't crawled for long. Perhaps he knew he would be in less danger of being trampled upon if he was upright. He was feisty and attempting the stairs alone so I had to keep a close eye on him. He had started to babble 'da', 'ba', 'ga'. He knew his name. He was reaching all his developmental milestones on time. He was already very different from his brothers at the same age.

His brothers would always have each other and they might not be good playmates for him in the future. A sibling for him would complete our family perfectly.

As always, I truly believed it would be fine but it wasn't, yet again, it wasn't. I had another miscarriage, my sixth, a few months later. This particular miscarriage was a physically painful and messy one. Jonathan rushed home from work and drove me to hospital for an emergency operation the same afternoon. That evening I was home again, feeling very sorry for myself as it had all happened so quickly and I was feeling very weak, too. Again, we hadn't really told people I was pregnant which meant not many people knew or cared about the miscarriage. We cared though, we cared enormously. The pain was not diminished by having gone through it before, if anything it was cumulative. I was expected to pick myself up and carry on looking after my three boys without any help. Jonathan couldn't take time off from work; he needed his holidays for all the appointments we had to go to so I only had another pair of hands to help when he was home during the evenings and weekends. I never really had any time to rest and recuperate. There was too much to do.

We had received the final statements of special educational needs for both the boys in early October. We were not surprised at all that they named a local specialist autistic nursery on the statement as to where the boys should go. As we had anticipated, there was no mention of the therapy we were using.

We had visited the autistic nursery a few months before. There were six boys, all non verbal, sitting almost silently in a row. The nursery environment was purposefully very plain, to avoid distractions and sensory overload. The children did what they were told with no meltdowns, unlike Thomas, but there was no joy, no noise. I had left the room mid way through the visit in tears. Was this how my boys were going to be? Joyless? I knew that this was absolutely not the right environment for them. If they couldn't learn with the additional distractions of the everyday world around them, how would they ever manage at school?

We appealed officially against the statement and got a date for tribunal hearing at the very end of January 2003. In preparation we booked a private educational psychologist to assess the boys and provide a report. We would need to fight hard and prove that the nursery provision they were offering wouldn't be as effective for our boys as the early intervention programme we were providing was.

After four months, Thomas was starting to combine two words together like 'want flower' and 'in boat' but when he wanted something he still grabbed his tutor's hand rather than calling him by his name. He was only co operative for a few minutes at a time. The educational psychologist wrote in her tribunal report:

'Although Thomas' expression and comprehension are both severely delayed, his spoken language is increasing fast.'

'Thomas' drawing skills are only at the 18 month old level.'

'Thomas is generally not yet compliant although his behaviour is variable.'

Benjamin now had a few words like 'juice' and 'water' and was less inclined to meltdowns than Thomas. His play skills were much better than Thomas' and he liked to play with a greater variety of toys.

She wrote:

'Benjamin has just begun to talk. He mainly uses single words but does occasionally put two words together. His language is suddenly developing fast.'

'Benjamin's cognitive abilities are almost certainly within the 'broadly average' range, although he may not be able to access and use all of his cognitive skills until his language develops further.'

The reports were often upsetting but reading that particular comment was a bright moment, 'average cognitive ability'. We were more determined than ever to help Benjamin talk.

In September, the boys started at local mainstream nurseries part time accompanied by their tutors. They had both briefly started at a Montessori nursery during the summer term. Benjamin returned to the same nursery as the structure and routines there suited him. Thomas had left the Montessori nursery as he was very reluctant or unable to follow direction. He would object and yell fiercely if asked to do something he didn't want to do. He needed free play and very little structure so we found him a different style of nursery in a local church hall. Sometimes they only went to the nursery for an hour during their morning sessions but it was vital that they were exposed to mainstream children in preparation for primary school in a year's time.

Thomas never attempted to play with the other children but observed what they did and then copied it after they had left. This was a significant improvement as he had no real play skills at all and copying play was the first stage of playing. He didn't attempt to talk or make any social advances to any of the other children in the nursery but at least he tolerated being around them for short periods.

Benjamin happily mixed with the other children, playing alongside them if not with them. He would sit in a circle and wait for his turn. He would attempt to do whatever task was given to him and was happy to be there.

I was determined to tackle potty training. The boys were now three and a half and still in nappies. We were aiming for mainstream school. The stigma of sending them in nappies might make them stand out even more from the other children and who would change them if I was not there?

A local neighbour with an older boy with autism told me he had potty trained his son while he was non verbal and it was like 'a light in the darkness' to achieve it at a young age. If he could do it, so could I.

I started with Benjamin as he was the most co operative at the time. I don't think I realised what a huge task I was taking on. The tutors were very reluctant to start potty training so one Friday evening, after they had finished for the week, I started it myself. As the boys were quite big, I decided that they would start with a proper adult toilet and no children's potties. Our boys were being taught most skills by imitation so it made sense that they copied and did what the rest of us did. I had to take the boys with me into the toilet whenever we were out anyway and always had to leave the door open when I was at home so they knew what a toilet was for. Now I just needed to teach them that they could use one too. The word 'just' implies ease, but it was far from easy.

Benjamin took over a year to fully toilet train and it was a very dirty year. Due to his sensory issues, he loved the feel of mud in his hands and unfortunately for us, poo for him was a great substitute.

Benjamin liked to smear it. He would remove his clothes and his nappy and then smear it everywhere, walls, floor, over his own body. I found some large all in one sleep suits like the ones they had worn as babies, which I secured with a nappy pin at night so that he couldn't undo the zip and get at the contents of his nappy. During the day we just had to watch him vigilantly and hoped to catch him when he did a poo and change him immediately. Not so easy. He was quite resourceful and would hide behind doors. When we tried to leave his nappy off to toilet train him, he would poo behind a door unseen. He seemed to sense that it was wrong to poo everywhere but he didn't care.

One day I walked out of the kitchen to find him naked, covered in poo in the hallway. He was, I think, attempting to clean the evidence of what he had just done. He had a slightly shifty, guilty look on his face. He had removed his clothes and in trying to remove the poo from them had just made matters much worse. He had found some baby wipes which he knew I used when clearing up mess like this. There was poo all over the carpet. Hector was crawling by this stage and about to crawl straight into it. I didn't know what to do first. I scooped up Hector and put him safely in his cot. Then I ran a bath, dumped Benjamin in it and showered him down. He wasn't remotely bothered by any of this. To him, poo was poo and something to play with. Finally, I cleaned up the hallway. My nursing training came in handy sometimes. I was not fazed by poo in any way!

We finally managed to potty train Benjamin after a year using a method I found online. Whenever Benjamin pooed on the floor,

I would pick it up with one hand, take him by the other hand and walk to the toilet with him repeatedly saying 'poo in the toilet' and put it in the toilet. I didn't shout at him, I didn't tell him off, I just walked backwards and forwards several times calmly repeating 'poo in the toilet'. He really didn't like it, I don't know why he didn't like it but it worked. After a week or so, he finally stopped pooing anywhere but in the toilet. It had been a long year.

Thomas' toilet training was a complete contrast. He didn't like to be wet or dirty. If his T shirt got wet, he would take it off. I had started the potty training with Benjamin first as I couldn't face doing both boys at the same time. When it became obvious that it was going to take a very long time, I started Thomas too. He was dry within a few days which was absolutely amazing. He couldn't bear the sensation of being wet so that was that. As soon as he knew how to use a toilet, he used it. For another year or so, I put pants on underneath their pyjamas which mostly helped them stay dry overnight.

Autism affected them both uniquely. They say when you have met one person with autism, you have met one person with autism. It's so true. They were twins and yet so different. Thomas needed to be encouraged to drink to keep him hydrated. Benjamin would drink constantly. Thomas only ate when he was really hungry. Benjamin ate constantly as he never felt full. They were polar opposites in many ways.

A psychologist once remarked that:

'They are like one typically developing child and one with autism. They each have an equal half of both. So one has one aspect of the autism and his twin has the opposite half.'

Life was full on and exhausting, physically and emotionally. When we could, Jonathan and I walked and talked, while the boys sat in their buggies or ran around. We kept our relationship together by always trying to make time to talk things through. The statistics of marriage breakdown in families with disabled children are sadly very high. We did not want to become another casualty. Perhaps because we had no other real emotional support except each other it meant that we clung together, like life rafts, through everything and it made us stronger. Our lives revolved around autism so we had little time for much else. We couldn't keep up with many friends or do things on our own together like going to the theatre. Our lives, as we had known them, were basically on hold.

My life, in particular, was to stay on hold for a long time to come. I could not work. I couldn't rely on the tutors turning up each day in order for me to be able to work. Tutors called in sick, went on holidays and had other things in their lives which meant that we were not always their first priority. I dreaded the sound of the phone ringing between 7.30 and 8.00 am. It invariably meant a tutor calling to say that they would not be in that day. It was a rare week when all the tutors turned up as planned.

I learned the hard way, as most parents running their own programmes do, that tutors can be amazing, dedicated, hard working people who love their jobs and can change a child's life, or, they could just be filling in time. I felt a bit more in control once I worked out that the best and most reliable tutors weren't necessarily the ones with previous experience, but often those whose personalities felt right. Years later, I still got it wrong from time to time. It was a huge responsibility to employ and manage tutors but I felt very privileged to be in a position to be able to choose who worked with our family.

Chapter Five

'We don't want childcare, our boys need education.' – Me, speaking at tribunal

The New Year began with reports, reports and more reports; so many assessments and meetings all building up to the fearful tribunal hearing. Both hearings were to be on the same day at the end of January, one in the morning and then hopefully the other in the afternoon if we didn't run out of time.

We were absolutely dreading it. We were dreading both the actual day and the possible outcome. I had heard horror tales of tribunal panels giving parents a truly hard time. Parents are supposedly able to represent themselves at tribunal, but in reality, they can't. It's stacked against them. The panel consists of three high ranking professionals in the education system. The local authority has a lawyer to represent themselves against you, the family. They also send another expert witness. In our case, this was the speech therapist who was running the specialist autism nursery which we were appealing against our boys going to.

How could we as parents represent ourselves against experts? Jonathan was a government lawyer and had no experience of special educational needs. We had no option but to pay a special educational needs (SEN) solicitor to represent us at a high cost. We also needed expert reports from both an educational psychologist and a speech therapist. And of course, it was all double the cost with twins. On the tribunal day itself, we had to pay three experts to attend including our programme consultant. The expense was eye watering and we winced every time we opened another bill. There was no other option but to pay up. We had to prove the very real progress our boys had made in the past seven months in order to stand any chance of winning the funding we desperately needed.

The tribunal was held in a room, but to me, it felt like we were going into court to fight for our boys' futures.

A week before, the local authority Richmond decided to withdraw its in house solicitor and instruct a specialist education barrister against us. We were told this was quite unusual and meant Richmond LA was making a big effort to win against us. Suddenly, we had to find a barrister and brief him at short notice to represent us. I didn't really understand why we needed a barrister too but that is how it works. It meant even more money to find. Going to tribunal cost literally thousands and thousands of pounds and we had to weigh up the risks. If we lost, we would have spent a huge sum of money on legal costs which could have been spent on another year's therapy. Even if we won, we would not be able to recoup any of the tribunal costs or the costs of the programme until that date. No wonder there weren't many families doing their own therapy; they couldn't afford to.

The mental toll was costly. Jonathan and I were sleeping badly, all our thoughts were consumed by the tribunal and while we tried not to dwell on the 'what if we lose' calculations, they were ever present in our heads. We would sit down at supper time and however hard we tried to avoid them, the circular conversations would continue:

'Do you think the supervisor's report shows enough progress?'

'What if we win funding for Benjamin, but not for Thomas?'

'If we lose, shall we sell the house?'

I was mindful that however hard it was for us, there were other families who would not have either the financial or mental resources to fight as we were doing and that their children had little chance of ever getting what they really needed.

We believed that money spent on the boys now would mean they would need less social care and less support in the future. It shouldn't be just about money though. For us it was about our children's future quality of life.

Years later, our boys needed far less support than was predicted. The long term costs of their lifetime care will be so much less than anticipated. Their happiness and accomplishments cannot be measured in any monetary way but are monumental. Early intervention transformed their lives.

'What will you do if you lose?' I was asked. 'Will you continue with your programme?'

Yes, we would continue; how could we not, seeing the progress that the boys had made? We had no money left and we would have to sell our house if we lost. But we needed to go in fighting and believe that we were going to win. All our lives were in the balance depending on the outcome of that one day.

We won.

It was one of the worst experiences of my life. At times, it felt like cross examination. We were even accused of lying at one point. I said that we used verbal praise, time on the computer or a toy as rewards for the boys but never gave them food as rewards. The speech therapist contradicted me saying we bribed the boys with chocolate to make them speak. Later, talking to my tutors, one of them said that on the morning when she visited us, she had been teaching Thomas the word 'chocolate' and had been giving him little pieces. My credibility was questioned; unknowingly, I had lied.

We took photos of the boys to place in the centre of the table. We wanted to remind the panel we were talking about our children and not names on a piece of paper. The process was dehumanising and brutal. We were fighting for our children's futures. The local authority was fighting to save money.

They asked us why the boys needed the programme. I thought

I would be nervous, but the need to represent them gave me the courage to speak out confidently and positively.

I had to be the voice for my boys that they didn't yet have.

During the afternoon, Richmond hurriedly offered us some nursery sessions to make up the hours to the statutory recommended 20 hours which the boys required, as the nursery placement they had offered was only four mornings a week. At this point, I retorted that my boys needed education and therapy, not childminding.

It was an anxious two week wait for the tribunal decisions. They came by post. We could hardly bear to open the envelope.

We had won. From then onwards, the costs of our programme would be paid by the local authority.

The relief was enormous. Jonathan and I opened a bottle of champagne that night after the boys had gone to bed. We could finally sleep again and stop stressing about the tribunal which had taken over our lives. Our boys had funding for the therapy they so desperately needed. We didn't have to sell our house. We had been through unnecessary stress. We should not have been forced to fight so hard for our boys' education. It was our first real taste of fighting for what our children needed. Little did I know that this was the first major battle of many more to come. Advocating for and fighting for our children turned out to become a constant thread throughout their lives.

It was exactly a year since they had been given the autism diagnosis. What a year it had been.

Life returned to whatever 'normal' now meant for us.

For me, that meant my longing for another baby returned. I had two young boys, both with high needs and a young baby. I was exhausted caring for all the boys but I felt like time was running out for me. I was now 41 years old.

I had another painful, horrible miscarriage a few months after the tribunal. I can't believe I am writing about my seventh miscarriage. Seven. A shocking number. It wasn't caused by the stress of the tribunal. Stress doesn't cause miscarriages. I wished I did know what caused them so I could have done something, anything, to stop it happening. I had stopped telling people each time I conceived. The distress of having to tell them later that I had miscarried again was too awful. I couldn't bear to hear their platitudes. We all have our own paths to go down and I was determined to carry on down mine, no matter what other people thought or said.

Another three miscarriages in a row meant I could be referred again but to a different recurrent miscarriage clinic this time. Again, after months of testing, they found nothing wrong; there was no cause, so there was no treatment. The consultant's advice was to give up. I wasn't ready to give up. I think by this stage, Jonathan wanted to move on and put the miscarriages behind us but I couldn't. I was like a gambler, each time believing that this pregnancy would be successful.

We were constantly hearing about therapies or interventions which might help the boys. Now that the tribunals were over, we had a little more time and energy to investigate some of them. They varied from giving nutritional supplements and restricting certain foods to physical therapies like osteopathy. There were so many, it was hard to know which, if any, to try.

Removing gluten entirely from all the food they ate helped some autistic children. There were various theories about why and how it exacerbated behaviours such as hyperactivity. The boys had lived on pureed food until their autism diagnosis due to their enormous, recurrently infected tonsils. By the age of three they needed to start learning to chew to develop their muscles for speech but when we stopped feeding the boys meat, chicken, fish and vegetables in pureed form, they refused to eat them. Thomas would only eat bread, pasta and pizza. Someone said:

'He is addicted to gluten. If you remove it, he will eat other food.'

'They get 'high' on gluten, they will calm down if they don't eat it.' I heard from another parent whose child's behaviour had changed drastically since becoming gluten free.

It wasn't easy to implement but it was definitely worth trying. Being gluten free meant Thomas just ate grey, bland pizzas. He still didn't want to eat anything else but bread and pasta. No change at all. If it wasn't the gluten he liked then maybe it was the texture? Or maybe he liked bland foods? The gluten free bread tasted like cardboard and was barely palatable unless toasted, but he still ate it.

It made no difference to either of them. There were no changes at all in their behaviour or their preferences for different foods. We did a six month trial before we abandoned it. Being gluten free obviously helped some children, but not our boys. When we reintroduced gluten slowly back into their diet, we noticed no difference either. In some ways, I was secretly quite relieved that it hadn't made any difference. We could go back to trying to get them to eat a more varied diet but of course, if it had, we would have stuck with it.

In July that year, I was filmed for a BBC Newsnight TV programme in our house. Luckily, it was just a very small film crew so it wasn't too imposing or scary. They recorded me talking about the tribunal and how much it had cost us, financially and emotionally. It was quite a long slot and we stayed up 'late' to watch it as it was past our bedtime in those days. We were in a few newspaper articles, too, that year. I wanted to make people more aware of autism and its difficulties so I was always willing to talk. One article was about how the boys ran around in supermarkets while people looked at us in disapproval. The thing was, they looked just like every other child, and there were no physical differences in their appearances, only in their behaviour. People often wrongly assumed that they were naughty and we were bad parents.

One afternoon in Osterley Park, Thomas ran off and was chasing Canadian Geese. He was having a great time, giggling as he made them run away. I had Hector in the buggy and Jonathan was with Benjamin. I was watching Thomas intently. A woman came up and remarked crossly:

'I suppose you think he is clever, chasing geese. You should stop him.'

I explained that he was autistic and that I couldn't easily 'stop him'. She then responded

'You should keep him on a lead then' and strutted away.

There were no words. I didn't respond. My child was not a dog. Remarks like that have stayed with me forever.

Our boys brought us so much joy. They were so happy, interested in everything and curious about their world. They were not 'shut off' from the world around them, in the way people often thought autistic children were, but trying to make sense of it. Without language, it was much harder for them to do so. They got frustrated when they couldn't communicate. That frustration caused anger and sometimes meltdowns. How else were they to make their feelings known?

Everyone says they just want their children to be happy; that was so true for us. Thomas had long meltdowns where he would throw himself to the floor and scream and scream. If anyone tried to touch him, apart from me, he would kick and hit, not to hurt people but to keep them away from him. This was his method of communication until we could give him an alternative one.

He instinctively liked or disliked people and tended to make his preferences known. There is no grey area with him. To be liked by Thomas is a wonderful thing, he is loyal and loving but to be disliked by him made life hard for whoever was in the firing line. His grandmother, Liesel, didn't know what to make of this little boy who was unpredictable in so many ways and not the grandchild she expected. He picked up on her wariness and would scream when she came in the front door. It upset her greatly and made her increasingly even more wary of him, a vicious cycle for them both. Eventually, we worked out a way of pairing her with something positive. She would arrive and immediately hand him a mini bag of chocolate buttons. It worked. He stopped screaming when she arrived. She relaxed a little after time and he became easier around her. But, they never developed a close relationship. She tried her best on an intellectual level by reading articles and books about autism in a quest to understand the boys but on a physical level, she couldn't cope with their not being able to talk or behave as she expected little boys to behave.

It was sad for all of us. The boys were unaware they were missing out by not having doting grandparents or uncles and aunties. They knew their tutors better than any of our family. It was only us parents who grieved the lack of family support. I could empathise with Thomas at times. When the LA refused to pay for the boys' therapy, I wanted to scream and shout, too. How satisfying it would have been to refuse to stop screaming until they agreed to pay. Jonathan and I are both very reserved in some ways. We have been taught to repress our anger and to be civilised in any situation. We held onto our stress and internalised it. Perhaps it would have been healthier to have expressed our frustration a bit more like Thomas did. I don't think many of his colleagues at work were aware of Jonathan's situation at home. There was little allowance made in those days for people's private lives, certainly it wasn't encouraged to talk of anything very personal. He needed two very separate personas and a strict dividing line between the two which was his cycle ride to and from the office.

I didn't want to suppress Thomas' feelings. I wanted him to be able to express himself better which meant giving him language to do so.

It would have been easier to let him carry on as he wanted to. Not to battle with him, to leave his hair uncut, to let him walk around in socks and no shoes, to let him eat anything he wanted. We didn't know how he felt; he couldn't tell us. We all teach our children to wear a coat when it's cold, to eat with a spoon and not their hands, to use a toilet. Those things are necessary for comfort and health. Although teaching them to Thomas was often hard, it would make his life much easier in the long run.

We met another family with a little boy of a similar age with autism. Their son sat on the sofa the whole visit, saying nothing and doing very little. Our boys in contrast, picked up every toy they could find, charging around making a lot of noise and mayhem. The parents observed this and then asked us:

'How do you manage to take them out? What hard work it must be having boys like yours.'

They felt sorry for us. Their child in comparison was easy to manage. I felt the opposite. I felt sorry for them. To me, it appeared that their son had little interest in other people and anything around him. In contrast, my boys were engaging with their surroundings albeit in an uncontrolled and socially inappropriate way. We could work on that.

We had adjusted to a different daily life, a different way of living. We weren't angry. I don't think we were angry that they were autistic. We were angry, though, with a system that wasn't prepared to help them. And, we were sad at times. We were still grieving for the children that we had imagined they might have been, for the things we hoped they would do. That grief would come and go at different points in their lives and often surprise us with its intensity. Sometimes, it was for us and what we felt we were missing out on, but at other times it was for the boys when they were missing out and they knew it. Witnessing their distress that they didn't have friends like they wanted to have, or were unable to do things their peers could do, was heart breaking.

Alongside our boys, living in a leafy, affluent area of South West London, we had so many examples of typically developing children surrounding us.

'Will they ever talk properly? Will they be able to work? Will they always live with us?' were questions that the comparisons threw up.

I stopped going to playgroups. I couldn't bear to hear the other mothers speaking proudly of what their children could do.

'He's so clever, he can read and he's only just turned four.'

'Well, we wanted him to be bi-lingual so he's learning French at nursery.'

I had to withhold the urge to scream 'I wish my boys could speak one language.' We felt like we didn't fit in at all.

Outside of therapy hours, we couldn't leave the boys with anyone else who might jeopardise their hard won progress. Once they were able to ask for an item by name, we needed to be consistent and encourage them to try to say the actual word. We didn't actually have any offers of help and couldn't afford to pay the tutors for additional hours, so it meant that I had no real help at all for a few years. We did try a few live in au pairs, but they didn't work out. Mostly, they just wanted board and lodging in London. They were perhaps too immature to grasp the situation. In the end, it was less work to look after the boys myself than to have another person in the house that also needed looking after, albeit it in a different way.

The boys couldn't be left alone for a minute. Ideally, we needed one to one help for each of them all the time. Incidents did happen, like the summer afternoon that Benjamin deliberately threw a small metal Thomas train through a large window. It wasn't the first window he had broken on purpose. He loved the instant smash and shattering of glass. He was jumping up and down, flapping his hands in excitement. For me it was a nightmare. I had three little boys who didn't have any idea of danger running around gleefully at the mess and laughing at the huge hole in the window. It was one of those situations again when I had to decide on priorities. I had to get them away from the glass but how could I keep them away? I put on a video to distract them and kept shooing Hector away. I swept up the glass and covered the hole with a big piece of cardboard. While I was doing it, Benjamin ran out into the garden. The video hadn't kept him occupied for long enough, his attention span was so short. He was trying to saw through a new Lilac tree sapling I had just planted with an eating knife. He managed to make quite a mess of the trunk while I was taping up the cardboard. I was furious but shouting had no effect on Benjamin. He kept sawing the tree. I think he knew I was angry as I was shouting and I rarely shouted. He didn't care. Objects were just meaningless things to him. My anger was meaningless, too.

He had wanted to break the window. It was hugely gratifying for him to see it smash. He wanted to cut down the tree. It was a hard concept for me to understand that he didn't care at all about my distress or anger. He did test my limits at times, but I am able to say truthfully that the worst I ever did in retaliation was to burst into tears of frustration, not that he noticed or cared.

Thomas was very much more aware of my emotions. It upset him greatly if he thought he had upset me in any way. He is still like that now, another example of the twins being polar opposites at the time. I am glad to be able to say that eventually, as a teenager, many years later, Benjamin became much more aware of others emotions and has become a very caring young adult.

I can hardly bear to write it again, but in the autumn I had another miscarriage, the fourth since Hector was born and now the eighth that Jonathan and I had suffered. The details are no longer relevant of how and where it happened, let alone why. But, the emotional pain was relevant; it added another layer on top of all the sorrow of the previous losses.

We had been married six years and in those six years I had given birth to three boys, the eldest two had been diagnosed with autism, we had started early intervention programmes for them and I had had eight miscarriages. Oh, and we had bought a house and renovated it with major building work.

During those six years, we carried on, trying our best to lead some version of a family life involving birthdays, holidays and maintaining some friendships, but it was not the life we had expected six years ago, saying 'I do' at the altar.

Friendship wise, it was hard going. We didn't have the time or energy to go out. We certainly didn't have the money to pay for babysitters. We never got to catch up or talk to any other adults if we had the boys with us. While other parents chatted to each other as their children occupied themselves or played with other children, we just ran after ours. We mostly gave up trying to socialise.

One weekend, we took all the boys to a friend's party in Nottingham overnight. The boys were in strange beds in a strange house and would not settle at all. We took it in turns to sit upstairs with them. I had to eat my plate of food on the stairs outside their room as I couldn't leave them. What was the point of sitting on the stairs all evening not talking to anyone? It was of no benefit to any of us.

My new local friend, Mary became my closest friend. She had a son the same age as the twins and a daughter eighteen months younger, both very bright and able children. She was unfazed by my boys and totally non judgemental, something we had begun to realise was rare in people who did not have or work with special needs children. Her children accepted our boys for who they were, and they would all mess about happily together. I was so grateful to have a friend and a safe place where we could all go and just be ourselves. We spent many happy hours at each other's houses. My boys would not sit at a table to eat without the distraction of a video to keep them sitting still long enough to eat. I had a small nest of little coffee tables and children's chairs and they would sit in a row at one table each. Mary's children in contrast, would sit properly at the kitchen table to eat. Her children never questioned this and Mary never judged me or the boys. This was how things needed to be done and she instinctively understood that.

In the summer we were often in the garden with all the children and a paddling pool. One day Benjamin wandered inside naked.

'What is Benjamin doing? He's very quiet, he must be up to something.'

I went to investigate and caught him doing a poo on her living room floor. He looked a bit shifty but happily ran back into the garden. We just laughed and I cleaned it up.

Apart from Mary's friendship, I often felt isolated. There were not many support groups and nothing like the level of social media that there is now. I found one rather eclectic website online for autism parents to ask and answer questions. Late in the evenings, occasionally a thread would be hijacked or veer off topic and become a witty exchange. These became my favourite threads. Autism parents seem to share a similar dark sense of humour. I think we need it to get through some hard days. We have to laugh sometimes or we would cry and we do enough of that.

Chapter Six

'All my attempts to engage him in a reciprocal social interaction failed' - the paediatrician writing about Hector.

Mainstream school in September for Thomas and Benjamin would be a huge step and a challenge for them. They would be four and a half by then. We had a preliminary meeting with the head teacher and a member of the LA.

'What will happen if one of your tutors is off sick?'

'The boys won't come into school. I will keep them home with me.'

'You will end up in court if your children do not attend enough school.'

It didn't bode well, but by then, we were already committed and had the school named on the boys' statements.

The boys only went in to school for short periods with their one to one tutors as they couldn't sit still or concentrate for long. Having very little language meant they weren't able to access much of the curriculum. The tutors taught them academic skills quietly at home often using different methods from those at school. Thomas started writing words and then painstakingly adding the little connecting loops afterwards to make an exact copy of how the joined up writing they used at school looked. We asked and were granted permission to teach him straight forward single letter formation.

From a social aspect, it was really beneficial for them to integrate with other children. Understanding social cues and being able to socialise was one of their targets to work on. Left alone, they observed other children playing but didn't attempt to join in. Once settled in school, the tutors set up games like tag in the playground which didn't require any language so the boys could run around and play with their classmates. We even managed to arrange a few play dates at our home in the first year.

I sometimes wondered how life would have been if the boys didn't have autism. I imagined dropping and picking them up from school every day, perhaps forming friendships with the other mothers as we all waited in the playground. We lived in a middle class area where most parents were eager for their children to succeed and play dates with barely verbal, socially different children were not on their agenda.

In the youngest class at school, the unspoken rule was to invite the whole class to birthday parties which did mean our boys were usually included. However, I would always have to stay with my boys at any party and usually ended up helping. I felt resentful at times, that I helped, while the other mothers left their children and had a few precious hours to themselves, which I craved. As we had decided it would be better for the twins to be in separate classes, we recklessly invited both classes of 30 children to their 5th Birthday party, held in a recreation centre. That was the one and only time they had a combined birthday until they were teenagers as it was chaotic despite some of the other mothers staying to help me in return. In subsequent years, we gave them a party each on consecutive Saturdays. Mostly they were swimming parties or those run by the instructors at the local gym club, parties where it really didn't matter how much language you had.

Their school wasn't a special needs school; it was firmly mainstream and none of the parents had any understanding of autism. A few mothers talked to me but most avoided me. Did they think my boys were disrupting their children's education?

Or did they not know what to say? Over the years, we stopped attending Christmas and class drinks as I invariably came home and cried after spending an evening listening to people talking about their children's achievements. Our lives were such a contrast to theirs. The boys had lovely tutors at the time who were kind to them and fun. They enjoyed their hours at school and were unaware of being socially excluded. We, in contrast, were rarely made to feel welcome by either the school or the parents and were very aware of it. Autism affected all of us, not just the boys.

I booked Hector into the crèche at a local art college. I joined a weekly calligraphy class in the hope of having a few hours where I did something for myself and not housework or admin. Disappointingly, one of the tutors who worked on Tuesdays frequently took the day off at the last minute for various reasons. It meant I lost my precious 'me' time. She didn't realise or care how important those few hours were to me. Months later, I had to dismiss her as she wanted to be away travelling more often than she was at work. We were no more than a job to her to fund her holidays.

I set up a monthly local book group, one of the criteria being that we would try to avoid talking about our children. It became a very tight knit group for many years and provided a much needed outlet for me. Reading has always been a big part of my life. Regrettably, many years later, a new member joined who made it very obvious that she disliked me and the books I recommended. She made me feel so uncomfortable that I felt I had no option but to leave the book group. I couldn't face any more conflict or personal rejection. I mourned the loss of that group for a long time.

Halloween and Christmas were occasions that we did our best to join in with, despite the boys not really understanding what was going on. We wanted them to experience their childhoods like we had as children and like the children around them did. Mary and I took our children 'trick or treating' dressed in Halloween outfits. None of them could bear face paints or wear masks but were alright with wearing a basic black cape or skeleton top and trousers. We knocked on the door of a local friend who had a daughter the same age. Ingrid and I had spent hours and hours talking and walking our babies round Richmond Park in the early days and their house was very familiar to the boys. When she opened the door, Benjamin ran in to watch their television having no idea that it wasn't a social visit. How could I explain the concept of knocking on doors for sweets, but only once a year? Thomas hung on to the buggy handle, not understanding at all what we were doing or why. Hector, who was not yet two, happily ran up to doors shouting 'trick or treat' and waiting for sweets. It was a glimpse into what life was like for a child without autism. It was poignant, though, to see my little boy able to do what his older brothers could not, although he was nearly three years younger. Moments like that made me grateful for Hector's abilities but sad at the same time for Thomas and Benjamin.

Would they ever be able to join in? How would it affect Hector's life to have two autistic brothers? Would he end up becoming a carer for them later on? That was a sobering thought; my little toddler perhaps destined to be a carer one day.

The twins needed to learn to swim for their own safety. Hopefully, they would enjoy it too. After many months, with the help of a special needs swimming teacher, they were eventually able to swim doggy paddle style and most importantly, keep afloat. The water was blissfully warm in the local hydrotherapy pool, so it was easy to encourage them in. I always got in too and we encouraged them to swim between us, gradually increasing the distance apart. Thomas hated rain or getting accidentally wet in any form but he loved his baths at night and he loved swimming. Was it because he could anticipate the water and felt in control? Or was it the prickly sensation of rain on his skin that he intensely disliked? Either way, it was a relief that he really enjoyed his swimming sessions.

Walking could be hazardous too. There were terrifying times where we lost the boys. That sounds awful, doesn't it? How could we lose a child? But they were so swift. They could disappear silently in moments. We would be walking along pushing Hector's buggy with the boys beside us, just behind or just in front. Suddenly, we would realise one boy had disappeared, often behind the nearest tree but on rare occasions, nowhere in sight. We would call their names, but they never responded to their names, so that didn't work.

We regularly walked in Kew Gardens because there was no traffic, no roads, no dogs and no cyclists. Once, Thomas literally 'disappeared' into thin air. We called and called, making ever widening circles to find him. I tried my best to stay calm but as time went on and we couldn't find him, I started to panic. Where could he be? Had someone snatched him? Was he hurt? He had no language at the time. I wanted to run but I didn't know in which direction to run. I shouted and shouted his name while my heart beat wildly.

Fortunately, Kew Gardens have their own police. They alerted the gate keepers and contacted their own officers within the grounds. We didn't have a mobile phone in those days. It was hard to know whether to stay where we were or to walk further away looking for him. By the time he was found by a stranger, he was a good twenty minutes walk away. He must have run all the way there. When we were reunited he just smiled at me. He was totally unconcerned, whereas I was a sobbing wreck. The social mechanism which usually means a child needs to know where their parent is didn't apply to our boys. They had no anxiety about being lost. They just expected us to turn up. Thankfully, we always did.

The worst incident at Kew was when we were having tea one afternoon inside the Orangery. There was a wall with a gap either end masking the toilets behind. The boys were running in and out of either exit in a circuit, playing. It wasn't a problem until Benjamin didn't appear for a while. We checked the toilets;

he wasn't there. The staff checked the kitchens; he wasn't there either. That's when we started to panic. How could he have run past without us seeing him? It wasn't possible. The police were called and started searching the grounds. He was non verbal at the time; it was cold outside and he wasn't wearing his jacket. I had to stay with Thomas and Hector who was asleep in his buggy in case Benjamin returned. Jonathan went to join the search. It was the longest imaginable half hour. I was weeping, I was terrified by then. There were ponds and he couldn't swim. How could he have got out without us noticing?

Finally, an alarm went off. Benjamin was found in a conference room, also hidden by the wall but only accessed by a key code. He was too small to even reach the code box high up on the wall, so they hadn't looked in there. An employee had gone in. She obviously hadn't noticed the small boy following her in. She had left, turned the lights out, and closed the door. Somehow he managed to set the alarm off. Again, like Thomas, he wasn't distressed. He was handed back to us and seemed totally unfazed. He just grinned, like nothing had happened. I never wanted to experience that level of fear again.

But, we did manage another terrifying episode the following year. Thomas 'disappeared' while we were walking on Wimbledon Common in quite a remote area. The police mustered a helicopter as the common is totally open, vast and surrounded by busy roads. It wasn't like Kew, which was 'safe' and contained and where no child could get out of the gates unaccompanied. We were terrified. He had very little language. He had no sense of danger, he could be anywhere. As I gave his description to the police and told them what he was wearing, my fear grew. Fortunately, as we were calling his name loudly some walkers heard us. They had walked past him while he was hanging on some railings, happily watching some horses. The helicopter was cancelled just in time. Thomas greeted us with a big smile. He had no awareness of the panic he had caused. He didn't know that he had been 'lost'.

We went on self catering holidays to Cornwall or Devon sometimes taking tutors with us, partly for the need of another pair of hands because of the 'running away and getting lost' factor. It wasn't ideal for many reasons and we realised that holidaying on our own as a family was the only way to get some sort of break. Staying in a hotel wasn't an option as the boys needed to be safely locked inside with us at night.

It was good for the boys to experience new places. We would hang around in the unfamiliar holiday house for the first day, while they adjusted to the change. Increasingly we went out for longer periods each day. Although holidays were really hard work, we told ourselves that the more we persevered with exposing them to new places and new surroundings, the easier it would get each time. At least, that's what we hoped for.

One unusual thing we had to manage was that the boys absolutely refused to get in an unfamiliar bath, and would scream if we tried to put them in one. Some holidays it meant that they didn't have a bath at all. Once, in desperation, bringing Hector back to the house covered in sand and salt, I knew I had to do something. All the boys had eczema and couldn't tolerate soap or bubble bath. Salt and sand would irritate his skin too if I didn't wash it off. I had an idea. I filled the bath and got in. Jonathan handed Hector to me and he tolerated sitting on my lap while I washed him. Years later, I ended up with all three boys squeezed in with me in a small standard sized bath. I don't know how we all fitted in, as there certainly wasn't much space left for any water. I had Benjamin in front of me with Thomas in front of him and Hector on my lap. We sang 'row, row, row your boat' as the water overlapped the edges and flooded the floor. It had become our thing, to bath together on holiday.

In late December, Hector turned two. He was a gorgeous, happy boy who had many single words by now and a smile for everyone. His angelic face suited his personality. I was so grateful to have him in our lives, my little ray of sunshine. When I felt low, I only had to see him to instantly feel cheered.

That Christmas, he ripped open his presents and those of his older brothers. The twins didn't get the point of presents. Why didn't they want to tear the paper off? If we helped them to tear the paper and they had a new toy in front of them, why weren't they excited to play with it? Presents were received like a lead balloon; they didn't want them. They had very limited play skills so toys were of little interest. Hector was three years younger but already far ahead of his brothers developmentally and socially. He happily took control of all the presents.

I had longed to have a family of my own to share Christmas with. Christmases in my family had not happened for many years due to my parents' divorce. Jonathan's family did not celebrate in any major way either. He and I had gone away together for a week to Scotland with the walking club the first Christmas we met. So I had free rein to create Christmas myself. Christmas with the boys for many years wasn't really Christmas as I had imagined it. Christmas lunch? They were still eating pureed food at the age of three. What were crackers? Frightening things that made you jump when you pulled them. Who was Father Christmas? How do you explain him to a child with no language? Why would they want to 'talk' to a strange, scary man with a big white beard? They wouldn't wait in a queue for anything. They certainly weren't going to queue to see him. But I hung out stockings for all the boys and we left carrots for the reindeer on the fireplace. I was starting family traditions even if they didn't understand them.

This was the first year we took them to see the Snowman ballet. It was visual and needed no language to follow the story. I had the video and we played it daily for weeks before we went so the boys were familiar with it. When we got to the actual show, thankfully, it was faithfully reproduced exactly like in the film. We sat close to the stage so the boys could see it all really well. Hector wanted to get off my lap and run. I clung to him and kept him occupied pointing things out to him. The boys loved it; the magical flying scene and the train whizzing across the stage were the high points for them. I was making memories for my boys and creating our own, new family traditions.

Going to see The Snowman on the last Saturday before Christmas every year became one of our most sacred family traditions. Hearing 'walking in the air' made me tearful every time. We took them sixteen years in a row until finally, the boys declared they were too old for it. By then, I am sure any of us could have stepped up on stage to join in as the choreography never changed a step from year to year. Benjamin knew the exact moment the train would appear and would shriek with anticipation.

Hector had a two year toddler check with the health visitor. Everything was fine. He was meeting all his milestones on time. He could speak! For us, that was like a tiny miracle. He had 50 – 60 words and was starting to combine two words together. We had a typically developing child. He would be able to do the things we had dreamt that the twins would do. He would go to nursery and school alone, without tutors. He would lead an independent life. Who knew what he would grow up to do? It didn't matter. He could be whatever he wanted to be.

Towards the spring, we noticed that Thomas and Benjamin were learning new words every day, but Hector seemed to be losing them. That couldn't be right, could it? He learned new words but then he forgot them quite quickly. He was also losing familiar words he had used for a while. Surely you couldn't 'lose' speech for no reason?

Hector was regressing slowly right in front of our eyes. No one else noticed for a few months; even I wasn't sure I wasn't imagining it. I didn't want to even think about it. I started to keep a list of the words he knew and used. The list was slowly dwindling away. Both the health visitor and speech therapist thought he was progressing well. When I said I was worried about him, someone at an assessment said:

'Don't worry. Look how good he is at puzzles. He's fine.'

That was not reassuring to me. My older boys were severely affected by autism in many ways but I knew how good they were at puzzles. To me, that was a warning light.

Some days I thought his eye contact was fine, on other days not. Mary and I would spend hours observing him, constantly trying to pin hope on little things he was still doing.

'He looked at you, phew, he's alright.'

Although the changes were slight on a daily basis, over the months they added up to a devastating change.

Jonathan and I were by now extremely worried. His parents thought we were being overly anxious. To be fair, everyone else thought so too. I started looking up symptoms online and then I couldn't bear to read what it said; that too familiar 'A' word started to appear. Autism. I stopped reading. I wasn't going to consider it. This excruciating cycle of worry and denial started at Christmas and continued for five very difficult months while we watched and waited.

Hector had been seen by an audiologist. His hearing was declared to be well below normal limits. He had glue ear like his brothers. Maybe that was why he was no longer talking so well? When the glue ear was treated, he would start to talk again, wouldn't he? I was determined he would.

In February he had his ears drained of fluid and grommets inserted under a general anaesthetic. We were able to take him home the same day. I remember putting him into his cot late that afternoon. When I went to check on him 20 minutes later he was doing a headstand with his legs up against the cot sides. He was happy and back to his usual self. He seemed totally unfazed by his operation.

He was very quiet over the next few weeks. Was he shocked by the level of noise around him now that he could hear properly? I think we were determined to remain in denial.

The speech and language therapist wrote in April:

'Hector's eye contact is fleeting and is still only used on his terms.'

'I noticed the use of three words 'bubbles', 'open' and an approximation for juice.'

'Hector has fleeting, self-directed attention skills.'

By late spring, we could no longer pretend to ourselves that there was nothing to worry about. We knew there was. I could not bear it. I could not bear to 'lose' him. I was losing him to autism. I didn't want to believe it. I wanted to believe that he would start talking again, that I had not 'lost' my precious child as I knew him.

He no longer looked at us. He had started to jump rigidly in front of the television. All the signs were there. He hadn't been autistic but there was no longer any doubt to us that he was now.

It was really a formality to get a diagnosis for him. We saw the same private paediatrician in June who had diagnosed his brothers, so there was no need for long explanations about our family history. We left him on a Sunday morning for an hour and a half with the doctor while we took the older boys away for a walk. We avoided talking about Hector during that walk. It was too painful to think about.

The paediatrician confirmed what we had dreaded hearing; that Hector, too, was autistic. Hector had tripped at one stage and fallen over but had not sought help or become distressed that we weren't there and that he was with a stranger. He was in his own world.

The paediatrician wrote in his report:

'All my attempts to engage him in a reciprocal social interaction failed.'

'Hector presented as a self-directed, unaware of danger and active boy.'

'Very little in the way of spontaneous imitation of others actions, no pointing to express interest.'

It had been a slow decline which we had hoped and prayed would be temporary. It was not. It was permanent. The realisation that we now had another young child with classic autism was too much to bear.

I really can't put into words how devastated we were. We had two five year olds barely able to talk and needing full time attention and a huge amount of therapy. We were going to have to do the same for Hector too now.

His whole future loomed ahead in parallel to his brothers. We knew what was to come and we knew how hard it already was. I had first read about regressive autism after the twins' diagnosis. I had thought how cruel it must be to have a child who 'lost' skills. It seemed so much worse than if they had never had them in the first place. Now here we were with our third child experiencing it ourselves.

We told our families and received very little of the sympathy which we so desperately craved. I remember someone ringing a week later. She asked casually how I was. I replied:

'Not so good' to which she then said:

'Oh, are you still a bit down about Hector?'

A bit down? My son had just been given a diagnosis which we knew only too well would impact severely on his life from now on.

I think we would have got more sympathy if he had been knocked down by a car and brain damaged. Maybe then people would have understood a little of what we were trying to come to terms with.

The most heartfelt reaction I got was from a fellow mother at school who rang me as soon as she heard and just said:

'Oh Sarah, how f***ing unfair, I am so sorry.'

That was what I needed, some empathy, but few knew how to give it to us.

Often, people said very thoughtless things.

'Well it's good that it's you as you know what to do about it.'

How could it ever be good that we had all three boys with autism? And no, actually, it's worse that it's me as I know only too well how hard his life and ours is now going to be.

We were more than devastated. We had got through the twins' autism diagnosis not feeling angry. We were worried about their futures and ours, but we didn't really know at that time what to expect and how things would turn out for them. Autism had been an alien word. That sense of the unknown had kept me going and made me determined to do everything we could to help the boys. I dug my heels in and got on with it and any anger I felt was channelled into setting up a programme and going into action mode. But with Hector, I was raging. Why me? Why us? Why our third child too?

I became very angry at what life had thrown us. The fact that he had been developing typically until now felt like a trick had been played on us. It was cruel and it wasn't fair. That is how I truly felt at that time. I had been so grateful for one of my boys to be able to talk and have the chance to live his life as we expected and now it was snatched away from us.

I felt I had been brave about the twins' diagnosis and hadn't allowed it to engulf me in grief. I was no longer brave. The grief overwhelmed me. It was not to leave me for a long time. All I could think was: why us? Why all our boys? What did we do to deserve this? I knew I should be grateful to have had my boys at all after all the miscarriages, but I can't deny how I felt at that time.

One friend said to me:

'You are learning valuable lessons in life and your boys are here to teach you and others around you.'

Yes, but surely two of them with autism would have taught me enough? It didn't need Hector too. Oh, I couldn't bear the platitudes we were given by other people who were certainly not walking in our shoes. Jonathan and I pulled together once again in the absence of family support.

By the time he was diagnosed, Hector had learned and lost possibly hundreds of words and, with them, nearly all eye contact, too.

I had managed somehow to retain a dozen vital words that Hector could still use for things he really wanted. I was familiar with how to teach language word by word so I used that knowledge to ensure he kept those words. It meant he had some basic communication for a biscuit, juice, crisps and his beloved sheet. His 'sheet' was a muslin with a silky label that he liked to feel between his fingers. He had one with him wherever we went. None of the boys had had a special toy, no favourite teddy. We learned this is quite common in young children with autism. The boys formed attachments with inanimate objects like a twig or a discarded toothbrush holder, but even those cherished items would change on a weekly basis or even sooner. There was a favourite purple seal at bath time. I would find teeth marks in its neck, bitten lovingly by Thomas. It was part of a set of small bath toy animals and squirted water out of its mouth when squeezed. I ended up with numerous sets as the purple seal was regularly beheaded. I wouldn't call it a comforter though; it was definitely treated as an object.

Autism to us meant a daily struggle for the boys to learn to speak, to learn to interact with others, to learn to play. It meant a lifelong struggle to learn most of the things that others take for granted that their children will learn. They did learn things but with so much more time and effort and patience than other children needed. Of course, when they did learn something new after great effort, it was a cause for celebration, to hear them finally say 'Mummy' when I had wondered if they would ever be able to say it. Those moments made all the hard work worthwhile. But, it was unbelievably hard at times.

I could now see an altered future for Hector, a future that followed the same trajectory as his brothers. I wondered if I could do it.

I had to do it.

People sometimes ask if it is cathartic writing about the boys. I can honestly say that writing this and having to re read it still brings back overwhelming feelings of pain and distress. My heart is beating faster. My hands are sweaty and there are tears in my eyes. I can never forget that painful period and the profound grief it brought with it.

Chapter Seven

'Why do all three of our children have autism?'

Groundhog day. We had another early intervention programme to recruit tutors for, and to finance. How could we not do for Hector what we were doing for his brothers? We could see the results in front of us. Thomas and Benjamin were our living proof that early intervention worked.

We kept an increasing list of every word they learned 'biscuit' 'train' 'juice' which meant they could ask for wanted items. They also had some abstract words 'up' 'in' 'out' and 'push' which they could use on the swing or to go out to play.

I wondered if they realised what an enormous leap they had taken in learning that words had a meaning and could be used to get what they wanted. We certainly did.

They still had tantrums when they didn't get their own way, but also meltdowns which differed from tantrums and were very much part of their autism. The meltdowns often looked similar to those who couldn't tell the difference but were often sparked by sensory overload. Thomas couldn't tolerate noise which he didn't make himself, so something as seemingly simple as someone singing, could greatly upset him.

Would Hector progress in the same way that the twins had? He had been able to talk. He had eye contact for the first two years of his life. Now he had regressed to where the twins had started from. His autism was different from theirs. Theirs had probably always been present. His had not been. We didn't know if he would improve like they had or not, but early intervention felt like our best chance for getting his speech back.

We had 'lost' our little boy and we wanted him back. We would do everything we could to find him again.

We had to do it. We had no money left and we couldn't remortgage again. We hadn't paid back the additional mortgage we had taken on for Thomas and Benjamin. Years later, we have never paid it off. How on earth were we going to fund his therapy?

We already had a lodger. There was no possibility of me being able to earn any money while looking after three young autistic boys. Our only option was another lodger but we also needed tutors. The logical step was to combine the two. I advertised for a trainee tutor/special needs nanny to live in. The pay was quite good, and all training was free so it was a good opportunity for someone to train as a tutor.

To free up a bedroom, we moved the twins to the smallest bedroom and squeezed a small double bed in there. At night, I put Benjamin in there to sleep and put Thomas into our bed to fall asleep. They wouldn't go to sleep together, too much giggling and messing around. It was great that they could amuse each other but not at bedtime. Later, I would carry Thomas asleep from our bed and lay him down in the bed with Benjamin. It hurt my back. He was six now, a big boy for his age.

We couldn't afford the full 35 hours a week therapy for Hector that the older boys had. He was only two and still had daytime sleeps so as long as he had a three hour session a day that would have to be enough. I was so familiar with the techniques and the programme that I could help him too. I never formally trained up as a tutor myself. I knew some parents who did, but with all three boys, it just wouldn't have been practical. I never formally trained up as a tutor myself. I knew some parents who did but with all three boys, it just wouldn't have been practical. I also wanted to be 'Mummy' and for all the boys to know that I would always be 'Mummy' and not turn into a tutor for a few hours mysteriously. Sessions are quite intensive. Sometimes, you need to be dispassionate and not affected by a child crying because they don't get what they want. For a tutor, this is part of the job but for a mother it is harder. The boys were all very perceptive. I didn't want to blur the two roles

People sometimes think that children with autism don't have empathy for others; that they cannot read emotions. Our boys certainly could. It was their reaction to those emotions which was sometimes different. Benjamin might know I was angry, but he didn't care: breaking windows was fun. Thomas disliked certain people. He thought if he screamed at them they would go away. His method usually worked. Hector by now was in his own world, not reacting to what was going on around him at all. He looked bewildered and confused most of the time.

The one thing all three boys could show us was love. They hugged me. They wanted to sit on my lap. They loved to be kissed and cuddled. They made it very obvious which people were special to them.

We started to plan for the cost and stress of the inevitable tribunal for Hector. We were not intending to fund Hector's programme ourselves in the long term. We didn't have the money.

We wrote to the LA requesting formally that they assess Hector for a statement, a preliminary process which takes six weeks. At the same time, I also rang the nursery he would be attending in September to say that he would need one to one support there. The lady, Janet, who ran the nursery attached to the Baptist church was a lovely woman and very supportive. A special needs panel at the LA (local authority) agreed to fund the nursery's staff for one to one help for him for the three mornings a week he would be there.

The same head of that panel sat on the LA panel a week later considering the need for a statement of special educational needs.

He declared Hector didn't need to be assessed for a statement. So why had he agreed to one to one support if he didn't think Hector had any special needs at all? The game playing had begun.

Hector had been seen by the NHS developmental paediatrician back in April when it was still unclear if he was autistic or not. She had written:

'He is an active boy with a receptive language delay. It is possibly related to the history of mild hearing loss and glue ear'. That old red herring, glue ear.

By June, only three months later, it was very clear that he was autistic. But the statement panel looked at the earlier report and ignored our newer one with a definitive diagnosis of autism. So now we would have to fight to get the assessment.

Were they annoyed that I had spoken out against the LA on Newsnight about going to tribunal for the twins? Did they just want to delay the whole process because they knew we would request the same therapy again? We didn't know why they had refused to assess him when it was obvious they needed to, only that it meant a delay in getting a statement. It was all additional stress for us adding to the paperwork and expense. We appealed against their decision not to assess and a date was set for a tribunal hearing. As soon as they were notified of the date, they backed down and agreed to assess him. The tribunal hearing was cancelled. They had succeeded in causing a four month delay and therefore we would have to find an extra four months programme costs. We were struggling to find the money we needed already. How were we supposed to find the money for those four months that we hadn't budgeted for?

And how was Hector? The Hector we had known had disappeared. Our happy, chatty, inquisitive boy was no longer. He was now almost silent. His eye contact was fleeting with anyone but me. He still played with toys but he played alone. Other children were no longer of interest to him. He couldn't bear noisy places and would hold his hands over his ears when it got too much for him. He had retreated into a world of his own. It was a world where it was hard to reach him. The contrast from six months before was utterly heartbreaking.

I wanted 'my' Hector back. I couldn't bear it. I was in shock still for most of the time. I couldn't believe this had happened to him. Most days, I sobbed. I had to hide my sorrow from the boys so I didn't upset them too. Jonathan was devastated but he had to hold it all together. Now more than ever, we needed his salary. Work for him was respite of a kind. He could switch off and concentrate on something other than autism. I could never switch it off. At times, I was jealous of him going off to work. He could mix in the outside world. I had to live and breathe autism 24 hours a day.

I met a new friend that summer who was to become substitute family for me and the boys. Sally had recently retired and was holding a 'community open house' art show in her house around the corner from us. I wandered in one afternoon and wistfully admired her small but exquisite garden. I told her how pretty it was with all the flowers. She asked me:

'Do you grow flowers?'

'No,' I replied. 'I grew some beautiful tulips but after watching them for weeks until they finally bloomed, my boys snapped their heads off. There is no point in having flowers, except in a vase, our boys trample and trash our garden.'

She says now that she always remembers that conversation and me standing alone looking out onto her garden. It was the start of a wonderful friendship. She has been a huge support to me emotionally ever since. She adores the boys and is there unfailingly at every birthday and party for the boys with big hugs for us all and total acceptance.

I am so grateful for rare, true friends like Sally in our lives.

We went on our last holiday to France that summer with Jonathan's parents and his Uncle Ulli from Australia. We ended up sharing our bedroom with Hector, who as all the reports had said, was a very active child. He was up and down all night. We were sleep deprived all holiday. The brochure had a photo of a lake which didn't exist. We found a 'pond' an hour away to take the boys to. It was exhausting as we couldn't sit down at all for even a moment. We had taken a tutor to help with Hector but she mostly wanted to lie on her towel in the sun, another holiday that really wasn't much of a holiday for us. Jonathan's parents were unable to look after the boys at all and it was even harder for us, managing the boys with other people around than it was when it was just us on holiday on our own.

Another poo story. On this particular holiday, I was trying with little success to potty train Hector. I knew from past experience with Benjamin that it might take a long time so thought I might as well start early. Hector liked to strip naked and climb up the climbing frame in the garden there and then poo from a height onto the grass. There was also an ancient mangle outside which he liked to swing upside down on naked and poo off too. Liesel, Jonathan's mother, was fairly appalled at all of this; she thought we should put him back in nappies. We just laughed and picked up the poo. If we had succeeded in toilet training the twins, we could certainly train Hector. It might require more effort and take longer than it did for other children, but we knew now that most skills were possible to teach with the right support and a great deal of patience.

Shopping on holiday was an interesting challenge. The hypermarket was enormous. There was no way we could chase three small, swift boys and do the shopping. The solution was using two trolleys, one to put all the boys in and one for the groceries. People stared at us with three boys crammed in one trolley, jumping up and down and shouting. Was that how the mad English behaved? It was hard enough explaining to people at home why the boys behaved as they did, but we had no chance in a country where we could speak only school level French. We just ignored the stares. Our boys were enjoying their outing, we didn't care what strangers thought.

That was our last joint holiday. After that, we holidayed alone as a family. It was easier than having to cook and cater for additional people.

We desperately needed practical help but for various reasons, our families weren't able to give us any. We appeared so capable, we always managed somehow. We were perhaps too good at hiding our feelings from anyone but each other. We didn't want to beg for help, so we coped on our own, sometimes badly, but we did cope.

Hector started at nursery. It wasn't an ideal set up as the nursery didn't want our tutors with him, only their own support staff who were funded by the LA. One of our tutors called him 'Little Lord Hector' as the nursery coddled him and had few expectations of him. Unsurprisingly, he didn't learn as fast as his brothers had at the same age. He couldn't interact with the other children. He wasn't lonely but he was alone. It was so sad to see, my previously friendly little boy, not joining in.

Annual reviews were terrifying as we knew the LA was always looking for a reason to pull the boys' funding. We had to fight continually to keep it by proving how well the boys were progressing. This meant keeping massive amounts of data. The head teacher of the boys' school really disliked our programme and the fact that our boys were in her school. At their annual review in October, in front of a table of people, she addressed me very coldly:

'I hear Hector has also been diagnosed with autism, what are you going to do about it?'

She didn't have the grace or empathy for a private conversation or even a sympathetic, 'I'm sorry to hear about Hector.' She really didn't like us.

We had to revisit the local autistic nursery; the same one we had argued against at tribunal for the older boys. It was not what we wanted for Hector either. I didn't cry this time but I knew I didn't want him to go there. He needed more. We had fought at tribunal twice. If necessary, we would fight a third time.

At home, the boys were all very active and they could still only follow basic instructions to sit down or get their shoes. It was a battle to get them all to eat, to get them dressed, to get them to bed, in fact to do anything. They were joyful in themselves which kept us going, always laughing (sometimes inappropriately to themselves about nothing that we could see) and intrinsically happy. I don't think they realised that they were different in any way. They didn't have that insight at the time.

They all loved to watch videos, in particular 'The Wiggles', an Australian children's band who wrote their own songs which they danced and did actions to. The boys and I would join in and copy the moves. We lived on a busy street where our living room window was close to the pavement. Passersby must have laughed to themselves seeing me Irish dancing to encourage the boys to join in!

When they were particularly hyperactive, I would put on the Hungry Caterpillar or Fantasia which had calming music. Benjamin would watch Thomas the Tank Engine videos on a loop if allowed. He watched so many that I too learned the names of all the engines. When he got very excited, he would jump up and down, flapping his hands rapidly. It is one of the known aspects of autism called 'stimming', shorthand for self stimulatory behaviour. Other people, including children, would regard him as 'odd' when he did it. He also made strange high pitched noises when excited.

Hector would stand very close to the television. If he was over stimulated and excited, he would go rigid. He would also jump, very rigidly too. He never flapped his hands. He was totally unaware when he was doing this and was almost surprised by himself. He can tell us now that it was totally involuntary, he couldn't control it and he didn't even know he was doing it until the urge passed and he realised he must have just been jumping.

Thomas' form of 'stimming' was passing objects back and forwards closely in front of his eyes. He would use his hands and stare at them almost cross eyed if there was nothing else available.

Sometimes, he would get really close to something random like the corner of a table and stare intently at it while moving slowly towards and away from it.

'Stimming' meant something different for each of them. There was no text book statement about autism which could be applied to them all.

Late one Sunday afternoon, Hector fell over. Smacking his chin on the edge of a table, his teeth bit through the flesh just under his lip. He went very quiet. I asked Jenny, a neighbour who knew all the boys well, and occasionally babysat, to look after the twins while we took Hector to hospital. As soon as we entered the children's A and E department, he started to scream. He was inconsolable, utterly bewildered, frightened and in pain. Eventually, the staff told us to take him back to the car and they attempted to treat him there. He would not let them touch him, so it was agreed we would bring him back starved in the morning and they would sew the wound while he was under general anaesthetic. As I had been an A and E nurse myself, they gave me glue and steristrips to take home and try to apply later when he was calmer. I put him to bed and managed to stick the wound together. By the morning, it was starting to heal, the edges were aligned and on arrival at hospital, they cancelled his procedure.

The boys loved to run, jump and climb. They played in the garden digging up my plants and making mud craters in the lawn or clambering up the climbing frame and whizzing down the slide. We took them for long walks at the weekends. Being outside seemed to calm them and was good for us too. We could escape everyday life and its problems for a few hours and just be us, a family. Sometimes, we even managed everyday conversations.

'Where shall we go on holiday this year?' 'What do you fancy for dinner tonight?'

Jonathan and I needed some normality, discussing the usual mundane day to day stuff. We couldn't live and breathe autism every moment. We couldn't let it engulf us.

We knew the boys were happy most of the time except when Thomas had a massive meltdown, throwing himself on the floor, flailing his arms and legs and screaming. The rest of the time, though, he was a sunny little boy. It was always lovely to see him skipping along, which he did when he was happy.

But I was still very sad and I was angry. I couldn't stop the feelings of:

'Why me? Why all my boys? What have we done to deserve this?'

The shock of Hector also being autistic was too much for me to cope with emotionally. I couldn't stop crying. I wondered how I would ever get through life like this. Jonathan was more accepting than I was. He was desperately sad about it but he didn't rage against it in the way that I did. It was hard for him too but he didn't have to live with autism twenty four hours a day like I did.

I found a local spiritual church which offered hands on healing. I would lie down and someone would place their hands on me and all the held in grief and emotion would come pouring out. There was no judgement and no misunderstood sympathy there. I was allowed to break down and cry in a safe place. I desperately needed to do that. No one there knew about autism personally but they knew how to support me.

I read something recently about sympathy and how it means people often start with 'at least' when attempting to offer consolation.

'At least, you can afford therapy for your boys.'

'At least, you have had children and not just miscarriages.'

The worst one being about Hector:

'At least, you know about autism.' The implication being that it was alright for me to have a third child with autism. It wasn't alright. It really, really wasn't alright. It wasn't my turn.

People tried to make it better by offering what they saw as a positive angle. Actually what I needed was empathy, an attempt to understand how I felt or if they didn't, to admit it and offer a shoulder to cry on or a cup of tea.

I don't agree with the notion: 'you are only sent what you can handle'. Are special needs parents 'chosen' for that role? If I was chosen, I didn't want to be. I didn't want all my children to have autism.

When one of the healers, Verity, asked me what was going on in my life and I told her, she arranged some counselling for me at a centre where she worked herself. We didn't have enough money for the boys to have therapy, let alone for me to have therapy.

Verity was wonderful and taught me to say no when I needed to. I needed to stop worrying about hurting other people's feelings. I was hurting my own feelings and I was too fragile to do so. At that time, I was on a contact list for others to ring when they needed to talk about twins with autism. A lady used to ring weekly about her sister's twin girls. When it reached the stage where those girls were starting to talk and Hector was regressing and losing his words, I had to say that I couldn't do it anymore. I could barely cope with my own grief. I was not able to take on other people's pain too.

It takes a lot of strength sometimes to say no when it is much easier to be a 'people pleaser'.

Verity also said something very valuable about the boys' autism. It is something I have held onto. Instead of saying:

'Why me?' she asked me to look at it from Hector's point of view. She said:

'He chose the mother he wanted and needed, so he chose you.'

The next Halloween I will never forget, as it was so heartbreaking. I am reminded of it every Halloween when we take the boys out trick or treating. It is embedded forever in my memories and just thinking about it, I can see him now. Hector just sat in his buggy with little interest or awareness of what was going on. He didn't attempt to get out. The contrast with the year before was shocking. It was hard to remember how he had been then, a happy, talkative little boy running up to doors and knocking on them saying' trick or treat', being delighted to be given sweets to put in his bucket. A year later, he scarcely knew what was happening and just sat there looking confused. It felt totally wrong that he was dressed in his orange pumpkin outfit from the last year which I had squeezed him into.

From a report in November:

'Hector is very quickly highly aroused resulting in him being 'hard to reach'.'

'Hector can be immersed in his own agenda and difficult to engage due to either the distracting environment or an emotional 'upset'.'

From our supervisor's report:

'At the start, Hector had 15 words of which 4 were used consistently, he now knows 66 of which 22 are used consistently'. In five months, he had regained some of his words but was still far from where he had been before he regressed.

The LA Ed Psych reported:

'Hector does not seem to be aware of the other children within the nursery. He does not approach them or observe them.'

'Hector very rarely gives others eye contact but does use it with his mother.'

'At times, if the nursery staff need him to do something, they will lift him and carry him since he will not follow their instructions.'

'During my observation there were times when he just wandered around, hopping and running, without seeming aware of what others were doing. At times, he made excited noises and smiled, although this seemed inappropriate since he wasn't focused on anything in particular to provoke these reactions.'

Christmas came and went with another visit to watch the Snowman. We went to Jonathan's brother for Christmas lunch. Unfortunately, they served Christmas lunch about three hours later than planned by which time the boys were thoroughly bored and irritable due to hunger. The boys needed to be fed at exactly the same times each day and Christmas day was no exception.

Before pudding, Thomas left the table and found his coat which he put on making a statement which he didn't have the language for. He wanted to go home. We have had Christmas Day to ourselves ever since, arranging our day around them.

This year, Hector no longer rushed to open everyone else's presents. He wasn't interested at all anymore, but Thomas and Benjamin were now starting to learn what presents meant. It was another poignant reminder of the year before. The boys who couldn't do something last year, now could, and Hector who previously could, now couldn't. Our happiness for the twins' development was spoilt by our sorrow for Hector. Were we ever to get to a point where everyone could really enjoy Christmas?

The local church held a Christingle service where each child was given an orange decorated with sweets to hold, and with a candle in the top, lit while we all sang Away in a Manger. Benjamin blew his out singing 'Happy Birthday dear Spot' (from a video about Spot the dog) instead. The man standing behind us was not amused and grunted crossly at us. I whispered to him that Benjamin was autistic as I relit his candle. The man was very apologetic and kept relighting Benjamin's candle for him as he delighted in blowing it out over and over.

We got a proposed statement for Hector in January naming the local autistic nursery. We had expected that, but the games continued. The LA didn't want to finalise the statement, another delaying tactic. We sent a legal letter to enforce it before we could finally put in papers for an appeal. We were going back to tribunal.

By now, we really didn't have any money for full time tutors for him. The primary school had said I would be in court if my older boys missed school, so whenever a tutor took a day off sick or holiday, one of Hector's tutors who also worked with them, would step in and fill the gap. It meant that he wasn't getting enough hours and so his progress wasn't as good as it could have been but it was all we could do. His programme was also not as consistent as his brothers' had been due to his home tutors not being allowed to accompany him to nursery.

It sounds totally crazy to write that I still dreamt of having another child. I longed for a child that didn't have autism. It wasn't that I didn't love my boys. I loved them fiercely but I badly wanted to experience what I thought other mothers experienced; the miracle of a child talking with no help and no extra input. I thought of the things my boys and I might not experience in the future; college, relationships, living independently. For whatever reasons, I couldn't switch off that longing for another child no matter how hard I tried to look at our situation with perspective. We had three children with very high needs. I could hardly cope with the three of them. How could I cope with another child? Even the hideousness of the miscarriages was not enough to put me off.

We discussed our options and embarked on seeing various specialists. I met a doctor to discuss sperm donation. Removing one of us from the equation might reduce the risk of autism which could be due to the genetics in our family. Sperm donation is much cheaper and easier than egg donation so it was an option which might be financially possible. She said her team might refuse to treat me on ethical grounds, as they would be helping to bring a child into a family with three disabled children. She didn't think it was a good idea for us to have more children. I was so shocked I didn't respond. I got into the car to drive home and burst into tears. She had never met me or my children, but had made a judgement on my fitness to become a mother again.

We enquired about genetic sex selection where we would have IVF and a female embryo could be chosen. Although girls are also diagnosed with autism, the numbers diagnosed with the non verbal classic type that my sons had, were much lower than the number in boys. I was told that I was too old for the pioneer programme which was just starting to offer this for families like ours.

I then asked to see a genetic specialist at St Mary's in London. They could find no genetic reason to explain why all three boys had autism. There was no history of autism in either of our families. I am one of four siblings who between them have eight children all unaffected by autism. In Jonathan's family there was just him and his brother and no family history there either. It was very unusual for all three of our boys to have the classic type of autism. The chances of a sibling also having autism were usually estimated at around 8%. I had heard of other families having more than one child on the spectrum but that often meant one child with classic autism and perhaps another with Asperger's. We were given a scientific estimate of a 50% chance of another child being autistic based on us having three children who were already diagnosed. For Jonathan, that risk was just too high. He didn't want to have any more children.

I couldn't accept it and asked for a second opinion and we were referred to St George's. The doctor there thought that however many children we had, our future risk would always be 20% each time. I heard what I wanted to hear and decided to accept the St George's estimate and not the St Mary's one. It cheered me up a little and I managed to persuade Jonathan that we could keep trying for another baby. He knew how desperate I was to have another child, hopefully one unaffected by autism. I think he probably thought at my age and with the gloomy pronouncement from the miscarriage clinic that it was very unlikely that I would ever conceive again, he could feel safe in agreeing. We talked it over. It was a risk but I just thought 'it can't happen again'. A 20% risk meant an 80% chance of having a child without autism. The odds were in our favour.

There was really nothing anyone could do to medically to help us and so I tried to switch off my desire and sent up a silent prayer saying:

'Please don't send me any more pregnancies unless you are sending me a baby. I can't cope with another miscarriage.'

That seemed to be effective. I didn't conceive again for a long time.

Chapter Eight

'You must never, ever. Don't russy out' - Thomas aged five

As a toddler, Thomas had walked around repeating 'oh dear' and 'all gone' to himself, enjoying the sound the words made. It was 'echolalia', quite common in autism, clusters of meaningless words repeated over and over again. He would also quote lines from videos known as 'scripting', another form of echolalia. It sounded like he could talk but it wasn't real speech as he didn't understand what he was saying; he was just repeating it parrot style. He learned the ABC from watching a Maisie ABC video, which was enunciated beautifully and accompanied by clear pictures.

'G is for Green Grass.'

He knew the whole alphabet within a few days, but could only repeat it verbatim, word for word. I would say:

'G is for Girl', 'G is for Goat.'

Thomas would parrot back in a sing-song voice:

'G is for Green Grass.'

How were we going to un teach him what he had learned? It took weeks of saying 'G is for...' everything we could see beginning with G before he finally grasped the concept.

I used to scour eBay for old Thomas the Tank Engine (TTTE) collectible toys for Benjamin. They were his ultimate 'reinforcers', which meant if we asked him to do something, a 'Thomas' item would be his reward for doing so. Eventually, we had a house full of different train sets, the favourite being Brio, the ultimate wooden TTTE set but we also had other plastic sets which we would get out from time to time to try to offer some variety. I would spend ages building a track all over the kitchen floor only to break it up again at bedtime. Would the boys ever be able to build it themselves one day? An intense interest, bordering on an all consuming passion with Thomas the Tank Engine is quite common among children with autism. Benjamin could spend hours with his trains, either enjoying the 'stimmy' (stimulating) effect of pushing a train round and round repetitively or watching a video where trains whizzed up and down a track. The soundtrack became like an earworm in my head some days.

'Duh duh duh duh de da daa' and Ringo Star's voice on repeat.

'Thomas is a really useful engine, indeed.'

Our house felt like a shrine to Thomas the Tank Engine at times with all the books, videos and crates full of track and trains.

Hector liked Thomas trains too, but was not as fascinated by them as Benjamin was. He liked to have stories read to him from picture books. 'We're going on a Bear Hunt' was one of his favourites. We used to chant it when we were out walking. It backfired on us when we were walking through a tunnel in a cliff heading to Shaldon beach in Devon. We were shouting:

'It's a bear!' 'Quick, back through the tunnel.'

I was playing a game but the boys took it literally. They really thought that a bear was coming and were terrified. The following year, they refused to go in the tunnel in case the bear was there. We could not persuade them to ever go back to that beach again. But, they loved seeing the book come to life when we took them to see a production of it at the theatre months later.

Another of Hector's favourite books was 'Little Rabbit, Foo Foo' about a violent rabbit who goes around bopping everyone on the head. Hector had a wicked sense of humour and would giggle happily, a sign of his dark sense of humour developing which would see him through some difficult times in the future.

I was getting increasingly worn out. Some days I was tearful from sheer exhaustion. I needed help. I needed some respite. I didn't know who to turn to so I self-referred to social services. An unknown woman on the end of the phone asked why I needed help. I replied that my third child had just been diagnosed with autism and I was finding it hard to cope. She just said:

'Oh, we don't cover autism.'

Her implication being that only serious conditions were covered. Wasn't autism serious enough? I responded that my boys had full on non verbal severe autism. She said:

'You sound angry. I shall make a note of that.'

Of course I was angry and that remark made me even angrier. How dare she dismiss my boys' difficulties as being too trivial for their caseload? Eventually, after another call, we did get a social worker to visit. She was sympathetic and ensured that the boys were registered as disabled. They couldn't offer very much but after many months of repeatedly asking, we finally got funding for a few hours respite care a week for the boys, to pay for some after school help.

The paperwork was endless. I was collecting data for Hector's impending tribunal in the summer. I also had to complete some very long, detailed forms for DLA (disability living allowance) which took literally hours. I sat at the kitchen table allocating an hour at a time to fill in a few pages. It was all the time I could spare and it took me weeks to get them finished. It was so depressing, filling them in. The questions asked how much help your child needs with all aspects of daily living, how often they need help and for how long each time. For example:

'Do they need encouragement, prompting or physical help to: wake up/get out of bed/get into bed/settle in bed and then for each sub section 'how often each day' and 'how long each time'. Then there is a box to write more detail.

What do you write about a hyperactive child who refuses to go to bed, won't stay in bed and continually gets out again? How can you quantify time into a neat box? There were 55 main sections with subsections, plus additional boxes to write in on the main form alone. Section 2, entitled 'Help with getting around' was a little shorter but needed more explanations in writing. The biggest obstacle in those forms was explaining that:

'Yes, my child can walk very well. No, he doesn't have a physical problem walking but...because he can run so fast and get across a road in seconds, without looking, he is a very real danger to himself and those around him.'

The boys still had no sense of danger at all. I hadn't been able to run in two directions when I had the twins. Now, I had three to run after. It was impossible to go out alone to places involving streets and traffic. I kept Hector tightly strapped into a buggy until he was way too big for it and his head was hanging over the top edge of it. I needed to explain this very clearly on the paperwork.

The DLA paperwork was to become a recurring headache. It needed redoing every couple of years plus occasional 'spot checks' where all the forms needed rewriting just in case one of the boys mysteriously, miraculously no longer had autism and no longer needed support. Didn't they know that autism is a lifelong diagnosis?

We needed the extra money the DLA provided. It helped to pay for things like their swimming lessons. Apart from all the therapies, other expenses including repairs to the house like smashed windows and replacing the vinyl tiles three times in the bathroom were costly. After paying to have the lounge carpet cleaned several times owing to food stains, we tore it up and had wood flooring put down. What had I been thinking of? A cream carpet was never going to be a good choice.

Benjamin managed to rip the radiator off his bedroom wall when he was only three, somehow snapping the copper pipes at each side. We were in the living room, directly underneath their bedroom, when we noticed water running down the walls. We went upstairs to find the radiator lying on the floor and a small flood. Both rooms needed redecorating once the damp had dried out.

The boys often damaged things by accident as they didn't look where they were going or think about the consequences. If they wanted to throw a ball inside the house, they did it; in a split second they could break something precious like a china bowl or a picture. After a few accidents, we placed most things well out of their reach. We also avoided taking them to their grandparents' houses, which were a minefield of dainty glass ornaments and prized trinkets waiting to be smashed. Their grandparents were always nervous in the boys' presence, anticipating an accident. The boys intuitively picked up on this energy, making them equally jumpy and even more likely to break something. It was better for everyone if they visited us at home.

Benjamin liked hiding in the curtains, wrapping himself in them by turning round and round until he was so twisted up that quite often, he pulled them down. It was a regular job for Jonathan to screw back the lounge's curtain rail into the wall. Mary, my good friend, lent us her immaculate flat in Poole for a few days. While making a cup of tea, we left the boys alone for just a few minutes and walked in to the living room to see Benjamin lying in a pile of curtains on the floor. I rang Mary. We had to find a handyman as her parents in law were on their way to the flat the day after we left and we needed to leave it in perfect order. Hours later, after the damage had been fixed, we caught Benjamin happily twirling in the curtains again.

The twins were just about coping with a few hours at a time of school inclusion. It wasn't easy for them as they were not able to follow much direction. Most of their learning still needed to be on a one to one basis. If Thomas had a meltdown and start yelling and screaming, his tutor would have to try and get him out of the classroom, while he continued to yell. It didn't endear the boys to the school or the head teacher.

Benjamin was very taken with a little girl who he wanted to sit with, talk to and play with but sadly, she wouldn't tolerate him anywhere near her. How could we explain to him that she didn't want to be friends with him and he needed to leave her alone? He then made a friend of a tiny, little girl who was electively mute. They were comfortable with each other as neither of them needed to speak.

The boys learned that other children were unpredictable and that adults were safer to be around as you could anticipate what they would do next; adults would co operate with them when children often would not. Adults also made an effort to understand what they were trying to say. When the children at school didn't understand what the boys were trying to say or do, they tended to get bored and wandered off, leaving the boys puzzled.

Thomas' talent for art started to show itself. At school, he drew a beautiful Chinese dragon on a red envelope for Chinese New Year. The other children asked him if he would draw theirs for them too. It was a social breakthrough for Thomas; because his peers respected him for his art skills they were more accepting of his severe speech delay. He began to create exquisite, detailed models with playdough, mostly animals. We bought him some coloured polymer clay which needs to be baked in the oven to harden. He made tiny, delicate creatures using a single lump, gauging the exact size and pulling out each limb so each animal was made from one single piece. He was so patient, concentrating hard while he made them. It calmed him.

Finally, in July, we had our third tribunal, for Hector this time. He was doing mostly repetitive activities at nursery and he really wasn't learning any language or developing any social skills. It was time we got our programme officially on his statement so that the nursery would allow our own tutors to accompany him and he could start learning vital skills. We found out through the grapevine that Hector's supposed place at the autistic nursery had been given to another child with the caveat that it might only be temporary. It meant they didn't waste the much needed place. It also meant that we had to go to tribunal to fight against taking that place, so it was a calculated tactic on their behalf. If they had been officially 'full', we might have avoided tribunal.

Our solicitor recommended a barrister from the outset as the borough were up for a hard fight. It increased our financial costs. We had to pay for an educational psychologist assessment, a speech therapy assessment and an occupational therapy (OT) report too. We resented paying for a very expensive tribunal process to get what Hector needed. All these reports were unnecessary and we couldn't afford them. Why did the system work this way? What about other parents who couldn't afford to go to tribunal? It meant their children would probably never get the therapy they needed.

On the morning of the tribunal we walked in and the lovely lady who had been made to speak for the LA, against us, was there. She had been advising Hector's nursery on his management and approved of our programme. She and I got on well and the LA had put her in a difficult position. I went straight over to give her a hug which produced some strange looks. You don't hug the opposition when you are about to go into battle.

Minutes before we went in, the LA offered to settle for an amount which would barely cover our legal costs and it was only on an annual basis, so could be withdrawn. It certainly wouldn't pay for Hector's programme. Our barrister suggested that we accept it. He thought we had no chance of winning as he told us the chair of the tribunal panel that day didn't support early intervention programmes. How were we to fund Hector's programme if we accepted the money? I nearly burst into tears, but somehow I held it together. Jonathan and I said no, without any hesitation. There was no question of us settling. We were going in there to fight for Hector and what he needed.

I was asked by the chair of the three person panel why I wanted the early intervention programme. Due to the adrenaline rush caused by our barrister trying to back out, I went into fully assertive, articulate mode and talked convincingly at length. If he wasn't going to fight for us, I was.

My killer line was:

'Hector already lives in a special needs nursery twenty four hours a day. We want him to experience mainstream education with children who are not autistic as he does not have this at home.'

I think the panel accepted that I knew how to run a successful home programme because our older boys were doing well with theirs. We had to wait a few, very anxious weeks for the result. We had no backup plan. If we lost, as our barrister had predicted, we would only have the same option as before, to sell our house. Hector had to have intensive therapy and we would have to find the money somehow.

We won again. We were so relieved. We could open our bottle of fizz and celebrate but I felt angry too; angry that we had been forced through this process. The stress of having to go through a third tribunal hearing had been mentally, emotionally and financially draining. We had won, but it was a win that should never have been necessary.

From the written decision by the tribunal to award the programme that Hector needed:-

'We find that Hector's home circumstances are unusual...we find on the evidence in this case that this opportunity for social interaction is of crucial importance – it is a crucial need for children with autism.'

'As it happens Mr and Mrs Ziegel are particularly well informed with regard to autistic children. We have no doubt that the parental preference in this case is based on a sound foundation of accurate information and wise judgement.'

Not only did we win but the panel were behind us. It felt good to have validation.

We always self-catered on holiday as the boys still only ate a restricted diet and anyway, they could not have sat still in a cafe. They mostly ate lots of pasta but we had added sausages and smiley faces (frozen potato shapes), fish fingers and a few other items slowly over time. We took our own video player in the car with us; one time we even took a television to France and always packed a crate of Brio trains that were familiar to the boys. It made staying in a house away from home a bit easier.

Due to their sensory issues, the boys couldn't tolerate sheets that weren't 100% cotton so we also took their own duvet covers with us. If we tried to put them into t shirts or pyjamas with plastic transfers on the front they would pluck at the pictures with their fingers and pull the clothes straight off. Nylon, polyester and most synthetic fabrics were instantly rejected as too scratchy and irritating. We had many t shirts with holes in the necklines due to ripped out labels which were the ultimate offenders for irritation. Well meaning friends and relatives would gift them clothes which we would have to discreetly give away. It is still the same, two decades later: their clothes are chosen to avoid all sensory intolerances, although labels are now mostly accepted.

The boys loved to visit the seaside, the zoo and mostly outdoor activities while we were away. Taking them somewhere new and different each day could cause sensory overload for them. They would get agitated, irritable and more hyperactive which wasn't easy to manage. Familiarity helped. Going back to the same house time after time and doing the same activities, like visiting the same beaches helped to make it all less stressful. We started taking them on steam trains while on holiday which was Benjamin's absolute favourite activity. We would give them little flags to wave as the trains departed and they would spend hours in the station shop each choosing a new Brio train.

It was good for the boys to have a break from their tutors and for us to have a break from our everyday lives. It would have been much easier to stay at home but we all loved fresh air and walking so a week in the countryside did us all some good and it was precious family time.

In Cornwall one summer, we visited a seal sanctuary. It was pretty dull, two old swimming pools filled with seals. We didn't think it was going to be much of an exciting outing until the keepers came out, armed with pails of fish to feed the seals. Throwing the fish was strictly keepers only, until one of our boys grabbed a fish and threw it. Thomas was delighted and shrieked with joy as the seal leapt for his fish. The keepers handed over the buckets to the boys and we all watched while Thomas and Benjamin spent the next half hour throwing fish. Their joy was contagious. They thought it was hilarious and laughed loudly every time a seal caught their fish. For once, they didn't seem to notice the smell or the sensation of dead, cold, slimy fish on their hands, they were having too much fun. Their little matching cream fleece jackets with embroidered sheep on the front (a gift from Grandma) were covered in fish blood but they didn't care at all. Spontaneous moments like this kept us all going.

We missed travelling abroad. I longed to lie on a beach in the sun, to swim in warm water. It was impossible now. We had no one who could look after the boys for us and if we took them with us, there would be no chance of lying on a sun bed. We certainly couldn't look around galleries and museums with them. Our only attempt at culture on holiday had been to visit the Bayeux Tapestry in France. We had been loudly criticised for the boys running around and had to leave. Jonathan had always gone on skiing holidays before we were married, but he never went again after the boys were born. He said he didn't miss them but I think he did miss exploring new countries. There was no point in hankering after what wasn't possible so we made the most of our breaks in England.

September meant that finally, Hector's tutors could accompany him into nursery. Now that the LA was paying for his tutors, we could afford to only have one paying lodger in our house. We asked our live in tutor to move out so that we could split the twins up and give them a bedroom each.

We were the only family in the country that I knew of running three full time home based therapy programmes. It meant we now needed to fill 30 sessions a week with different tutors coming and going. If a tutor left who did certain sessions, say a Tuesday and Thursday morning, I could never find a new tutor who had the exact same sessions free. They were juggling their timetables too. Recruiting three full time tutors was our best option. The downside was that if one went off sick or on holiday then I had to cover all their sessions. It meant I often had a boy at home with me full time for weeks. The priority was still ensuring that the older boys' sessions were always filled as their school was waiting for an opportunity to make trouble for us. That 'you will end up in court' weighed heavily on my mind.

Our tutors were young people in their twenties, often with psychology degrees. We chose them for their personalities. The boys were very lively and interactive. They needed people who could think fast on their feet and keep up with the speed at which they learned. We had some great tutors who stayed with the boys for years. They took the boys' successes personally and were justifiably proud of the work they did. The not so good tutors would not last very long. They might phone in sick frequently or even leave us for another family who would pay them more. When things got tough and one of the boys had a meltdown, they would decide it wasn't for them.

It was hard trying to manage staff issues as the tutors were so personally involved with us all. Some did not see me as their 'boss' which was great when things were running smoothly but not so easy when issues arose. I was accustomed to people coming and going in our house and no longer felt it was invasive. I was just so grateful to have them and appreciated the changes they were making to our boys' quality of life. Some of them became close friends and part of our extended family. We are still in touch with many of them from years ago and they are as proud as we are at the progress the boys have made over the years.

Jonathan's brother, Nicholas, married Stella that November. Hardly any children were invited to their wedding, which included our boys. We had to pay for two carers, a big expense, to look after the boys at home as one person was not enough for three boys unless it was one of us, in which case we of course coped alone. We were always grateful for the gesture if people did invite us with the boys to social events but often it wasn't practical to take them with us. A few tolerant and caring friends like Liz and Peter their God parents, my friend Mary and a wonderful ex boss of Jonathan's, Roland and his wife Claude insisted on inviting all of us regularly to their houses and always made the boys feel very welcome.

The film, Polar Express came out that autumn. It was the twins' first outing to the cinema. Fortunately, we were able to take them to an autism friendly screening. They were thrilled by the film. As the train raced along the tracks they jumped up and down in their seats causing the whole row of seats to rock. Benjamin was flapping his hands madly in excitement and squealing loudly in delight. To see a film on the big screen like that was magical for them. They couldn't sit still for a moment. No one complained, and no one else's children could keep quiet either. It felt great to be able to take them somewhere new without any judgement from those around us. We bought the DVD and they watched it on a loop for years, the train racing along being Benjamin's favourite part. Every time, no matter how many times he watched it, he was as excited as the first time he saw it.

I took the boys to a Christmas party at a local soft play centre. One of my tutors was no longer able to come with me at the last minute. I'd promised the boys a party so I didn't want to disappoint them. As it was indoors, I thought I could manage all three boys alone. How wrong I was.

There was a magician who the boys were totally uninterested in and food which they couldn't eat; I was trialling a dairy free diet for six weeks as casein was thought to negatively affect some children with autism. It meant no milk products so no cake, no chocolate, no butter. I steered the poor boys away from the party food feeling like a cruel mother, but I felt the need to check some of these theories out. The casein free diet made no difference at all and by Christmas Day, they were back to biting the heads off chocolate reindeers.

The boys all loved the big bouncy castle. Benjamin got a bit over boisterous and jumped on another child. Of course, he didn't do it on purpose but the child was smaller than he was and started to wail. The child's mother was furious with Benjamin and started to shout at him. I explained that he was autistic and couldn't understand what she was saying. She got more flustered and said:

'If he is autistic, what is he doing on the bouncy castle?'

I tried to get him to get off which was not easy with all the other children bouncing away. He of course didn't want to get off and evaded me. Eventually, the woman got so cross that she started yelling at me to take him away and shouting to all the other mothers that:

'She shouldn't be here with her children. That child is dangerous.'

'How dare she bring them and endanger ours?'

Benjamin hadn't meant any harm. He hadn't deliberately hit or bitten her child or even injured them. I had been accused of being a poor mother many times by now. It was hard to be shouted at while trying to capture all three of my boys without help. My saviour was another mother, Sue, whose son was at the same nursery as Hector. She stepped in to defend me. I was in no state to defend myself. I was too upset and too occupied trying to get all the boys away as quickly as I could. She told the woman to stop shouting at me. The intolerance of strangers was sometimes quite startling. I was shaking by then with a mix of anger and sorrow that we were so obviously not wanted at a children's party. Where was her Christmas spirit? The best result of that afternoon was that I had found myself a new lifelong friend and supporter in Sue.

Benjamin couldn't sit still at all; he continually moved and twitched and fiddled. He couldn't pay attention for long enough to learn very much. He also couldn't control his impulsive need to break things or to do whatever he felt the overwhelming need to do. We saw an NHS developmental paediatrician for a diagnosis. He had ADHD (attention deficit hyperactivity disorder). One of the tutors and I filled in identical forms. When the doctor compared them, she said it was unusual for a parent to score a child lower than an outsider did. My scores for Benjamin meant I had quite a high tolerance threshold. That was hardly surprising to me as I spent most days 'fire fighting' and had got used to all the boys and their actions. It was how life was. I didn't know how a child should behave. What was acceptable behaviour? We lived in a family where all our children had autism. My only point of reference was the occasional glimpse of other people's typically developing children. I really didn't know any different.

I was reluctant at first for Benjamin to take Ritalin, the drug commonly prescribed to treat ADHD, as I didn't want him to be 'sedated'. Fortunately, it helped and he was just as lively as usual but less impulsive. He could pay attention for longer periods. We could begin to teach him to read, something that hadn't been possible before as he couldn't stay still long enough. I accepted that he needed the medication for now but I didn't want him to remain on it for life. We agreed to try to teach him more coping strategies and work on his attention skills until we were able to take him off it.

I did a trial some months later to see if he could cope without it and it was a disaster. He became more aggressive and started hitting people including his twin brother, Thomas. The knock on effect was that Thomas thought that hitting was quite acceptable and so he started to hit too. We worried that Benjamin would get asked to leave their school. They all went to a local mainstream gym class after school which was great for teaching them to follow instructions and routines with very little language required. They could just copy what the other children did. Although we had OT (occupational therapy) on the boys' statements, in reality, like speech therapy, we never actually got any sessions so the gym class plugged the gap. It was an activity they all enjoyed. One afternoon Benjamin hit a child there, so that was the end of the trial. He was back on Ritalin again.

It was a year before we were able to wean him off it.

A few years later Hector and I got told off and threatened with expulsion at the same gym club when he was quite young. Someone left their crawling baby right by the edge of the foam pit. Hector could not resist the temptation to give it a little nudge to fall in. It was a cartoon moment but not a funny one. Fortunately, the baby was absolutely fine.

We refrained from teaching fat/thin for obvious reasons. Years later, we couldn't avoid it and the inevitable:

'Daddy, why is that man so fat?'

spoken by a not so small boy at a crowded swimming pool in earshot of a man with an enormous beer belly. The man turned round and glared at us. Cowardly, we pretended we hadn't heard anything and made a sharp retreat as we hurried the boys away.

When we were out with the boys, we often got negative comments from strangers passing judgement on our parenting skills. We were obviously just 'bad parents'. Sometimes, we explained to people that they had autism but sometimes, we just couldn't be bothered. Sometimes, we were just too busy managing the boys to care what anyone else thought. We developed a thick skin and tried to ignore others' comments and get on with our activities.

One damp, miserable afternoon, a man on Wimbledon Common threatened Jonathan who was trying to deal with Thomas having a meltdown on the ground. At home, we would have left him to calm down alone. But it was cold so Jonathan was trying to move him. He was resisting. This stranger thought Jonathan was treating Thomas badly. I had to run over and intervene and explain that the large child screaming on the floor was not being hurt by his father, he was having an autistic meltdown.

The boys were often judged as being too old to be having a toddler tantrum and that they should have grown out of it by their age. An autistic meltdown and a toddler tantrum are not the same thing. Tantrums might be caused by their frustration at not having the language to make us understand what they couldn't tell us. Meltdowns were often caused by sensory overload. It could be too much noise, too many people, just too much going on at the same time. Places like big gym halls which echoed were particularly difficult for all the boys so unfortunately if they were invited to a party in one, we invariably left early.

Over time, I learned to anticipate what might cause a meltdown. If we were out and I personally felt at all overwhelmed, I knew the boys would be feeling it so much more than I was. It was safest to only stay a short time at somewhere busy, no matter how much we had paid in entrance fees. We could always go back. If we had a bad experience somewhere, the boys would remember it and wouldn't want to return again. We never returned to the bouncy castle party place. I don't know if the boys associated it with a negative experience but I certainly did.

Chapter Nine

'Bank television' 'Bank television' – Thomas and Benjamin

Two voices were chanting in the back of the car as we drove to the cinema. We kept saying:

'Cinema, cinema' but they kept repeating:

'Bank television, bank television'.

Oh dear, how could we tell them where we heading. The boys were learning to talk and to use their language in a meaningful way. Sometimes it was more meaningful to them than to us.

We arrived at the cinema. Two gleeful boys shouted 'bank television!' and were delighted. Then it dawned on us why they were chanting 'bank, television' - you had to queue by walking between the purple ropes just like you queued in the bank. Behind the tills there were small screens on the walls that did look like televisions displaying the times of the films. The boys knew exactly where they had wanted to go and had described it to us perfectly. I don't know which one of them had first said 'bank television' but his brother knew exactly what he meant. They were so much more in tune with each other than we were with them.

Another time, Thomas declared he wanted 'home seaside', which meant going on holiday as we stayed in a house 'aka' a temporary home and went to the seaside. Just to be sure we understood, he drew a picture of a sandcastle with four bigger figures and one small one which was Hector. Although we understood him, it wasn't easy explaining why we couldn't actually go on holiday there and then.

They were becoming creative with their communication, using the words they did have and drawing pictures if they didn't. They were not choosing to stay silent in their own world. They wanted to talk to us.

Their autism came with a severe language disorder. But, by this time, it was clear that the boys did not have additional learning difficulties. They were able to learn and they picked up concepts quickly when taught in the way that best suited them.

We were infinitely grateful that they had some basic speech. I knew of other children, who like our boys, didn't talk at three but who never went on to acquire spoken language. Who knows whether our boys would have learned to speak as well as they did without the intensive early intervention which we fought to provide for them. When the boys were very young, we weren't as immersed in the autism world as we are now and so we really didn't come across many autistic children in those early years. There were no other autistic children at either of their schools. Slowly, I started to become aware of how broad the 'autistic spectrum' really was. It seemed to cover a huge variation in disability.

'Oh I have a friend who has an autistic son too.'

I would meet that child and wonder how the diagnosis could be the same one. Their child had been diagnosed at a much older age, was fully conversational and using sophisticated language which in my wildest dreams my boys would never get close to having. I knew they had their difficulties and issues too, but they were very different needs from my boys.

The absence of language makes an enormous difference to a child's life but the same label, autism is given. Because the autistic spectrum now covers such a range of ability it confuses everyone, including other parents. It's very hard for us when people remark:

'Oh, you were lucky to get your boys diagnosed so early.'

Lucky? They were diagnosed so young because their autism

affected them so severely that it was a straightforward diagnosis made in one appointment. I'm not sure I would use the term 'lucky' at all.

People who only meet our boys now didn't know them as they were at age three. They are almost unrecognisable. So in that sense, yes, we are very lucky.

We were delighted when two wonderful tutors who had worked with the boys for more than a year offered to look after them all for our wedding anniversary. We could go away for a night, something we had never managed before. That level of kindness was so unexpected but exemplified some of the tutors' level of support for us and our boys. I am still in touch with both those tutors, Adie and Tracy, who now have children of their own. We went to a very quiet hotel near Bath, to read, to walk, to catch up on sleep and to have precious time together which we had not had for years. It was wonderful.

Although I didn't work in a paid capacity, I 'worked' many additional hours doing paperwork and attending appointments on top of caring for all the boys. A night away on our own was desperately needed and much appreciated, even if we did find ourselves discussing the boys most of the time. We rang the boys to talk to them before they went to bed, even though they couldn't really talk back to us. They needed to hear our voices so they wouldn't think we had disappeared. The girls reported that they were surprised when they woke up in the morning that we weren't home but they weren't distressed.

We resolved to try and go away again more regularly. We needed it for our sanity and for the sake of our marriage. It was hard to remember at times that we were husband and wife, and not just full time carers.

Hector by now had many single words which he could use in context. Being able to label objects can be like a party trick but one which is totally meaningless, unless those words can be used for some purpose. He could say 'Mummy' and 'Daddy' which was so lovely to finally hear. Mummy seems to be one of the earliest words for most children. For those with autism though, first words can be quite random and often for food. Thomas and Benjamin had to be 'taught' by the tutors to ask for me by name. They started by showing a photo of me and saying 'Mummy'. Then they pointed at me, saying my name on a regular basis until the boys could label me when asked. Finally they needed to teach them to call for me when I was out of sight. It all needed breaking down and taught systematically in small steps. Now, it's all I hear. 'Mummy this' and 'Mummy that.' Sometimes all of them demand my attention at the same time and it's hard to remember a time when they didn't know how to use my name.

Hector stayed at nursery with his tutors until the summer. He had started to acquire more language now that his therapy was consistent. It was a huge relief. We had worried that he wasn't learning as fast as his brothers were at the same age. What if he never really improved? We knew how autism affected his brothers learning but we didn't know how it differed in a child with regressive autism. We were constantly observing and learning. In time, Hector's language skills would overtake his brothers. It was years later before we realised this, and as much as we can look back now and think we didn't need to worry, at the time we didn't have a crystal ball to see into the future so of course we worried.

Although Hector was potty trained by now, he still had accidents. Half an hour after being put to bed at night, he would get out of bed and poo on his bedroom floor. Eventually, I solved this by placing a small, sit-on throne like potty next to his bed and taught him to use that. Perhaps he didn't like using an adult toilet? It was always hard to guess why the boys did the things they did, but if the remedy to a problem worked, it worked.

We started taking Hector to the cinema too. To begin with, I would only stay for the first ten minutes or so, leaving Jonathan to watch the film with his brothers. Hector was restless and usually ended up on the floor within minutes, attempting to burrow under the seats. I would leave and wander round the local toyshop with him, returning for the final ten minutes. On each visit, we extended the times between leaving and returning until a year later, he was able to sit and watch through a whole film. It wasn't that he didn't like the cinema, he just couldn't tolerate the sensory aspect of the loud sound and the enormous vibrant screen. Recently, he has told me that he still finds it really hard to sit still doing nothing but look at a screen. He needs popcorn! In fairness, he needs something additional to 'do'. I can identify with this as I have to knit while watching TV and cannot just sit there either. He has ADHD (attention deficit hyperactivity disorder) like his brother Benjamin, although we have never sought a professional diagnosis for him.

Although Thomas and Benjamin's school was not very supportive, we decided we would still send Hector there. It was the best way to manage the administration and the staffing logistics, as the tutors tended to work with one boy in the morning and then swap to work with another in the afternoon.

This proved to be a big mistake. But, it was to be a catalyst for change, too, so maybe it was not a mistake at all.

In November that year, Jonathan and I flew to an IVF clinic in Barcelona to discuss egg donation. We left the boys with our two lovely tutors for two nights and departed for our first overseas trip alone since having the boys. It was incredibly liberating to fly again and read a book on the plane undisturbed.

We spent a full morning with an English doctor. We wanted to know whether we could choose to only put back female embryos. At the time, it was believed that the incidence of autism was tenfold in boys to girls. It was nearly all boys in the families we knew whose autism affected their speech and behaviour severely. In fact, I didn't know any autistic girls at that time. Putting back only female embryos would in theory lessen the chances of us having another child with autism. The clinic said we could do IVF but not select the sex of the embryo.

We could start the process whenever we wanted. They had donors ready and waiting. It all seemed surreal.

Meanwhile, we had a day and a half to ourselves to sightsee and we discovered Gaudi. In that small window of time we visited every building and garden he had designed and delighted in being alone together in Barcelona. And of course, we talked and talked and then talked a bit more.

Arriving home, Jonathan was keen to go ahead with the egg donation. I think he knew how much I wanted it. I had been through such misery with all the miscarriages. To him, our family was complete but he knew I yearned for another child. I loved him for supporting my wish.

Strangely though, I decided to leave it on ice. I felt better just knowing that at any time, we could be on a plane six weeks later to have an embryo implanted. It took away my desperation.

I had mixed feelings about a possible baby. What if the child was autistic too? And, what if this future child was autistic and I then felt it wasn't mine biologically? It would of course be Jonathan's child, as although I would carry and give birth, I wouldn't biologically be the mother. How hard might that be?

I had other worries too. What if we had a little girl who was perfect and didn't have autism? What if everyone adored her and ignored my beautiful boys? I almost couldn't bear the thought; that my boys might be rejected by others. I couldn't do it. I would need to resolve all these worries first.

But I could move forward and take strength from the fact that we had an option and that it was still there if I changed my mind. Barcelona had been good for us in many ways.

Hector hadn't even finished his first term at school when it was time for his first annual review. The school booked all three boys to have their annual reviews one after each other in a single morning which created a huge amount of work and stress for us and should never have been arranged in that way.

We knew that at any time, the LA could decide to withdraw

funding. The annual reviews were necessary to ensure we got funding for the next year. We always dreaded them but this time, we had good reason to do so. The meetings were even more awful than we could have imagined. Each meeting took about 45 minutes.

Thomas' review was first, him being the eldest.

His class teacher came in and said:

'I don't know why he is at mainstream school. He can't access education.'

Benjamin's review was next. His class teacher came in and repeated exactly the same thing about him, almost verbatim. She must have been rehearsed in what to say. It certainly wasn't the approach she usually took when discussing Benjamin's progress, which was usually positive and supportive. The stony faced head teacher also complained that his tutor couldn't swim.

'Swimming is the one and only thing Benjamin can actually do.'

At that point, I could have done with a break for a cup of tea and an opportunity to scream loudly. But we still had Hector's meeting to get through.

'We don't think he needs his tutors anymore.'

He had only been at that school for two months. We had gone to tribunal so he could keep his tutors for years, not months.

When I responded that Hector could only string two or three words together, the speech therapist said that he was at the same level as the other children in his class. She and the head teacher had also colluded together.

I felt like I was in a play, one where everyone else knew their lines and I had to improvise. I held it together until I left the meeting room and then burst into tears. We had won his funding at tribunal only a year before. Now they were trying to take it away already. We knew that the head teacher didn't think our boys should be at a mainstream school and wanted us to leave. If she succeeded, we would lose all our funding and be offered a special needs school. It was a nightmare. If we lost our funding for the programmes, we would never get it back.

It wasn't just Hector's funding that was in jeopardy, it was all three boys'. I couldn't believe we were in this situation after three successful tribunals. How could one head teacher wield so much power against us? We had to find another school to take the boys before we lost our funding. They had all improved so much. We could not lose it. We couldn't let that happen.

A few days later, I spoke privately with Hector's speech therapist. I told her that I was very disappointed in the meeting. I didn't think Hector functioned at the same level as his peers but closer to the speech level of a two year old. She agreed his speech was around the level of a two and a half year old. So why had she said what she did at that meeting? That he could speak at the same level as his peers who were rising five years old? I didn't challenge her, it was too late. The damage was already done.

We were back to the 'what if's?' Would we have to go back to tribunal if they took our funding away? How could we afford tribunals all over again for all three boys? What if we couldn't find another school to take them all? Would we have to home educate them? I had to try really hard not to keep worrying about what might happen and to get on with making sure that it didn't.

When we enquired, a different local school made it very obvious that they didn't want us either by citing they didn't have enough space to do one to one sessions out of the classroom. We were lucky to live in an area where there were more local schools to try, so we rang another.

A few days before the end of term, just before Christmas, we met the head teacher, David Ford at East Sheen Primary School. We couldn't believe our luck. We had just met the most inclusive head teacher in the borough. We started to explain our problem and he called in his deputy to join us.

'Of course we will take all your boys and all their tutors'

David said without hesitation. He had never met any of our boys. He didn't need to. He would accommodate them whatever they were like. We had been treated like second class citizens. Now, we were being treated with utter respect and grace. We couldn't believe the contrast between the two schools and the two head teachers. They were even pleased that we had our own staff in place as that meant they didn't need to recruit anyone. This was in total contrast to the current school that had really disliked the fact that they were 'my' staff and not theirs.

They couldn't fit the older boys into the classrooms straight away due to lack of space but they said they would take Hector in January and the twins hopefully a term later.

We would have to sit it out with the current school for the older boys. It was not a nice prospect but at least we had the promise of a place later in the year. I could have hugged them both there and then. Truly inclusive people are such a rarity and we had just found two.

What a wonderful early Christmas present. I was as relieved as I had been when we got the tribunal results. Time to open another bottle!

I always wrote a round robin style Christmas letter, not to brag about our children, but to educate friends and family about the difficulties of autism and how the boys were progressing.

I would spend all year trying to get a photo of all three boys looking at the camera at the same time. This was of course in pre digital camera days. I would take multiple shots in the hope that when I sifted through the packet of developed photos, I might be lucky enough to find one with all three looking at me. I took it as a personal challenge to get a perfect photo as it was a rarity. Invariably in most photos there was one child looking elsewhere or with their eyes shut. These days, with my digital camera, I take a series of photos as capturing all four boys in one place looking good (they don't want to be caught in an unflattering pose) is still elusive. Maybe I should have included a 'usual' photo as well, one where they were all doing different, random things. But, I wanted them to look cute and to have a photo of how I felt they should all look.

In the New Year, the day before term started, the new school's deputy head teacher, Helen, rang. Hector could start the next day and she had thought hard about the twins. It would be very awkward for us to keep them at their current school. She could take them now too. The classrooms were too crowded for an additional child plus an adult tutor but until they could swap classrooms, the boys could go to those lessons held outside the classrooms like PE and music. We couldn't believe how accommodating the school was and what efforts they were prepared to make on our behalf.

At the first meeting, a few days later, to meet the teachers and introduce our boys' therapy team, I tentatively asked whether there was any possibility that the twins could stay down a year as their birthday was in March and so many of the children in their current class were up to six months older than they were. Socially, being with slightly younger children would be helpful for them. The next day the school phoned to agree and said that the year two classrooms were bigger and therefore they could start straight away and attend all the classes. It was a win, win situation.

We gleefully told the old school we were leaving. The head teacher tried to call a big borough meeting as she felt that mainstream was not appropriate, the boys should leave her school but not to go to another mainstream school. They should be in a special school. Jonathan managed to persuade the Head of Education in the borough to cancel the meeting as we had already been accepted by another mainstream school. The change in school placement was officially approved and we were utterly relieved. Another battle won.

I bumped into a local mother a few weeks later who asked why we had left the first school. I simply remarked rather facetiously that the colour of the uniform at the new one suited the boys better! It was too complicated to explain, so we kept a low profile and didn't say very much to anyone about why we had left.

The new school was as fantastic and supportive as they had been from the first desperate meeting before Christmas. The teachers were interested in our programme and wanted to help as much as they could. Most of the teachers had worked there for many years and there was a real sense of community. Our tutors were welcomed into the teaching community, so for them it was a much nicer environment to work in.

The boys had no problem in settling in at all; they have a strong instinctive sense of whether they are liked or not. Their behaviour at school improved dramatically. Thomas' meltdowns and negative behaviours decreased rapidly. Perhaps he had been trying all along to let us know that he wasn't happy at the old school.

My father once asked:

'Why are your boys at mainstream school? Don't they disturb the other children's education? Why aren't they in residential schools?' He thought we were selfish in regards to the other parents in placing our boys with mainstream children. In his generation, children with disabilities were mostly locked away, out of sight. He, like many others his age, honestly thought that was the best place for them to be.

I wish he could see them now.

It was impossible to get to know three new sets of parents. There was more than one playground and I couldn't wait in just one as I needed to be in three places at the same time. I would dash from one pick up point to the next, never really getting time to talk to the other mothers.

By the end of that term, we had decided that Hector would repeat reception class and stay a year behind like his brothers. At that point, I abandoned getting to know parents in his class. By the time he started back again in September, it was his third new class in a year and the third set of parents, my brain couldn't absorb any more new names by then. As for Hector, goodness knows how he felt being continually exposed to new children but he seemed to cope with the changes. I wished I could have explained things to him but he was still using only single or two word combinations, good enough for him to be able to request things he wanted, but nowhere near enough language for complicated explanations.

The parents at the new school, like the new head teacher, were also a total contrast. Instead of the attitude that we were spoiling their children's education by having our boys in the classroom, these new parents were welcoming and inclusive and actually thought it was good for their children to learn about diversity and integration. The new school was fantastic in every respect. The boys were much happier there, the tutors were happier and Jonathan and I were certainly much happier.

We were never, ever challenged again by any of the staff. We only ever met with compassion and welcoming arms. It makes me tearful writing about this, that such a caring community can exist and does and is physically only yards away, but light years away emotionally from the contrasting one.

We dared to go to parents social evenings again. Many of those parents from years ago are still our friends. It didn't matter if our boys were friends with their children or not: we were accepted. We had felt like outsiders as parents at the previous school. Now we were treated and included like everyone else. The boys were able to have play dates and were sometimes invited back to other children's houses. The next four years of school were happy ones for us all.

We never had a member of the LA present again at an annual review. At one previous review, at the old school, they had invited the head of SEN for the whole borough. That never happened to any other family, as it was up to the school whether they felt they needed to invite the LA at all. East Sheen Primary never felt that need. Usually schools managed their own reviews, the presence of the LA spelt trouble. We had had a lucky escape from the first school in keeping our statements and our funding intact.

I conceived again in the New Year. I mistakenly had this belief that I could get pregnant and not miscarry.

I was totally convinced all would be fine. I am the eternal optimist at times or maybe I was in eternal denial. The miscarriage consultant prescribed me steroids and daily heparin injections, the latest new 'treatment' for recurrent miscarriages. I would try anything to keep this pregnancy. We didn't tell anyone that I was pregnant again, just in case.

It didn't work. I suffered yet another missed miscarriage, my ninth; the baby died early before twelve weeks and I had to have another operation under general anaesthetic. I was almost hysterical for a few days afterwards. It had taken me over two years to conceive and I was now 45. That had been my last chance and now it was over. I would never have another baby. All I could think was 'it's not fair' and 'why me?' Why so many miscarriages? I should have been grateful that I had managed to have three boys among the nine miscarriages but I couldn't turn it around that way. I just wept for the babies I had lost.

I purposely never tried to remember or mark any of the dates on which I lost a baby or to remember their due dates. I would never have been able to put it behind me with all those dates in the calendar. Perhaps with one miscarriage, the dates remain imprinted in your heart but with nine I made a conscious effort not to remember. I sometimes buy a bunch of white roses to remember them all but not on any particular day, just when I feel the need to remember those lost babies privately. We don't discuss the miscarriages now. They are in the past but they will remain in my heart forever.

Thomas started mainstream pottery classes after school with his adored tutor, Adie. To begin with, he couldn't bear the dry feel of the clay and had to wear thin plastic gloves, but, eventually he managed to desensitise himself. He was able to create everything that the other children did and often better than some. Thomas is very talented in all mediums of art, but we think this is a familial trait and not some sort of savant talent that people sometimes think those with autism must have.

Benjamin still had no fear. One afternoon, my sister and her family had come over for a barbecue in our garden. We heard

Benjamin shout. We looked up. He was on the flat roof leading out from the loft window, leaning over the edge, waving to us. Our lodger had left his room unlocked and the window open despite our frequent reminders not to. Nicola grabbed a sheet off the washing line ready to catch him if he jumped. I shouted to him:

'Back! Back! Inside! Go Inside!' Only single words would have any impact.

For once, he did what I said and backed away. I raced up to the loft and rescued him. I had been absolutely terrified. He was nonchalant as usual and grinned at me as I grabbed him and hugged him fiercely. Sometimes I think we must have angels keeping watch over us. We have had so many potential accidents and incidents, but the boys remain unharmed.

I no longer cried about my boys, they were happy, they were thriving. They didn't know or think that they were missing out on anything. If I cried, was I crying for them or for myself, for what I felt I was missing out on? It had taken years for me to accept their autism. I accepted it but I would never stop fighting for them. Crying was wasted energy. I needed that energy to keep fighting for what they needed.

Chapter Ten

'Wherever we are, it's not Holland' - Me

There was an outbreak of nits in school. Combing through each boys hair every night in the bath took ages. They hated it. It hurt them. Cutting their hair had slowly become less traumatic but nit combing caused a new anguish. I had a Kiwi rugby player, Richard, who came after school some afternoons to help with the boys. He was my 'nit' saviour. He would walk in with a big grin and offer to delouse the boys. It lasted for months. We would get the boys clear and they would go back to school and catch them again from another child. We called the nits 'insects'. I offered the boys rewards for how many 'insects' we could catch as we pasted them onto folded squares of white toilet paper.

Tugging a nit comb through Hector's ringlets was the worst. When he had a haircut, me and his fantastic tutor, Mina, would say his shorn locks made him look like a 'little sheep'. He would not like to hear that now as a cool young adult. Mina worked with all the boys for three years, full time and was excellent. I believe she is one of the reasons Hector improved so much and so rapidly.

An early intervention programme is only ever as good as its tutors. I realised after a few years, the better the tutor, the more a child improves. It made me even more careful about finding the best people I could, who would make a real difference to the boys. We lived and breathed the therapy. I mostly had great tutors but part of the success of the therapy was because we embraced it as a family. We had to maintain whatever the boys were learning outside of their hours. This might be using new words that they were learning or practising self help skills like dressing. We sought out opportunities to practice these skills in the house. It wasn't difficult. It became second nature to label every item as we used it and verbalise whatever we were doing.

The boys went to the youngest scout group, Beavers and then, as they grew older, to Cubs in the church hall conveniently next door to our house. They all managed to repeat the cub promise which was a proud moment for us all. We sent one of our regular babysitters, Esther, to help them join in with the other children there, some of whom they were at school with. I don't think the cub leader ever fully understood the boys and how their autism affected them. She was astonished one day during a park trail with activity stations. Thomas was able to name the countries of all the flags pictured on a quiz sheet in minutes. I think she had presumed, like many did, that he was unable to learn because of his severe language difficulties. But, he acquired and retained facts easily. One memorable interest of his was the Titanic. He adored the film and knew so many facts about the sinking of the ship. For years afterwards he would build a model of the Titanic with Lego and draw pictures of it.

We decided it was time to get a pet for the boys. A kitten was the obvious choice. She was tortoiseshell and we gave her to Thomas. The boys all had a tendency to squeeze her with love so she spent the first few months in our bedroom with regular, safe visits from the boys accompanied by us. I wanted Thomas to name her. After weeks of asking him:

'What is the baby cat's name?' and him replying 'baby cat', our tutor Tracy announced that she looked like a Margaret so that's who she became. She lived for 17 years, never becoming particularly friendly but definitely a member of the household.

There was a piece of prose which was often sent to me by well meaning people titled:

'Welcome to Holland'

It was written by a special needs mother and is an analogy about when you are expecting a baby. You are anticipating life with your new baby to be your dream trip to Italy. You are really looking forward to going to Italy. The reality with a special needs child is that you find yourself in Holland and not Italy. The essence of the piece is that Holland may be different but you need to appreciate the good things Holland has to offer. You should not mourn forever that you didn't get to Italy or you will miss the special things that Holland has to offer.

Many people are comforted by it, but it never comforted me at all. It made me cross. The timing was all wrong when I first read it, I was still too angry; angry at my children's diagnosis; still at the why me? Why us? stage. I was angry at all the barriers we had already had to face, battling at tribunals, trying to fund therapy ourselves, having to jump schools. Where was all of that mentioned in Holland? One summer, an online friend and I had a brilliant email exchange on this topic. The emails were rants.

'It's not Holland, it's like a war zone some days'

'We are dodging bombs daily'

'It's like living in Beirut' (which shows our age as this was a long ago conflict).

We compared our lives to being anywhere but Holland. Holland was not where we were at all. We were not living in a peaceful, easy country. It was like civil war some days, both inside the house and when fighting the authorities.

'We are treated like unwelcome refugees by many of the other inhabitants of this country.'

'Wherever we are, it's not Holland.'

So where were we? In an unnamed place that we should have just accepted as it was? That was never going to happen in our family, that calm state of acceptance.

Although Jonathan and I accepted the boys were autistic, we

didn't accept that we should do nothing about it. Leaving them potentially to remain non verbal with minimal communication and maximum frustration? We love our children unconditionally and we have always wanted to do all we could to make their lives easier for them. If that meant ongoing battles to get them the right therapy and the right schools, then that is what we would do.

Thomas was still a picky eater. I hadn't wanted to add food battles to all his other issues, so we hadn't tackled it within his programme and we just carried on feeding him his limited diet. In the end, we really didn't need to do anything drastic. He watched the other children eating school lunches and one day he decided himself that he wanted to try what they were eating. Eventually, he was eating school lunches like everyone else. Peer pressure can be a useful thing at times. He was always naturally a healthy eater, instinctively choosing fruit and vegetables and loudly objecting to fast food. Once, in pouring rain on holiday in Cornwall, we dived into a fast food chain for lunch. He absolutely refused to eat anything and sat there, virtuously eating an apple while the others ate burgers and chips. Benjamin and Hector were 'sugar monsters' and would devour anything sweet. They drank juice. Thomas would only drink water.

Benjamin seemed to have no regulation for feeling full. He would eat and eat if we let him. At a friend's house for lunch one day, we realised he alone had drunk a whole litre of apple juice. He exploded spectacularly later that night, not a visual picture you would like me to describe in detail. We needed to limit what Benjamin ate. We wanted him to maintain a healthy weight so we taught him that he had to ask for every food item he wanted. He still occasionally asks now. He was always much heavier and larger than Thomas until a few years ago when he made a decision by himself to lose his excess weight. He succeeded and is very proud of himself to have kept it off ever since.

His behaviour spiralled, and not in a good way, whenever he had too much sugar. We banned fizzy drinks and artificial sweetener in the house and kept a close eye on how much sugar he consumed. But, we never stopped treats, one ice cream was fine, three were not.

Thomas had to be reminded and persuaded to eat and drink. He only eats to 'fuel' and not because he loves food. Hector ate most things and we didn't have the food problems we had with the twins when they were little. He moved from pureed food to solid food without a fuss.

Italy was where Jonathan had proposed. For our 10th anniversary we went to Rome which neither of us had visited before. Our supervisor, Amanda, offered to look after all the boys for us for three nights. Three whole nights away! Without our team of tutors and carers, we would never have been able to go anywhere. How lucky we were to have them in our lives, not only for the radical changes they made to our boys' lives, but for their support. It was a whirlwind visit, cramming in everything we wanted to see. We never paused for a cup of tea to watch the world go by. We needed to be in the world for a change, not watching it pass by.

A few weeks after arriving home, the little blue line on the pregnancy test turned blue. Italy had worked its magic on us again. I was pregnant at the age of 46 against all the odds. I immediately saw the miscarriage consultant who wanted to give me every medical option he could as this really would be our final chance of a baby. I felt calm and serene as I turned it all down. It hadn't helped last time so I had no faith in it working this time. I would take my chances. It just felt right.

We tried not to get too excited. Thomas had been asking me for a baby for a while now. I had told him so many times that I couldn't have one. A few weeks before the Italy trip, he had left a pregnancy book open on the sofa at a page with a picture of a baby growing. I thought it a bit strange at the time that he had taken the book from the shelves. Had he known something? Now he started saying:

'Can we have a baby for Christmas?'

How did he know? I hadn't told him I was pregnant. I didn't want to risk his disappointment as well as my own. We didn't tell any of the boys.

I felt sick and tired which was all good, but not so good when looking after the boys. I existed from scan to scan, feeling reassured after each one, but then nervous again awaiting the next. I had become quite involved in the spiritual church by now and although we didn't tell anyone, a few people there somehow psychically 'knew' I was pregnant. They unanimously said it would be a girl. We desperately wanted a girl as we thought it would lessen the risk of another child with severe autism. I also wanted a girl as I already had three boys. A daughter would be perfect. I became utterly convinced I was expecting a girl.

We had CVS (chorionic villus sampling) due to my age and previous miscarriages. It was unpleasant but necessary, a needle through my abdomen directly into the placenta to take some sample cells. The consultant thought it would be kinder for us to know if the baby had a genetic condition at 12 weeks rather than perhaps finding out weeks later and losing the baby at a late stage in pregnancy. It was New Year so the results were delayed for an additional few nerve wracking days.

I was at Sally's house, drinking tea, when they phoned with the results. The baby was fine, no chromosomal abnormalities and it was a boy. No, that bit must be wrong so I asked them if they were sure.

'Yes, you have a healthy baby boy.'

I put the phone down and was nearly sick. I was in shock. It couldn't be a boy. I had been 'told' it was a girl. I rang Jonathan in a dreadful state. He left work and cycled straight home.

By the time he arrived, I was nearly hysterical. We couldn't have another boy. He would have autism. For the next 24 hours, we both cried and ranted and talked endlessly back and forth. In my mind, all the time, was the memory of the paediatrician who diagnosed our three older boys, saying that if we wanted another child unaffected by autism, he recommended finding out the sex at 12 weeks and considering termination if it was a boy.

I rang Verity, my counsellor friend, who very generously came over the next day and talked it through with us. We had not slept. We had spent the night talking and crying. What should we do now? I desperately wanted us to make a joint decision and not one that we would regret. If this baby had autism like his brothers then we both needed to accept that risk. Why had we not discussed the possibility before that we might have another boy? It was utterly miserable. After nearly six years of trying to have another baby, we finally had a viable pregnancy and should have been celebrating, but now we weren't even sure we could go ahead.

We didn't know if he would definitely have autism, the risk was still only 20%. There was an 80% chance of him not having autism. It seemed a fair risk and I don't think we could have actually gone ahead with a termination but we did need to talk it through.

I was as terrified of having to run another early intervention programme as I was about the possibility of having another child with autism. It was the one thing that really improved our children's lives, but it took such a toll on me. The main stress was finding, training and keeping decent tutors. It is a stress that leads many families to abandon home programmes. I made a pledge with Jonathan. I could go ahead with this pregnancy but I needed his word that he would never expect me to run another programme if this baby was autistic too. How awful that sounds. I could face the prospect of a child with autism but not of running another programme. I can truthfully say that running the programmes has been the hardest thing I have ever had to do and has worn me down terribly over the years. I wonder now though how we would all have fared without them. If the boys had stayed as severe as they were when first diagnosed, I'm sure my stress would be way, way worse now than it was while running the programmes. Most families ran one programme; we ran three: our stress was always going to be high.

I was pregnant and the baby was healthy so we tried to forget our fears. I knew a wonderful lady, Cathy, who did some EFT, a tapping therapy, with me. She somehow tapped my fear away so I could enjoy the pregnancy or at least, not be anxious about it. Jonathan carried on stoically without the need for therapy. He doesn't say much but has a quiet, strong faith in God which I don't possess. I need to look elsewhere for faith which leaves me at times, like it had when we suffered so many miscarriages with no answers.

We didn't start telling people until I was nearly 20 weeks pregnant and looking slightly fatter. By then, we were happy again that we were having another baby and we weren't going to dwell on the 'what ifs?' Most people were sensitive enough not to ask whether the baby was autistic or not.

The boys were all involved in this pregnancy, Thomas was delighted. His prediction of a baby at Christmas had been right as we were able to tell the boys just after New Year. When we told Benjamin, he asked me to open my mouth and then shouted down my throat:

'Hello baby!'

His reasoning being that if you have a baby in your tummy, you must have swallowed it.

When I picked the boys up in the playground, Thomas would lift my top up if I didn't grab it back in time and speak directly to my tummy. He would lie down next to me on the bed and try to feel it kicking. He loved this baby already. We didn't want to go into too much biological detail but we did explain to the boys that this baby was being cut out of my tummy and not being born out of my bottom like they had been. The twins were eight and I needed to warn them that I would have a big cut afterwards so they wouldn't be scared when they first saw me. Thomas started asking every pregnant lady, stranger or not, whether they were having their babies out of their tummies or their bottoms. They were mostly amused, but they didn't always know how to reply!

Considering my age and all the stress I was under, the pregnancy went well. I never got very large. I did get sciatica towards the end which the physiotherapist could not help me with. I could barely walk so I went to the church. A healer 'asked' the baby to move and the next morning, my sciatica and pain had gone.

We named him Marcus Isaac before he was born. His middle name Isaac, means 'he who laughed' and comes from the story of Sarah in the old testament who had a son, Isaac when she was too old to have a baby. That was me too. Marcus meant a warrior which he certainly was, to survive and thrive as he had done. He was transverse, lying across, so I was booked in for a C-section a few weeks before his due date. The consultant didn't want to leave anything to chance. He also wanted to deliver my baby himself. It was a perfect touch that his name was Isaac too.

It was surreal to walk into the theatre, lie down and 20 minutes later to be handed a very tiny baby. It was a moment I never thought I would experience again, a new, perfect baby. How could I have even hesitated six months ago? This little boy was meant to be here. He was small but very beautiful. His brothers were all very excited to meet him. He was blonde like they had been when they were born. They all trooped in to see him the next day and took turns in holding him. We had four boys now, enough for a five a side football team if Daddy played too.

Our first family outing when he was a week old was to Grandma (my mother)'s tree in Osterley Park. Her ashes were buried under an oak tree sapling. The tree was big by now. It wasn't a concept that the boys could understand. They had never met her. How could she be under a tree? We visit it regularly and it is known to the boys as Grandma's tree.

A few days later, being only about ten days post section, I gingerly pushed his buggy to his brothers' open day at school, where he was admired by everyone. One little boy asked me in a loud voice if he was autistic too like his brothers which really upset me. At that moment, he wasn't. I didn't want to think about the possibility and tried to cast it from my mind. It was hard to do so at times with those constant little reminders and remarks.

I thought I knew how to look after babies. Hector had slept through from about ten weeks old. I knew nothing. Marcus screamed and screamed and never slept. He had dreadful colic and so many dirty nappies. The health visitors were unconcerned. My only respite was when Jonathan would nurse Marcus while watching the Beijing Olympics for a couple of hours in the middle of the night and I could sleep. I was like a zombie for the first twelve weeks, seriously sleep deprived as I had been with the twins.

I had recurrent mastitis. Marcus just wanted to feed continuously night and day, probably to soothe his colic but it didn't help him or me at all. It probably made matters worse. One bout required three types of antibiotics to avoid an abscess but I was determined to keep going.

I had done some research before he was born. We didn't know if autism was preventable but I would try and do whatever might help. It meant no formula. I would only breast feed him. I expressed milk every morning as I was so tired by night time that I could barely feed him and we could top him up with that morning's milk.

He cried whenever we lay him down flat. The only time he slept was in his car seat or when carried around upright in a baby sling. It was a long, exhausting twelve weeks for everyone.

Finally, I discovered the culprit. I had been drinking fresh orange juice to increase my vitamins intake to benefit him. His colic was caused by oranges and all other fruit. I stopped eating vegetables too for the next year as hours after I ate them, he would get colic from the traces in my milk. Marcus finally started to sleep for short periods after I put blocks under one end of his cot so that he slept at an angle, next to my bedside, so I could reach for him in the night if he woke and screamed. The other boys by now were all really good sleepers and slept through the night; fortunately Marcus never disturbed them.

I really feel for those parents whose autistic children cannot sleep through the night, who are alert and wide awake suddenly for hours in the middle of the night and cannot be left unsupervised. Sleep deprivation is one of the hardest things to cope with. No one seems to know why autism interrupts sleep but it does and it's real. I had years of broken sleep but eventually it did improve. I know there are some families who will never sleep through the night again.

Jonathan wrote a prayer for Marcus' christening which had everyone in tears. He talked about all our lost babies and how blessed we were to finally have Marcus. The children sang 'Twinkle twinkle little star' to him. It was a truly special day. My three treasured friends, Mary, Sally and Sue agreed to be his Godmothers. They were my greatest source of support and it made them part of our family.

Marcus was my hardest baby to look after with his colic, but infinitely precious after years of trying and losing so many. Jonathan had persuaded me to give away most of the baby things a year before. Each time I had a miscarriage they were a physical reminder that we weren't having a baby and it upset me to see them. I hadn't quite managed to give it all away though and kept a treasured bag of the first year of baby clothes hidden away in the loft. I was so happy when I was finally able to wash them all, taking a photo of the tiny vests and babygros hanging in the sunshine on the line in the garden. When I dressed Marcus in them, I recalled each of his brothers wearing them. He was spoilt with new clothes too, as I couldn't resist the delight in finally being able to shop again for baby clothes. My mantra was that we had saved all that money from not having to pay for IVF, so I could buy a few new not strictly necessities couldn't I?

From the start, Thomas was Marcus' 'best' brother. Thomas adored him before he was born and has been his best friend ever since. The twin bond is meant to be stronger than a mother and child bond but in Thomas' and Marcus' case, their bond overcomes all others. Thomas is the doting older brother. That special bond has helped Thomas too. Thomas had almost no play skills himself as a young boy, but he learned some finally at a much later age, not for himself, but to play with Marcus.

Years later, at Kew Gardens, Thomas was playing with Marcus in a children's play area reserved for young children. Thomas' voice was loud and he was tall by then. A woman told him off for playing there with the little children. I went over to explain that he was autistic and that he was helping Marcus to get up and down the equipment. She apologised very nicely to us. As she walked off, Thomas followed her apologising himself to her over and over again. I think she felt quite bad as Thomas was obviously so mortified at being told off.

Conversely, Benjamin did have good play skills but he couldn't play with Marcus. Everything had to be on his agenda and he wanted to play with the toys in his way. He didn't understand how to play with someone else or that he needed to let a much smaller child have a turn. He would even grab toys off Marcus if he wanted them for himself.

Hector wasn't particularly interested in a small baby who didn't do anything interesting, but he tolerated him.

I was too tired for an English self catering holiday so we went on a resort holiday for the first time, taking a week off school in September when it was much cheaper and quieter. The holiday company allocated one to one nannies for the boys. They could go into the kids clubs and we could get a few hours break. Greece was hot, the sea was warm and it was all inclusive. It was the first holiday we had where we didn't have to shop, cook or wash up. Some evenings the boys could go into club to watch videos with the nannies and other children. We could have supper on our own. Perfect, except for one small ten week old baby with colic who couldn't sleep. I spent most of my time feeding Marcus in the hotel bedroom and trying in vain to get him to sleep in his buggy on the beach. It wasn't exactly a rest, but it was a great holiday for the boys. Having the nannies to look after them was a serious luxury. The three older boys slept in a row in a room next to ours with an adjoining door in the middle so we could see them and monitor them safely through the open door.

The holiday was such a success that we budgeted from then on and have been on an all inclusive active family holiday nearly every summer since. The boys had extra help if they needed it to go sailing, paddle boarding and swimming during the day. They still got time with us too. The holidays catered to the mainstream, so the boys got to mix with an able peer group. We rely on those holidays now for our respite. It's the only week or two of the entire year when we parents get a break from our caring role which is still intense even though it has changed so much since the boys were small.

I enjoyed my new baby all to myself for the next year. There had been a reason that I didn't go ahead with the egg donation. Here he was. My instinct had been right.

Someone asked me if I was 'surprised' to have another baby so late in life. After a few people asked, I responded with 'the only surprise was that I have a baby after so many miscarriages'. He was one of the most wanted and longed for babies and certainly not a random, accidental conception despite my age.

We tried not to watch for every stage and every milestone wondering if Marcus had autism. I really tried just to be a mum with a new born baby with no worries for his future but it was so hard to switch that fear off. I didn't begin to wean him until he was six months old because I wanted to do 'the best' for him and current advice at the time was not to wean until six months. I kept Marcus gluten and dairy free because some people thought they might be a possible cause of autism or exacerbate it. I myself had been gluten free due to very painful intolerance for at least five years by then, so it wasn't too hard.

Whenever he reached a milestone on time, we were reassured. I'm not sure I really knew though what a baby was expected to be able to do and when. Perhaps I falsely reassured myself that all was well. I certainly didn't want to think of the alternative. I took him out for walks and to cafes. He and I went to a music group every week in the library and sat on the floor banging instruments together. He loved to go on the swings and we took him swimming with all his brothers. He was a happy baby, always smiling and curious about everything around him. I made a friend around that time, Ali, who had also just had a baby girl. Her older daughter was Hector's age and she had suffered recurrent miscarriages too during the same six years that I had. She and I would meet up with our precious babies.

A week before Marcus' first birthday, Jonathan's mother, Liesel, died unexpectedly after a very short illness. Sadly, I don't think the boys missed her terribly as she had not been very involved in their lives. Jonathan was understandably upset, but pragmatic. He knew she would have hated a slow deterioration in her health and that this had been a kinder option for her. After more than 50 years of marriage, his father was alone. Jonathan would need to support him emotionally.

Only six weeks later, my father died at the end stage of vascular dementia. His death was a release for him after many years of intolerable illness, so I couldn't really mourn his passing. We had lost the real him years before. Again, the boys didn't suffer any real loss, as they hadn't known him well. Theirs had been an unusual childhood, not being close to either set of grandparents despite them living within easy distance of us.

Jonathan and I had both lost a parent in a short space of time. Life was changed by their deaths, but our lives with the boys continued as before.

The boys were very happy at home with us and each other and we were who they relied on emotionally. I sometimes worried that when tutors who had become very close to the boys left, the boys would be inconsolable, but they seemed to take it in their stride. They didn't understand the concept of someone leaving forever, so when the tutors left, the boys would happily wave 'bye bye' fully expecting to see them again the next week.

We held a first birthday party for Marcus in our garden. It was a perfect sunny afternoon with the paddling pool and trampoline out for the children. He was passed from each doting godmother to the next. He was a happy baby, he smiled, he was curious, he helped to unwrap his presents. All was well.

He began to make some sounds but no clear words. At sixteen months, he too was diagnosed with glue ear. He had started to wave bye bye at a year, but no longer did this. Some early signs of autism were there all over again, but we tried to ignore them and pretend they weren't significant. Being in denial was becoming my default mode.

I tried to avoid him needing grommets and spent the next few months doing everything I could to clear the glue ear. He had regular sessions with an osteopath. I burned specialist ear candles in his ears every other day which was as scary as it sounds. We would lay him on my lap and I would burn the candles in his ears, singing his favourite songs all the while to keep him calm and distracted. It didn't work. We kept him free of all dairy. Nothing worked. Eventually he was booked in for surgery to insert grommets.

Within days of surgery, at the age of twenty months, he finally started to walk independently. His balance had been badly affected by the glue ear. He had only been able to 'cruise', that is, walk holding onto the furniture or a hand from thirteen months old. It had been hard over the winter not to allow him get out of his buggy to crawl when it was wet and muddy outside. He was pretty heavy to carry in a sling, so we only carried him when absolutely necessary if visiting somewhere that couldn't accommodate a buggy. The grommets got him up and walking, they cured his glue ear temporarily, but they didn't get him talking. Hope is what keeps us all going and we had desperately hoped that this time, with this child, the glue ear was not masking anything more serious.

Marcus' eye contact was poor, he had no words and by 22 months, the speech and language therapist agreed with us.

Like his brothers, Marcus probably had autism too.

Chapter Eleven

'It is paramount for local services to take account of the fact that Marcus is one of a family with four autistic children and the considerable impact that this has on the family as a whole, and the parents in particular'. - Developmental paediatrician.

We needed to find a secondary school for the twins before the LA picked one for them. They were so happy and so settled at their primary school. How were we ever going to replace that nurturing, safe environment?

Choices in London were remarkably limited. Mainstream secondary was not the right option, with a one to one trailing them. Mainstream schools weren't able to differentiate the curriculum in the way that the boys needed or offer alternatives to GCSEs, but the boys were capable of learning. They were caught in a void, not able enough for mainstream, but too able for many of the special schools. I had one school in mind that catered for children with speech and language issues. The head teacher did not want to take our boys, but the LA actually offered to pay for their places, so she had to agree to an assessment day. She rejected them, making the excuse that the year group was full but a few weeks later, she accepted a local, very academic girl, who we knew. She just didn't want our boys, despite them fitting the entry criteria and even having the funding. I had set my heart on that school.

Local friends were also trying to find school places for their mainstream children. There was a wide choice for the academically able and an even wider choice for those able to afford independent school fees. They had choices and their children would find schools. Our choices were so limited in comparison.

In many ways, we, as parents, were more isolated socially than our children were at that time. I don't think Thomas and Benjamin had yet realised that they were different from the other children around them. They were included at school in all the activities; Benjamin went to an after school drama class which he loved and Thomas had his pottery club. But we knew they would not be able to take GCSEs or meet friends independently like their peers were already starting to do. I have to confess, we were envious and sometimes resentful when parents were disappointed that their children were offered their second choice of school and not their first. Oh, to have any choices!

At times, we even felt isolated from other families with special needs children. Many of them had siblings who didn't have autism. They could straddle both worlds; the mainstream one and the special needs one. We could only glimpse the mainstream world and know we would never be a part of it. It hurt still. We were so grateful that our boys had enough language now to prevent their frustration, but they didn't have enough for mainstream school or to read books or to join in abstract conversations.

It was time to leave mainstream behind. We had been included but our boys had never managed independently. They were not mainstream children and would never be.

We didn't want to send them to a residential school. I felt, very strongly, that we did so much ourselves as a family for them. I would continue to do everything I could for my boys to make their lives easier and more fulfilling for them. For us, that meant keeping them at home in their own local community. They were each other's friends and would have missed their brothers enormously if we had split them up. Because of their severe language impairment, most schools couldn't take them. I really didn't want an autism specific school. They lived in one at home.

I visited several schools out of London, but none were suitable for the boys at their level. The irony was that their early intervention programme had helped them so much. Academically, they were able to learn, but their limited language made conventional teaching inaccessible.

The LA would not provide an educational psychologist to assess them so we paid for one privately. Thank goodness we could afford to do so, I knew many could not. The last tests the LA had done for us were when the boys were under three years old. It really was time for an up to date assessment. The boys were 10 years and 11 months old at the time.

She wrote:

'Thomas has a very interesting profile of results. There is a huge discrepancy between his overall verbal skills and his overall non-verbal skills. Children with this discrepancy often experience a considerable degree of frustration.'

His word definitions scored him as 1st percentile.

His non verbal reasoning scored him at 99th percentile.

'Percentile rates are calculated as 100 children of the same age's scores, a score of 1 being the lowest of the 100 and 100 being the highest. Thomas has what is known as a 'spiky' profile.'

Now we could understand why he got frustrated. He had an extremely high score for intelligence and an extremely low one for language. The scores could not have been more contrasting.

Of Benjamin, she wrote:

'Benjamin has an interesting profile of results. He had a mixture of very high and very low scores within his profile. He did less well in recall of designs due probably to his dyspraxic difficulties.'

His word definitions scored him at 2nd percentile.

His non verbal reasoning scored him at 92nd percentile.

His scores also showed a huge disparity between his intelligence and his language levels.

She also noted that:

'He presented with significant difficulties with social communication in lessons. Due to his lack of awareness of social boundaries, turn taking in conversation and relevance of subject matter he gave the impression that he might be a management problem in the classroom.'

It was not just his lack of language that was an impediment to his learning.

They were briefly assessed for a day at More House School in Farnham, Surrey which catered for boys with specific learning delays and language disorders. On academic testing they scored fairly well. They were exactly 11 years old.

Thomas was assessed at 6 years for comprehension and 10 years 6 months for numeracy.

Benjamin was assessed at 7 years 6 months for comprehension and 10 years for numeracy.

The school could not take them. They needed too much support academically and it was glaringly obvious from their trial day that socially they would not fit in with their cohort.

An independent speech and language therapist scored Benjamin as having language skills in the 2nd percentile; 'a significant language disorder'.

She scored Thomas' language skills being in the 1st percentile, 'a significant language disorder'.

These results hit home. They were stark reminders of their language deficits which were severe. We were delighted that they could talk, having wondered at times if they ever would, but these results emphasised the gap between them and their peers. We were frustrated by the lack of schools which could meet their needs. How frustrated must they feel at times by their lack of language? We knew now that they had high IQ levels. We had to ensure that they were stretched academically and not bored or frustrated.

In the end, there was only one school who agreed to take them, so we accepted their offer. It was a small special needs school in

Clapham, south west London, Centre Academy. We knew very little about it. It did take a range of children with very mixed abilities. Vitally, for the boys, they could accommodate their academic needs. Alongside GCSEs, they also taught foundation levels. The boys would certainly be stretched academically and might be able to gain some academic qualifications. We didn't care particularly if they passed exams but we knew that they thrived on the stimulation that learning brought them in the classroom and which they couldn't learn from books. Our boys would be the least able verbally at the school but they had always been educated alongside others who had good levels of language and this was usually to their advantage.

With only half a term to go, they could start in September. It was a huge relief after nearly a year of searching. We gave their tutors notice that we would be finishing their programme in a few months time.

Hector was very much aware of his autism and himself by the age of eight. He started to ask:

'Why do I have a babysitter at school?' and

'Why do the tutors spy on me in the playground?'

He was angry when we told him he had autism and that he needed extra help. He said he didn't want the help. He didn't want to be autistic and declared that he didn't want tutors anymore.

It was so hard to hear his anger and his pain. We could only imagine how he felt. We knew how hard it was as a parent to accept a diagnosis of autism. How much harder must it be for him? He asked why he had autism and what had caused it. How could we make it go away? He said that he hated himself and that he was an idiot. When people say that autism is a gift or that autism is just a difference and not a disability, it makes me angry for those, like Hector, for whom it is a very real and defining disability. Some even liken it to a super power. For our boys, it really isn't. The struggles they have with language negate any super skills they may or may not have. Thomas' ability to recount facts is remarkable but it's not useful to him, except in a pub quiz. The boys have always needed additional support to learn academically, mainly because of their language disorder. I suppose you could argue that they don't need qualifications to be happy in life, but they do need to acquire the highest level of language they can. The wide discrepancy between their verbal and non verbal skills led to huge frustration for them all.

One day, in desperation, I told Hector that God had made him that way. I didn't know what else to say. A few days later, he declared that he had left his bedroom windows open so that a burglar could get in. When the burglar got in, he would kill him. The burglar would go to heaven and he could kill God for him. He hated God. It was such a powerful statement from such a young child and it was heart-breaking for Jonathan and for me to hear his anguish so passionately expressed.

We had to do something. He did not want one to one help anymore, but he could not manage at school without it.

More House school (hereafter MH) could not take the older boys, but we had been very impressed by the school and thought possibly it might be suitable for Hector, as they took boys from year 4. He was assessed at 8 years and 4 months.

His comprehension was 6 years and 9 months. His numeracy was 9 years and 3 months. They wrote:

'Hector was a chatty, friendly boy. At times he spoke rapidly and somewhat indistinctly so he was difficult to understand.'

They agreed to take him. It was a huge relief for us but especially for Hector. By now, his language was much better than his older brothers. He was able to verbalise what he felt and thought. Thank goodness he had been able to tell us that he no longer wanted to go to school with one to one tutors, so we could find an alternative which would suit him.

I was glad that Hector could tell us how he felt, but saddened by how miserable his autism made him feel. What could I say to make it better? He hated praise; he didn't believe us if we told him all the wonderful, positive things about himself. All he knew was that he couldn't read properly or understand what the teachers were saying, but everyone else in his class appeared to, so he felt he was stupid. No amount of telling Hector that he was far from stupid made any difference to him. We had to hope that the new school would be the right place for him.

It had been one of those joining up the dots moments; we had only come across MH school because of the twins.

It was a shock to us that it wasn't too difficult getting the LA to agree to all the placements. Perhaps it was because both More House and Centre Academy would cost less than their current provision did. There was nowhere in our small borough that could accommodate them and their needs. For once (or thrice) we didn't have a big fight. We were doubly relieved that we didn't have to go to tribunal, not only for the stress and expense it would cost but also because it would have caused a long delay of up to a year before they could move schools. Now they could all start at their new schools in September.

The current three full time tutors had been with us for nearly three years. My feelings were mixed as I gave them notice. I was truly sorry to see them leave as I had become very close to them, seeing them on a daily basis, but part of me was inwardly jumping for joy that our days of running a programme were over after eight year

Life however was about to throw us another curveball.

It was becoming increasingly apparent that Marcus, our precious baby, might also have autism. He was just two. While we waited to be absolutely sure that he did have autism and not just language delay, I decided to put together a little programme to try to encourage some speech. He didn't have the behaviours that his brothers had at the same age, so we didn't need trained tutors. I really didn't want to run a home programme ever again. Surely we wouldn't need to? Maybe he didn't have autism? I was again being the eternal optimist or perhaps once again in denial?

He wasn't like his brothers. He was keen to interact; he had some play skills and he didn't have the terrible tantrums or disconnection that the twins had when very young.

We had no formal diagnosis yet. We were still praying that he would be fine. He would start talking and any mention of autism would disappear wouldn't it?

That summer, we went to the cottage in Devon we usually rented for a week, the one with the bath intended for one, but which had to accommodate most of our family! I took a wooden tray with shaped pieces that fitted into it and sat on the floor religiously with Marcus two or three times a day. I kept saying:

'Sun' 'Put the sun in' 'Where is the sun?'

I would lift the wooden sun piece in and out as I said it. I also repeated it with the other shapes labelling them very clearly. Finally, towards the end of the week, something clicked. I asked, 'Where's the sun?' and he picked it out from the pile of shapes. I gave him the biggest hug and cheered him. My little boy had understood what I had asked. He had learned that everything has a label. It was a Eureka moment. We could start teaching him language.

It was a bright moment in what was beginning to feel like a very dark period once again. We could not remain in denial any longer. We knew without being told that our baby and the fourth of our boys was autistic. I wanted to scream:

'No, no, not him...Not Marcus as well...It's not fair.'

It wasn't fair. How could it be true? It was like being stuck in a recurring nightmare, where a doctor says:

'I have to tell you, your son has autism.'

Then you wake up, it's true, and the dream repeats itself until all four of your boys have autism.

We couldn't bear to hear it, but we knew we had to.

It was time to get a formal diagnosis and we weren't going to wait a year for the NHS to provide one. Early diagnosis was imperative to his learning and development. The doctor who had privately diagnosed his three brothers was no longer available so I booked to see another trusted paediatrician. The only positive for us was that, once again, we could afford to pay for a private diagnosis.

The consultant developmental paediatrician wrote in October:

'Marcus is an engaging, smiley little boy who showed some social responsiveness particularly to physical actions, although overall he showed poor response to social engagement and had very poorly integrated communication. He was however, very vocal with a lovely range of babbling sounds'.

And:

'It is paramount for local services to take account of the fact that Marcus is one of a family with four autistic children and the considerable impact that this has on the family as a whole, and the parents in particular.'

She knew that we were going to need all the help we could get.

We immediately started the statutory statement process which meant Marcus would be assessed by various professionals from both health and education departments.

It's hard not to question life and its meaning at times like this. I had so longed for a typically developing child, a child who didn't have autism; one who could grow up and perhaps support his brothers when we were no longer around. Another part of me, selfishly, wanted a child I could share things with. A child who would grow up and maybe go to university and live unsupported and so on and so on. One who would lead a different life to his brothers, a mainstream life. We wanted to experience what most other parents do, a child who learns to talk with no additional input, who experiences the world as we ourselves did as children. I didn't think it was wrong to wish for that.

It was hard not to rage but who was I to rage against? There was no one or nothing to blame for Marcus' autism. I was glad for that. I couldn't be truly angry, with no one to be angry with. I could allow myself some self pity. Why us? Why all four boys?

What were the statistical chances of that? A stranger who knocked at the door canvassing, on hearing I had four boys all with autism remarked:

'All four autistic? You must have done something bad in a past life.'

On difficult days, I sometimes believed that. It must be my fault. I must have done something wrong.

I wish I was given £1 for every time someone asks me if I know what caused their autism. I would be able to set up my own research project.

Do people really think that I know the answer but that I am keeping it to myself?

Of course I don't know! No one knows.

In some ways, we took the news better than we had when Hector was diagnosed. Hector's regression had been a horrible, unexpected shock. At the time, his older brothers were still severely autistic and we had no idea what their futures would be. The thought of a third child progressing in the same way had been awful.

With Marcus, autism had always been a possibility buried deep within our thoughts, even if we tried not to think about it.

We had gambled, but in truth, we hadn't lost. We had this gorgeous boy whom all of us loved and adored. Hector had progressed well in the last year and his speech had improved way beyond our original expectations. Thomas and Benjamin, while not speaking as well as Hector, were now so much better behaviourally. It was not as frightening to hear the word autism as it had been nine years before. We knew that things could change over the years with a great deal of support.

We had made it through the worst years of early autism. The boys no longer ran across roads without looking. We could go out and about with them all. We had a family life which was not ruled by autism. Yes, autism did impact on us all a great deal and there were many things we couldn't yet do, but we had hope.

We could look ahead and see a future for them all, and if we had to do the same for Marcus, then we could do it and we would do it.

I still couldn't quite believe that I had been looking forward to no more therapy programmes and my house finally being my own again. Now, I had to start all over again without even a break in between. The thought of recruiting and training new tutors, having to get a statement and fight for funding was shattering just to think about, let alone to do. I had vowed I would never do it again, no matter what. Now here I was, faced with the reality that Marcus did have autism. How could I not do for him what had changed his brothers' lives? I didn't really have to think hard about it. I had to do it. I had run three programmes, I had to run a fourth. Maybe it wouldn't be so bad only running one programme? To be honest, it was just as hard. The main stress was as always, managing the tutors. I trained up our lovely babysitter, Esther, who turned into such a wonderful tutor that she has made it her career. His other tutors were local Mums so we didn't have anyone with autism experience on his team to begin with. That actually suited us fine for the first few years, we could tailor his programme to suit his needs which were mainly around acquiring language.

September meant new schools for all three boys and new school uniforms. How proud Thomas and Benjamin were on their first morning in their crisp white shirts and school ties. Benjamin particularly liked the blazer with its crest on the pocket. Thomas didn't, but he was able to wear a plain navy jumper instead. Hector also had to wear a shirt and tie. It created lots of ironing for me as they could only tolerate pure cotton shirts and never polyester cotton mixes. They still had rip tape velcro shoes as tying shoelaces was yet to be achievable but they learned to knot their own ties.

At home, they each had a distinctive style of clothing that they preferred. Benjamin wanted only trousers that he could pull on and off with elasticated waists. No fiddly buttons or zips. He had a favourite dark green sweatshirt with a train on the front. Luckily I had bought it big to last and so it lasted for quite a few years eventually ending up with patches on the elbows. Thomas liked very neat clothes, pale blue rugby shirts with collars and smart cotton pyjamas with buttons. All his clothes remained pristine and I could pass them onto Hector when he outgrew them, unlike Benjamin's which went straight to the recycling as they were so worn out. Hector's favourite top was a blue long sleeved T shirt with an appliqué monkey on the front. He absolutely adored that top and it kick started his love of all things monkey.

All the boys travelled by taxi provided by the borough's special needs transport; the twins to Centre Academy and Hector in the opposite direction to More House School down in Farnham, well over an hour's drive away.

They moved from a large, bustling but incredibly supportive mainstream primary, where everyone looked out for 'the Ziegels' and took care of them and loved them, to schools where the students travelled huge distances and were not part of a local community. It had not occurred to us that they might be bullied by other children with issues themselves like low self esteem, low levels of empathy and behavioural problems.

All three boys struggled to adapt to a new environment with new teachers and new children. Hector was bullied in the taxi by two more senior boys. The bullying was severe and, at times, physical. The local authority refused to do anything about it. The school were powerless to discipline the offenders or to prevent it as the taxi service was not managed by them. These boys taught Hector appalling swear words. They used to throw things out of the windows and fight while standing up in the back of a black cab on the motorway. They didn't wear seat belts. We complained many times, but still the LA refused to provide an escort for the taxi.

I used to pay Marcus' tutor to stay on Friday afternoons, while I did a two and a half hour round trip to More House to collect Hector. It meant he got a break from the taxi once a week and time alone with me to download his worries. Sometimes my sister, Nicola, offered to have him overnight to stay with her as she lived near his school; anything to break up his week in the taxi.

My relationship with Hector was very open and fortunately, he told me everything. We had a system where he would tell me any swear words he had been taught so I could tell him which category they went into, as he had no understanding of how abusive or wrong they were as all the words were new to him. There were two main categories, one we called F words which were words that he should never repeat, the worst words. The other category was words which, while not pleasant, were not dreadful. Ideally he shouldn't use any of them but unfortunately, at school, the other boys used them indiscriminately out of earshot of the teachers and often without knowing their true meanings.

Finally, one day, Thomas came home in tears about school and a boy in his class who made it obvious how much he disliked him. Hector came home also in tears, terribly distressed about the taxi journey and I just broke down too. I howled for hours. I became hysterical. I didn't know what to do. Jonathan was away for the week with work and his phone was out of reach. I called a local mum, Abby who had done some tutoring with the boys on Thursdays, while we had our fortnightly team meetings. She knew the boys well. I needed someone to be with me as I was shaking and sobbing. Friends, not family, were who I had to rely on. She came and helped me make supper for the boys and provided a desperately needed ear, while I sobbed and tried to explain what had happened.

I rang both schools in the morning. The head teacher agreed to move Thomas into a different class to get him away from the boy making his life so miserable. The local authority still refused to do anything about Hector's taxi.

At 12 o clock on that Wednesday I went into the menopause.

I couldn't sleep, I couldn't function. I was having severe hot flushes at least hourly from nowhere without warning.

Speaking to a friend a few days later, she told me about adrenal fatigue. That was what I had: severe adrenal fatigue, it wasn't the menopause at all.

I had been through nine years of severe, unrelenting stress since the boys were diagnosed. It had been exhausting, and I had had to fight so hard for so long. I had been running on adrenaline for too long. The stress had finally taken its toll and I had crashed. I had no adrenaline left. Was it a nervous breakdown or a physical one brought on by the mental toll? Whatever it was, I had to carry on.

I couldn't afford to crash. Who would look after the boys and sort it all out? I can only explain it as feeling like permanent jet lag. I woke up exhausted from intermittent sleep. I felt sick most mornings from the tiredness and I had to crawl out of bed and keep doing all the things that I needed to do.

Marcus still had afternoon naps after lunch. I would get into bed and sleep too. It didn't really help, because on waking up I often felt worse than I had before I lay down.

It was the start of me trying many therapies as there was no conventional medical help on offer. I tried Chinese herbal medicine for months with little effect. I did homeopathy, reflexology, then I saw a nutritionist who advised more food restrictions and more supplements. She did a test which showed that I woke up with nonexistent levels of adrenaline and struggled through the day on a flat line of hardly any adrenaline. A standard reading would show a high level on waking and gradual decline through the day until the lowest level at bedtime.

GPs don't offer alternative medicine or healing. They don't acknowledge adrenal fatigue either. I had a terse appointment with a locum GP who tried to prescribe me hormone replacement therapy (HRT) and insisted I was menopausal. Finally, after requesting it three times, a blood test for hormone levels showed that I was not menopausal. I was thankful that I knew enough to refuse the HRT, which would have made me more ill.

I was to feel ill for years. I don't think I will ever be 100% recovered as any severe stress still knocks me for days and I crash physically.

Amongst other suggestions was that I was depressed. I probably was, but I was also totally and utterly burnt out physically. I wasn't getting the practical support and help that I needed. It was too much for one person, four disabled children, but we had no other help, so it would always be me doing everything with Jonathan around at weekends to take some of the strain.

The boys had Nintendo DS hand held devices in those days. As well as playing games on them, you could take photos.

Early one morning I got a call from the headmaster at Hector's school:

'You and your husband need to come in as a matter of urgency. We cannot disclose anything over the phone.'

Jonathan had to cycle home from work and we drove anxiously to More House. All we knew was that there was yet another 'incident' in the taxi, but that Hector was unharmed.

The headmaster placed a Nintendo on the table between us. 'Does anyone know how to turn this on?'

There was a photo of a boy's bare bottom. From the pulled down trousers I knew it was Benjamin's. The boys had been taking silly photos the day before. Hector had shown his companions in the taxi and the driver had overheard them. It was a potential child protection issue.

The result was that the following day we had an escort in the taxi. Hurrah for silly boys' games! After months of the transport department refusing to pay for an escort to protect Hector, he had solved the situation himself with Benjamin's threatening bottom.

From then onwards, a female escort was on every school journey and Hector was untroubled by the older boys. I continued to collect him on Fridays to allow us to talk things through. Over time, we also combined it with a stop at a doughnut shop half way, if he had a successful week at school. He found school hard as he was oppositional and didn't like being 'told what to do'.

Having sorted his older brothers' schooling, we now needed to turn our attention back to Marcus.

'Marcus is a lovely two year old boy with significant receptive and expressive language delay who also demonstrates some autistic behaviours' - from the NHS developmental paediatrician's report in October.

'Marcus is a delightful boy with a diagnosis of Autistic Spectrum Disorder. He displays associated difficulties in particular with his language and communication, social interactions and play.' - from the LA's educational psychologist in November.

And, most thrillingly:

'Marcus' learning will need to be carefully monitored. He would benefit from a structured, small-step approach to his learning, with frequent opportunities for repetition and generalisation of skills.'

In other words, she was endorsing our programme!

In April, we got a final statement for Marcus and it named our programme. It was incredible, to see it written there in black and white. We didn't have to go to tribunal. The borough had agreed to fund his early intervention programme.

There was nothing else they could offer us, because he was still only two and a year too young for the autistic nursery (the one that we had gone against at tribunal for three times for his brothers). We had beaten them time wise and they had no option but to agree to fund his programme. We had paid for less than a year of therapy ourselves this time. We didn't have to waste money that we really didn't have on yet another tribunal. We had also escaped the stress of a tribunal which I think would have finished me off at that stage with the adrenal fatigue at its worst. We should have been dancing for joy, but we were too worn out and worn down by then. We just accepted it gratefully and kept going as usual.

I had put Marcus' name down for a nursery place when he was six months old. I had explained to the head of the nursery at the time that his brothers all had autism, and that we didn't yet know whether he would be affected. I rang to tell them that he too had autism but he did not have any serious behaviours and we had help in place. He could attend with his tutors.

A letter arrived a few days later, explaining that they didn't have a place for him despite him being at the very top of the list. They had too many boys, the head said.

'Sorry, we can't take him.' 'We only have space for girls.'

I had to find another nursery. Of course they were all full by now.

A week later, my neighbour who hadn't got round to putting her son down for any nurseries at all, announced gleefully that she had found him a place. It was at the very same nursery we had just been turned away from.

It had happened again, obvious direct disability discrimination. We could have made a complaint but we were shattered with no energy for a legal battle. We had to let it go. How could people discriminate like this? The head of the nursery hadn't even met Marcus and yet she had decided she didn't want him in her nursery. Perhaps I should have challenged it, if only to teach the head that her attitude was not acceptable but I couldn't take on the world on my own. All my energy was spent helping the boys. I had none left to educate people about their prejudices.

It was almost the same story as with the first nursery. The coincidence of knowing both mothers who were offered my boys' places both times was uncanny.

This was life in the special needs lane. Our boys had been rejected by two nurseries and one primary school. They hadn't been excluded because they did something that endangered anyone. They had been rejected because they had autism. There was so much fear and ignorance about what that word meant. My boys couldn't talk when they were little. They did have some behavioural problems but they weren't dangerous.

A new Montessori nursery was opening and they had places. The lady who ran it was totally inclusive and welcoming. He could go there.

We had ended up sending our four different boys to four very different nursery schools.

The three older boys by the end of that first school year were finally settled into their new schools. We had been right to stick with them, but what a difficult transition it had been.

The first summer holidays without tutors were a shock to me. Years of them being taken out every day meant that the boys were continually asking for outings and treats.

Suddenly my days were more than full. I thought that I was busy before. Now, I really didn't have enough time to do the basics alongside having three boys at home all the time. We had trips to the zoo, to Legoland, the Science Museum, the cinema, the park and I was shattered. I was still struggling with adrenal fatigue and now had all the boys to look after too. On Saturday afternoons I would go to bed and sleep while Jonathan took them all out for a long walk.

My only break all year was our family resort holiday with childcare. No shopping, cooking or cleaning for a week and no admin either. I could read a book on the beach, swim in the sea and try to de stress and rest. We were a phenomenon wherever we went on resort. 'It's the Ziegels' people would say. We had four boys, all autistic, we stood out.

The boys were big, lively characters. They laughed, they joined in. In the children's clubs at the resort, they were often the first to do things; they didn't hesitate. They never whined or complained. They all have this unbridled zest for life, a true joy.

I have videos of them on holiday doing dances which the children's clubs choreographed. The boys are at the front, doing every move, loving it. Marcus came to watch, he ended up joining in wearing his pyjamas. The nannies wanted the boys in their groups. They brought happiness with them. At times like these, we felt blessed. So what if our boys couldn't talk very well and were a bit 'different', actually a lot 'different' at times. They loved their lives and we loved them unconditionally.

Chapter Twelve

'I no longer want to be your friend. I haven't liked you for a long time.'

We had dabbled with music for Benjamin before, with a local friend's daughter teaching him piano, but finally I took the plunge and bought him a second hand drum kit when he was around thirteen years old. He was a natural drummer. Although he is left handed and dyspraxic, which usually means he is quite uncoordinated, it didn't affect his drumming at all. While drumming, he was totally focused. The ADHD which often meant he couldn't concentrate for long, vanished when he played. He had developed a love of 70s bands like the Beatles, Elton John and the Carpenters and they became his musical influence. It was perhaps unsurprising, as that was the music from our youth and what we tended to listen to in the car. He had grown up hearing ballads. It made listening to the drums being played on a wooden floor more palatable being played along to music we enjoyed too. To begin with, we found local teenagers to teach him some basics, but it soon became apparent that he did have talent. He needed the expertise of a qualified drum teacher and someone who would turn up reliably as booked which wasn't always the case with teenagers.

The boys all still found it really hard to deal with when someone cancelled at short notice or worse, didn't turn up at all.

They took it very personally and were often very upset by it. It was hard to strike a happy medium. They needed forewarning that someone was going to come round, but at the same time, I learned to avoid telling them if someone was popping round who might well cancel. People really didn't understand how disappointed the boys were if they cancelled on them.

Martin hadn't taught any special needs children before, but he was patient and thoughtful with Benjamin and soon understood how he ticked. He is still teaching Benjamin ten years on. Benjamin really only wanted to drum. We persuaded him to do just 15 minutes a week of a piano lesson on an upright piano that I found on a free website. I felt that if he were to become a musician, playing the piano would help. Now, he loves playing the piano, picking out rock songs on it, by ear, to sing along with. He learned to play by ear without the need to read music.

Thomas was not very interested or very musical so he didn't stick with his piano lessons for long.

At thirteen, Thomas continued to demonstrate his artistic talent. He now went unaccompanied to art lessons locally to the same teacher he knew from pottery lessons many years before. He produced some fantastic art in many different mediums. He could draw cartoons. He could sculpt. He could paint. Somehow he managed to grasp quite abstract concepts too. Nikki, his teacher, would teach the children the same class about artists and their work that she taught adults. She showed them a famous painting of a train coming out of a fireplace. Thomas interpreted this and painted a bedroom with a bed and chair afloat in water with a picture of the Titanic on the wall. Everything was at an angle in his painting, he had combined his love of all things Titanic into his art. It was a sophisticated concept for a young child, but one he could accommodate. When he was unable to write about historical figures at school, he compensated by using his talent for drawing and would draw cartoon stories, sometimes with speech bubbles. They were intricate, expressive drawings.

Hector quite enjoyed playing the piano but he didn't like practising so he abandoned lessons after a few years. He started playing the trombone at school at the age of ten and had a natural aptitude for it, but he didn't like practising that, either. He was easily distractible and couldn't stick at anything for long. He wanted to do everything perfectly the first time without the need to learn it or practice it. He was very hard on himself, calling himself names and saying how useless he was. No matter how we attempted to explain that no one could miraculously play an instrument or learn a new skill without practice, he wouldn't listen. He found life harder in that way than his older brothers did. While they were able to go over and over the same things, improving slowly, he wasn't. His impatience prevented him from achieving skills which he would have enjoyed.

Hector was unhappy. He hated himself, he hated his autism. At school he would threaten to stab himself with scissors as he thought he was such an 'idiot'. He was often in trouble, with the other boys at school. At heart, he was a gentle child who refused to hit back, but he got very angry, very quickly. He could be 'wound up' in seconds by another boy.

Hector had all the classic signs of ADHD. His inability to control his emotions was extremely poor. He acted impulsively, with no prior thought or consideration. It was painful to watch him struggle with who he was. It was terrible to have a child who was so hard on himself. We couldn't reassure him. We tried to tell him positives about himself but he didn't believe us. I couldn't take away his difficulties. We had to be gentle with him. His self-esteem was brutally low. He had great self awareness of himself and his autism. It would have been easier for him if he didn't. His older brothers were mostly unaware of their own difficulties. They didn't even know the word autism or what it meant.

Hector would download his frustrations about his day when he got home. The taxi journey was still torment to him despite him having a DVD player to watch films on. He resented having an escort in the taxi. He felt that the escort was there because of his 'autism', so he hated it more. Boarding at school wasn't an option, because home was his safe place where he was happiest and he needed to be able to talk to me. His processing delays made talking on a telephone challenging, so a mobile phone would not have helped.

He was slowly starting to make friends at school. He was often invited to birthday parties at the weekends. We couldn't do reciprocal play dates easily as we lived so far from the school and his classmates mostly lived close to it. The school proved to be a great learning environment for him and he was much happier learning in small classes where he felt the same as everyone else, no longer needing a one to one. It improved his self esteem not to feel different. His form teachers were also speech and language therapists, so his language continued to improve.

Marcus was happy at nursery. He babbled away, making lots of sounds and smiling all the time. He couldn't yet talk but was doing his best to try to communicate. He didn't have the difficult behaviours that his brothers had had and was happy to follow directions and do what people asked him to do. His autism was most obvious in his lack of speech. I was so, so grateful that his autism wasn't as severe as his brothers. It could have been so very much worse. I don't know how I would have managed if he had behaved like they did as very young children. He was so much easier to look after in comparison to them. He was co operative. He didn't run away. He wanted to join in, when he could, with any activities. I didn't want to compare them but it was hard not to, fourth child along. One thing for sure, he definitely didn't have the ADHD that Benjamin and Hector had. He slept every day after lunch. While he napped, I could rest too. I needed the rest as much as he did.

We finally had to stop his naps only because he started school at just four. Being summer born meant he was one of the youngest in the year group. He also went to bed at night without any problems. The only legacy of his colic was that he slept surrounded by dummies. We had gradually weaned him off them so he only had them at night but he would wake up and want one. To save me being woken, I left a handful of them in his bed. I was constantly buying new ones as he had a tendency to chew on them!

I was grateful. I was grateful for this beautiful, sunny child whom we never thought we might have. Although it wasn't easy, I knew he would improve. He did have the potential, with the right support, to learn to speak. I would do my best to give him every possible chance in life.

Jonathan and I were struggling. Our social life at this time was minimal. We were tired and socialising just wasn't a priority. Occasionally we had friends for supper but we had existed on the fringes of society for so long, that we didn't know how to mix back into it again. Babysitters were hard to find who were willing to look after all the boys but when we could get one, we went to the theatre which was something we both really enjoyed. We had each other, our home was cosy and we were certainly never bored. Along the way though, we lost many friends. The arrival of children changes many relationships. It affects partnerships. The strain of caring for special needs children is at times immeasurable and many marriages do not survive.

Some days I just wanted to cry down the phone to Jonathan. I would phone him at work and sob. He often couldn't listen. He had meetings, he was in an open plan office. He needed to get on with his work. I would feel resentful. They were his children, too. I needed him to support me. Sometimes, he couldn't. I would put the phone down and cry harder. It is difficult for those who don't live with special needs on a daily basis to grasp just how relentless it is. By the time he returned home, I would be calmer. I had to be, I had the boys to look after. I couldn't hold it against him, that he hadn't had time to talk to me. Autism didn't destroy our relationship although it surely challenged it. Perhaps it made our bond stronger? We were united against an often unsupportive world. People reacted in different ways to our boys. There were a few friends who stayed the course. We often went for picnics in Richmond Park with one set of godparents, Peter and Liz. We trained their children, who were a similar age, to round ours up on their bicycles when our boys ran off. It saved us running after them and gave them a bit more freedom. Our boys were always invited to their children's parties. They might not join in, often they stood on the sidelines watching but they were included. One party we had to leave within the first few minutes, as it was in a very large sports hall in which sounds were echoed and amplified. Thomas and Hector both put their hands firmly over their ears and refused to move. We had to carry them out in our arms, which wasn't easy while also pushing a buggy and doing our best to pacify Benjamin who couldn't understand why we weren't staying as he wanted to. But they always invited the boys, no matter what and we appreciated that.

Other people kept in touch with us but they didn't really want to get involved. We never got offers of practical help like babysitting. People were afraid of the responsibility and indeed, afraid of the boys themselves and what they might do.

One of my very good friends had been my bridesmaid at our wedding. She was also godmother to Thomas and Benjamin. For many years, she was really good to them. She would visit regularly and play with them. Although she didn't want children herself, she had many young nieces and nephews and liked children.

Their autism didn't bother her. But I did. I had changed over the years. We had been drinking partners, party girls. Now I was serious and boring. I had no time for fun. She didn't like the person I had become and so one day after a mix up where we had both been waiting for each other at a different place, she switched her phone off to calls and emailed me to tell me:

'I no longer want to be your friend. I haven't liked you for a long time.'

She refused to speak to me ever again. I am glad to say she

was the only friend who reacted in such an extreme way. I like to think that there was something in her own life which caused this. The fact that I was no longer the person I had been seemed too cruel. I was really upset for months. She had been a good friend. I lost her as a friend forever and the boys lost their godmother.

We lost close contact with other friends as we couldn't travel long distances to visit them and stay overnight. Often, other people's children didn't want to spend time with our 'different' boys. There were so many reasons that we no longer saw people. At a time in our lives when we really needed support, it often wasn't there.

It was hard, too, for me to 'lose' myself. This wasn't the life we had planned and anticipated. I had lost who I had been. We barely had time to think of ourselves. Our life revolved around our children and their needs.

It sounds a bit dramatic but we put our own lives on hold in order for our boys to develop theirs. Of course we were prepared to do that. We would do anything for our sons. The more we did for them now, the more they would be able to do in the future and we would hopefully be able to step back a bit one day. We had made some new friends among the other parents, once the boys' moved to the new primary school. I made a few very solid friends who supported me when I was going through difficult times. I was conscious to spread the load between them and would try to remember whose 'turn' it was to listen. I didn't want to overload them and lose them. I also made online 'friends' with other mothers within the autism community for mutual support. Most of those, I have never met.

We learned to try not to take rejection on a personal level. People often don't know what to say or how to react. If they got it wrong and upset us, we had to realise that perhaps they hadn't actually meant what they said and it came out wrongly. This was particularly true each time one of our boys was diagnosed. It was our most vulnerable time, when we really expected and needed people to say the right things. So often, they did not. They made ill-considered comments like:

'Well you already know what to do about autism, you must be an expert now.'

I wanted to answer back:

'We do know only too well and that's why we don't want it again.'

'You are lucky to have your nannies paid for.'

No, we weren't. They weren't nannies, they were tutors. They educated our boys; they didn't provide childcare.

We would be the lucky ones if we didn't need tutors. When asked how I got all the boys to their new schools in different places, now three different schools for four boys, I told them, that the older three boys went in taxis provided by the LA.

'Aren't you lucky to have your children picked up and dropped off?'

My response would be:

'I would be lucky if I had children who could take themselves to school on the train or bus.'

It did upset us. People didn't think carefully about what they were saying. They wanted to make themselves feel better by diminishing our struggles. We grew used to hearing thoughtless comments, but it didn't stop them hurting us. It was no wonder we avoided other people who we didn't know well or who didn't know us.

We were never offered any medical support for the boys. After the age of five, they ceased to have annual developmental assessments. Their autism was seen purely as something to be managed educationally but not medically.

Now that we no longer had to pay for Marcus' programme and we had avoided the expense of further tribunals, we could afford to spend some money on other therapies which might possibly help the boys. I wanted them to reach their own, full potential, whatever that was destined to be and would try anything that was not harmful.

I'm not cynical but there were many 'cures' to choose from. How did we know what might help? We knew that different things suited different children like gluten free diets. What one parent raved about, another would equally dismiss as a waste of time and money. I was willing to try treatments where there was some scientific basis. Early intervention of course was a known, proven method of teaching backed up by research.

We found one of the only medically qualified doctors in the country who actively treated children with autism for medical problems which might cause changes in their behaviour. He did blood tests and specialist scans. It cost a small fortune. We couldn't just treat one child; that wouldn't have been fair, so we had to treat all three. Marcus was progressing quite well with acquiring language and had very few behavioural issues, so we didn't include him. It was quite complicated and I often struggled to understand the science, despite being a nurse, but knowing he was a bone fide doctor meant we could trust him.

They had low levels of 5HTP in blood tests. 5HTP is the natural precursor to serotonin (the happy hormone) and can be taken as a nutritional supplement. Thomas was still inclined to burst into tears at any perceived slights or when he was frustrated. The 5HTP helped him manage his emotions.

The boys all had high (ASOT) levels of bacterial streptococcus infection in their blood, way higher than acceptable levels. They had enlarged, pitted and scarred tonsils from recurrent infections. The doctor thought it was probably causing sleep apnoea, as well as causing chronic infection. They most likely had a condition known as PANDAS (Paediatric Autoimmune Neuropsychiatric Disorders Associated with Streptococcal Infections). Taking nearly six months of very strong antibiotics did nothing. Their levels stayed unchanged.

Hector's behaviour worsened. I was called regularly by the taxi escort to calm him down while they were en route home, but I was often unable to do so. When he was angry and upset, it was impossible to talk to him over the phone. She rang once while I was buying vegetables in the supermarket. Goodness knows what people thought.

'Hector, sit down. Hector, calm down and the taxi will bring you home. I can talk to you when you get home. Hector, please sit down'. Spoken loudly and clearly down the phone to a very agitated young boy with little effect, but just hearing my voice calmed him somewhat.

We checked his ASOT levels, they had doubled again. We agreed that all the boys needed to have their constantly infected tonsils removed. It was the only way to eradicate the strep infections. For Marcus, too, it would hopefully put an end to recurrent ear infections and glue ear.

Because of the risk of cross infection, all four boys had their tonsils removed the same morning. We couldn't easily explain to the boys how it was going to feel afterwards but they trusted us and they weren't frightened. They didn't know to be frightened of hospital as they had no real previous experience of one. They had been too young to remember having grommets inserted. We knew they recovered swiftly from anaesthetics so that was one positive.

I spent the morning going from the anaesthetic room with one boy to the recovery room to be with the next. I went round in a circle until all four boys were safely through. The relief was huge but the day had only just begun. For once, my nursing training was of use. People often thought that as a nurse, I would be familiar with autism, but in all my years of nursing I had never come across a single child with autism. The surgeon confirmed afterwards that they all had actively infected enormous tonsils. As he still had glue ear, Marcus also had some more grommets inserted at the same time.

We stayed in the hospital for 24 hours. The boys were in a small ward together and I had a camp bed. Marcus climbed out of bed and went to sit next to Thomas and hold his hand, a beautiful expression of their love for each other. As we left, the play therapist waved us goodbye and said we were like the Von Trapps. The Sound of Music is my favourite film, but at that moment, I didn't feel much like singing.

We went home to quarantine for a week. It was more painful for the older boys post operatively but they were all stoical about it as they ate their ice cream, watching videos. There was a moment of real fear a week later. I was in the shower when Jonathan called me. Marcus had coughed up blood all over the kitchen floor. He was white and shocked. We called an ambulance and I hugged him tightly in a towel. I went into automatic 'nurse' mode and was strangely calm. I knew it could be life threatening if he didn't stop bleeding. I got in the ambulance with him and left Jonathan at home with the other boys. Fortunately, they didn't know what had happened as it would have frightened them too. Slowly, he recovered from his silent state of shock and by the time we arrived at hospital half an hour later, he was his usual self again. The doctors said it was probably just a big clot that had dislodged. We watched him closely for a few days but fortunately there was no further bleeding.

As they were all off school and the Queen was visiting Richmond Park, I sneaked them out of the house as the quarantine period was close to ending. Thomas was rewarded with a wave from Prince Philip as the car passed through the park gates. He still talks about that day and when Prince Philip sadly died, he wrote a letter of condolence to the Queen enclosing copies of paintings he had made of her some years before and telling her about the day Prince Philip waved to him.

We went into the park and saw the Queen at close range. They have never mentioned having their tonsils out since, but they do talk about seeing the Queen that day.

What difference did it make having their tonsils removed? Hector within weeks was a changed child. His temper improved; he was no longer so angry or irritable at the slightest thing. I never got calls from the taxi escort again, he could manage his own behaviour so much better. At his school annual review, a few months later, the teachers produced a bar chart from various assessments. It was unrecognisable from the previous year's chart as every score had increased dramatically. It was proof that for him, the operation was definitely worthwhile.

Marcus had had recurrent tonsillitis, ear infections and glue ear. From then onwards, he was fully well and free from infections. He didn't need grommets again and his hearing improved to within acceptable limits which in turn led to a significant increase in the number of words he acquired. We had also spared him from the chronic throat infections his brothers had suffered for so many years.

I asked the boys' doctor if he could treat me too and he did. He diagnosed something called MTHFR on a blood test, a genetic mutation that many people carry. I received the test results in the post. I typed it straightaway into the search engine expecting adrenal or chronic fatigue to come up. Instead, the first page of results was all about recurrent miscarriage. It all made sense but it was too late for my lost babies. He prescribed high doses of Vitamin B 12 injections three times a day. I never got used to jabbing myself with them but less than week later, I woke one morning feeling the nearest to well I had felt in years. That was the beginning of my slow recovery, a kick start which none of the other therapies had managed to do.

I was constantly asked to talk to other parents. Sometimes people gave out my phone number without asking me first. It was often a friend of a friend or a school mother who hardly knew me. It seemed all roads led to my contact details some days. Many local people had heard of us and wanted my advice. A close friend, Sharon, who works for a local charity once said:

'You are a local legend. You have won three tribunals.'

I often had to say:

'No, I am sorry but I am too busy with my four boys. I can't speak to everyone that wants to speak to me.'

I could only offer contact numbers of useful organisations. I knew people were desperate for advice. I had been in that position myself and I knew how hard it was to find all the information you need. Occasionally, someone would get quite cross that I wouldn't speak to their friend or acquaintance:

'But I thought you would understand. This mother really needs someone to talk to, why won't you talk to her?'

I couldn't be a counsellor for everyone. I couldn't be a one woman helpline. I certainly couldn't offer individual advice. I was not an educational psychologist and I had usually never even met their child.

I decided that I would no longer talk on the phone to people. I could spend an hour just talking to one mother, who would then want to speak to me again a week later.

But I could write a book to help people and pass on all the information I had spent years acquiring. I knew people also needed emotional support and while I couldn't offer that on a one to one basis, I could write about it.

I had limited time. When I got a spare hour, I would sit at my computer and write. It took years to finish that book but I successfully found a publisher and my autism handbook came out in July 2016.

Having only spent a year at nursery, Marcus started school at just four years and two months old. He was able to go to the same fabulous primary school that had been so wonderful with his brothers. How pleased I was to be back there. We knew so many of the staff and they welcomed us and Marcus' tutors with open arms.

School was a big, noisy, busy environment for him. He often experienced sensory overload and became easily overwhelmed. When that happened, he didn't cry or have a meltdown, but needed to retreat and find a quiet space to be in. As a toddler, he would climb into his buggy and fall asleep when it all got too much. For the first few terms he only went in to school for the mornings. In the afternoons he would sleep or work quietly at home.

Marcus lived at home with three autistic brothers. He

needed to socialise with neurotypical children; those who had age appropriate language and play skills. Mainstream school was vital for him to learn about life outside the special needs home he lived in.

The other children accepted him. His language was still severely delayed, but he could run around and play tag with them. He was in the right place.

We never let life stand still for any length of time. It was time to move house!

We had outgrown our house after fifteen years. Strange to think we had started off with three spare bedrooms and despite adding another two along the way, needed more space, but the house had become top heavy with only one living space downstairs which now had to accommodate all six of us and a drum kit and piano! I was also thinking ahead. I couldn't imagine how we would all live happily together in the years to come when the boys became young adults. I didn't want them pushed into assisted living. I wanted that to be a choice when the time came and not a necessity.

We couldn't really entertain friends at home as the boys didn't go to bed until we did. We couldn't go out often as we didn't have the funds or the babysitters available. Increasingly, our social isolation had crept back. The boys needed more space for themselves too, to have friends round, play on games consoles and watch different programmes from us on the TV.

We needed to stay living locally for the boys' continuity, to remain in the community they knew so well and to continue at their schools. Another vital consideration was that we had four statements now and changing boroughs could mean starting a fight all over again with a new LA who might challenge the boys' current placements.

We finally found an old house which desperately needed renovation, having been lived in by the same family for the past fifty years. I had grand plans for it. The hard bit was downsizing from six bedrooms to four bedrooms for at least a year and no bathroom for the first six weeks. The twins had to share a bedroom for the next two years. We also had to live there throughout major building work being carried out. To get round the no bathroom problem for the first month, their carers took them swimming every few days!

It was a brave, perhaps mad, undertaking.

We didn't have our usual resort holiday that year but we did sample CentreParcs for a few nights, primarily to have hot water and showers. The boys weren't safe on bicycles and apart from the fabulous swimming complex, there wasn't much to occupy them there, so we went on our usual days out to surrounding castles and for walks.

One of the first tasks was to cut down some dead trees to make best use of the large garden. We assembled a large wooden swing frame with a large round net swing which could take a combined weight of up to 90kgs, similar to those at the playgrounds. All the boys loved to swing, as it calmed them down and neutralised disruptions caused by the vestibular system in their inner ear. They would often run outside, needing the comfort and stabilising effect that the swing gave them. It's still in our garden but not used often by the boys these days. They have found replacement activities, like running instead.

Most of the winter, we had no hot water or heating as the ancient boiler broke down at least six times. The inside of the house was newly plastered but the weather was so awful and wet that the plaster would not dry. I bought the boys each a warm animal onesie fleece to wear in the house. They seemed to take it all in their stride, the damp, the lack of hot water, even the twins having to share a bedroom again after years of having their own space. As long as their lives and routines remained relatively unchanged, they coped. I was surprised by their ability to adapt. They never asked to move back to the old house which they had known all their lives. They just accepted what I told them, that, in a year the house would be fabulous and so much bigger.

For the next year the house was a building site. The stress of caring for the boys and fighting for their education had been a far greater stress than rebuilding a house was. It was just organisational stress, no emotions involved.

For Marcus' sixth birthday, we erected a trampoline in the garden after he had gone to bed the night before, so he woke in the morning delighted to see it magically there.

Finally, it was finished. Having grown out of Brio, Benjamin laid out his Hornby trains on his bedroom floor. He had space for his drums and piano in the front room. He was developing a real passion for music and getting quite good at it, too. He started to compose his own songs. The first Christmas in the new house, he surprised us with a song, 'Christmas Time Again'.

'The lights are on, and friends and family come to join the fun, let's celebrate, because it's Christmas time again.'

He had written it about our new house and friends from his primary school. I cried when I first heard it. We hadn't realised how talented he was. Hector filmed Benjamin playing and singing it and put it on YouTube. By now, Hector was developing his skills as a film maker, all self taught. Their individual strengths and talents were evolving.

Every Christmas, we had a party for all our tutors, carers, babysitters and anyone who cared for and supported the boys. We still have those parties now. The boys used to perform some music, mainly Benjamin on the drums and piano, Hector, more reluctantly, playing trombone, and latterly Marcus playing trumpet and piano. The highlight of the evening was always a dance routine to a Christmas song performed by all four boys. For the first few years, we were lucky enough to have carers who could choreograph and rehearse the boys. The last few years, I had to make up the moves and join in so I kept it very simple. There was always a huge argument over which song we would choose and the dance was consequently often made up very last minute. The videos of them dancing over the years are my favourite videos of them all. Finally, they decided that they were too old to dance anymore and although I kept it going for a few more years, they stopped when they became adults.

They were growing up fast. They still needed constant attention and an adult around at all times, but they were able to go off safely into different rooms within the house unaccompanied. It made a huge difference. The bickering and arguments between them lessened. Empathy is an emotion that cannot be easily taught. Although the boys loved one another and in many ways were close, they lacked insight into their own conditions. If they didn't recognise how autism affected themselves, how could we hope for them to be able to respect how it affected each other? The extra space really helped our family dynamics.

Chapter Thirteen

Why?' 'Why are we all autistic? Did you do something wrong when you were pregnant with us?' – Hector.

We took our boys out every day of their lives whatever the weather. In the earlier days, it was mostly for long walks which we varied. We had our favourites like walking around Virginia Water or Burnham Beeches. We went regularly to Kew Gardens and Richmond Park which are on our doorstop and other local parks like Osterley to visit Grandma's tree and Wimbledon Common where latterly Jonathan's parents' ashes are scattered.

As teenagers, we started taking them to the occasional exhibition at an art gallery or to see outdoor sculpture. They liked contemporary art, paintings they could engage with. Coloured squares and abstracts which needed interpretation were not to their liking, nor what they perceived as stuffy old paintings. Artists like colourful Matisse and pop artists were among their favourites.

We never overstayed, making our visits short, moving swiftly, stopping only to look at paintings of particular interest worked best. I would read the accompanying explanations on the walls and break them down, giving the boys snap shots of what the artist was trying to portray.

On holidays, we might visit stately homes but they were mostly too dull for the boys who much preferred the picnic in the gardens afterwards.

They became used to going to new places over time and now ask: 'What are we doing this weekend?' in the hope of something new and interesting to see.

Living in London opened up so many possibilities. There was always a new art exhibition or special event to go to. We wanted to stimulate the boys as much as possible. They couldn't read books, only written facts, and most theatre was inaccessible to them due to their difficulties in following the dialogue. Musicals like The Lion King or The Snowman were fine but plays with too many spoken words bored them and they became twitchy and agitated.

We took them to see a production of The Railway Children at Waterloo station. Marcus was still in a buggy which we had parked outside. Benjamin really only enjoyed the bits when the train moved up and down the track, way too few for his liking though. Marcus kept kicking and the seats were close together so Jonathan removed his shoes leaving them on the seat. Before the show even started, he had to take him out as it was obvious he was going to spoil the performance for everyone else. He never returned, taking Marcus home on the train alone with no shoes or coat. In fact the train journey had probably been enough stimulation for him on its own.

Apart from the mental stimulation, another reason to take the boys out was to occupy them in the absence of friends.

Hector's school was far away. Only one boy turned up to his birthday party the first year. From then onwards, I arranged parties close to his school so that the other boys would come. Sometimes I would arrange sleepovers. It could be quite challenging. I was used to my boys and all their different ways. It was really hard work if a child stayed who just wanted to play computer games all day.

Hector would ask why he couldn't go to the local comprehensive school only a few minutes' walk away from our house. He didn't want to be autistic and have to go to a specialist school. He saw his autism as preventing him from having local friends. He would ask me:

'Why are we all autistic? Did you do something wrong when you were pregnant with us?'

What was I supposed to answer? That I really didn't have a clue why? It didn't appear to run in our family on either side. Was it genetic? Was it something I did?

There was no obvious reason. We had enrolled in some research projects over the years but never heard anything about the results. The most recent one had us all spitting into test tubes around the dining table. We had genetic counselling before having Marcus. I think now there is much more sophisticated genetic testing available but we have no desire to do it. It is of no benefit to the boys currently. There may come a point in the future where perhaps one of them considers having children themselves and that will involve some careful conversations. As none of them have ever yet had a partner of any sort, we will worry about that when the time comes, if it ever does.

The twins' school was very small, less than 50 children in total between the ages of 10 and 18. Their class cohort was only six children. They never had friends round as again the distances were too great. We did have a couple of birthday parties for them, in particular a swimming one that was a great success.

I felt sorry for the older boys. They didn't have friends like Hector did. Benjamin has never been invited for a sleepover anywhere in his life but desperately wanted one. My sister was his only option, but he was frightened of her dogs so she couldn't have him.

It was hard for Thomas and Benjamin to be thrown together so much in the absence of friends. They had to travel together in the taxi to school. They had to sit together at school with only four other children. We had deliberately kept them apart from each other from nursery age. Now they had to tolerate being with each other most of the time. They didn't like it much. There was no other school to send them to and we had been lucky to be accepted by the one we had.

They bickered like an old married couple at times. How do you explain to a child with autism that his brother isn't being annoying, he has autism, when that child doesn't know or understand that he himself has autism? Their own self awareness was minimal. At thirteen, they didn't know that they were autistic.

Benjamin was always quite anxious. He would ask hundreds of questions continually. They might be very relevant:

'What time are we leaving?' 'How long will it take to get there?' 'How long will we stay there?' 'Who else is going?'

He needed constant clarification. He still does.

Then there would be the non relevant questions; non relevant to us that is.

'In the summer, when we go on holiday, what time are we leaving?' 'What time do I need to get up the day we go on holiday?' asked in February at 10.30pm about a holiday booked for August.

It drove us all mad. It particularly drove Thomas mad as he was in his company for much of the time.

Apart from occasional summer holiday activities run by local charities and groups, there was little for them to do. We had to keep them busy ourselves. Having four children could be an advantage. They might argue with each other but at least there was always someone else to do things with. It's more fun to jump on a trampoline with a brother than on your own. In the summer, running around the garden with a water gun required a moving, living target. They would choose films to watch together. They would build Lego together. Even bickering is interaction with another person.

Thomas made one good friend at a local summer activity group and despite going to different schools, they became friends. Fraser's love of football rubbed off on Thomas. He became a Fulham fan. Thomas embarked on teaching himself football facts. He read voraciously online, watched endless matches and became a footie expert. It was remarkable in someone from a non football loving home and proved to be a great social skill. He could talk football to anyone. No matter which team they supported, he could conjure up transfer facts and tactics.

He was the only one at all interested in sport. The summer of 2012 was a memorable one for all of the boys but the real highlight that year was the London Olympics.

We entered the ballot and successfully got one set of tickets for the athletics, the 100m men's final track race. We took Thomas and Hector for the day. The actual track events were quite lengthy and not that exciting for the boys, but they loved the atmosphere. I made collages of their entry and train tickets and photos of the day which they still have framed on their bedroom walls. Thomas witnessed Usain Bolt's gold medal victory win. He declared it one of the best moments of his life. He knew the names of all the runners in the 100m race, their countries, their winning positions and times and would excitedly tell them to anyone willing to listen. He was inspired to start running himself. It was a pivotal day in his life.

We knew leaving the stadium would be problematic. Hector couldn't tolerate crowds or a stranger accidentally touching him. We shielded him as much as we could and tried to get on a crowded train as quickly as possible. On the train I put my arms around him to keep others from leaning against him or even touching him; an impossibility in the crowded underground. If he came into physical contact with a stranger he swore loudly, spitting out all the worst words he knew. People stared. How could a child be so rude? We couldn't stop and explain to people why he was so angry and how he was suffering from acute sensory distress.

Every year at the local firework display, we had to queue to squeeze through a tiny gate, he would erupt, start swearing and push his way through people. He would not queue. He was incandescent with rage and inconsolable until he calmed down, within ten minutes usually. People thought we were awful parents with an equally horrible child. In his mid teens, his tolerance to unexpected touch lessened and he was able to navigate crowds so much better. We didn't do any special programme or therapy, it was just another of those things which eased over time with exposure.

At Christmas, we bought Hector and Marcus a scooter each. They were delighted but their brothers were so envious that within days we had bought another two and soon all four boys were scooting in the park. The older boys had finally learned to ride bicycles but we hardly ever took them out as they had absolutely no road sense at all. They were unable to look before crossing the road still and had to be watched and sometimes stopped at the last minute as they tried to walk blithely into the traffic. We couldn't let them cycle on the road and they were too big to cycle on the pavements. Popping a pile of scooters into the boot of the car was a much safer and easier option to cycling.

On New Year's Eve, Thomas said he was so sad that the year had ended. It had been the best year of his life.

The twins turned 14 in 2013. Their hormones erupted. It was going to be a rough few years. In many ways, they were still emotionally very immature but their bodies carried on regardless. They still watched children's videos but also had a new interest in women's bodies. It was a tricky combination while there were still behaviours, which they needed help to work through and hopefully improve upon.

Thomas' tolerance for others and his perception of how they treated him was still a big issue for him. He would burst into tears and run out of the room if he felt wronged or not in control of the conversation. This often happened at school, not just at home.

He felt persecuted at times and that people were against him. He thought people were staring at him when in fact they might just be looking vaguely in his direction. He could take a long time to calm down after these episodes and until he did, no one was able to talk things through with him. He was also rigid in his thinking, so it made it even harder to reassure him. At times, he was unable to listen or to take in what others were saying to him. He needed strategies to handle his own feelings. There was no quick fix or solution. When he became stressed, he would put his arm bent down on the surface in front of him and bury his nose into his elbow in the manner of a stork burying its head in the sand. It was an improvement on running out of the room.

Benjamin's ADHD seemed to be exacerbated by his hormones. He could fly off the handle for almost no reason. He would shout very loudly and stomp around. He is a big boy, and to some he could appear quite threatening when he was angry. He was easily provoked. Unfortunately, Hector realised this and would wind Benjamin up. The combination of all the boys having autism made everything so much harder for us all. Hector had little empathy plus he was having a hard time at school. He would take out his frustrations on Benjamin. The knock on effect could be horrendous.

If I tried to moan to anyone about the boys' behaviour, they would invariably say:

'All teenage boys are awful, hormones are awful and all siblings squabble.'

I'm sure they do. But I am also sure it was worse in our house because of the autism. I got very little sympathy. After all, everyone else had teenagers too.

Hector was frequently frustrated with himself. He hated being taught to do anything. He wanted to do it all himself. At school, he was oppositional and defiant at times. He thought he knew better than everyone else. His teachers were very tolerant with him. They appreciated his enthusiasm and his cheerful personality. It wasn't that he didn't want to do things; it was just that he didn't want to need to be taught how to do them. He was often in trouble, but not for anything serious.

His school had a reward system. Conduct points and warnings were given for poor behaviour. Reward points were given for good behaviour. Hector's Cs far outnumbered his Rs. I didn't tell him off. My job was to manage his behaviour at home.

He was always out in the fields at lunchtime building dens. I approved of his being outside and not stuck indoors playing video games. One day he came home in his games kit.

'I got a C3 today for going down a mudslide.' He grinned at me.

His clothes were absolutely caked in mud. He had not been allowed back into school in them. He had been warned by a teacher not to slide down, but he still did it. In his words:

'But the boys dared me to do it. I was cool. I was a hero. Wouldn't you rather be admired by your mates for being a hero than be a goody two shoes?'

He was a hero to his friends. For a child who was sometimes at the receiving end of negative attention from his peers, for him, that was a good day.

Despite leaving home just after seven am every weekday morning, Hector could still not settle at night. He didn't want to go to bed. He couldn't read in bed. Listening to story tapes was not an option as his processing delay meant he couldn't keep up with the words spoken at speed, and if he had kept up, he didn't get the gist of the story anyway. He was hyperactive and refused to lie in bed doing nothing which was fair enough. Our compromise was not to offer video games for him to play but to let him sit on the sofa with us, watching whatever we were watching, until we all went up to bed. It took very little to provoke him and there was no point in getting him into an agitated state before bed or he would never go to sleep. Fortunately, once finally asleep, he didn't wake in the night. He just didn't seem to need as much sleep as the rest of us.

Marcus was such a dear little boy. He didn't get cross; he didn't have any challenging behaviours. It was such relief to have a child who was happy nearly all the time. Like his brothers, he had started out with no understanding of language and no eye contact. But, he didn't have the behaviours that Thomas and Benjamin had as young children. He didn't have the anger that Hector had. Despite them all having autism, they were all very different.

Marcus tripped up a lot. The walk to school was 15 minutes. He might fall over up to six times on the way. I always dressed him in long trousers, never shorts, to avoid grazes on his knees. We managed to get him some sessions with an OT (Occupational Therapist).

His therapy involved sitting on a big bouncy ball, trying to strengthen his core muscles. It did help his balance. We hadn't been able to teach him to swim either because his core strength was so poor. He would bob vertically in the water with his legs dangling straight down. Hector had had the same problem when he was young.

Autism affected many aspects of the boys' lives from their severe problems with speech, difficulties with social communication, behavioural problems and sensory processing issues. But, it also affected them physically. Hypermobility meant their joints were over flexible. Benjamin liked to shock people by dislocating the tip of his index finger, Hector was the worst affected; his knees cracked like an old man's. He and Marcus had weak core muscles which made them floppy in the middle and made balance harder too. They struggled learning to ride bikes, to swim, even to walk up and downstairs one foot on each alternate step, clutching the banister rail as they did so.

None of the boys played team sports. They found it hard to run well due to dyspraxia in Benjamin's case and hypermobility in all of them bar Thomas, making them prone to turning their ankles and twisting them. I broke my foot twice as a child with weak ankles, so I was wary of them doing the same, but they never did. It wasn't only the physical aspects which hampered them. They couldn't anticipate another's moves in football, they wouldn't know where the ball was coming from and where to kick it, if they managed to kick it at all. Understanding the strategy of playing team games was impossible for them.

Apart from Thomas, who only started to follow football because his friend did, none of them were in any way interested in watching sport either. I'm not either, so it's one thing I don't see as a big loss.

Thomas and Benjamin's school did very little sport, just a weekly visit to the local sports hall to throw a ball around. Hector did a weekly sports session. One of the reasons Hector stuck with playing the trombone was that he played in the school's brass band and was therefore one of the 'musicians' as opposed to one of the sporty boys, giving him an identity and a tribe to belong to.

Every December, Thomas and Benjamin took part in the Canbury School cross country race. It was held in Richmond Park for a group of small, local schools, many also being special needs schools. Thomas came about 50th out of over 100 children the first year at age eleven. He vowed he would win it one day. Benjamin hated running and stumbled around the course, grateful that it was only once a year that he had to run. Hector was sometimes chosen to run for his school too, arriving by mini bus. He wasn't a good runner. I suspect they chose him because it meant I could be there to cheer the boys on and take him home afterwards, a five minute drive from our house, saving him over an hour in the taxi for that one day.

Thomas decided he wanted to start running. At age fourteen, I took him to a local running shop which was advertising evening runs. The manager Ricky agreed to take him out with the group. Thomas was really keen and able to keep up on his first night out. Ricky had no personal knowledge of autism but embraced Thomas from first meeting him. I was humbled by his attitude and his willingness to look after him. He supported him by turning up and cheering him on at every subsequent cross country and other local races. Thomas ran with the group weekly for the next five years and became part of the local running community.

Occasionally, unexpected people turn out to be true saviours. We may not have gone looking for them. We aren't expecting them, but they appear in our lives. Ricky is one of these people.

Because Marcus only went to school in the mornings in his

first year, he missed numeracy in the afternoons. He was young for the year so the school agreed with us that he should stay down a school year like his brothers had. In the summer term, both we and the school wrote to the LA to request his repeating a year in reception. It was supposed to be a formality.

The LA refused our request. Worse still, they wrote an aggressive letter declaring that if we felt he needed to stay down, then 'obviously' our intervention programme was not working. We were now suddenly at risk of them pulling funding for the programme. I took legal advice but we decided that we wouldn't fight this time. We knew at some point they would force Marcus to miss a year. The LA had made both the twins and Hector skip and go back up a year when they left primary school to make up for the repeated year. By now, the other children's level of language was so much more sophisticated than Marcus'. He had a lot of catching up to do, to keep up with his current class. He was quite shy with the children at school as he couldn't understand much of what they said. We would also have to catch up on the maths he had missed.

'Room on the Broom' was one of Marcus and my favourite bedtime stories. As soon as he was able to read a little, he delighted in reading his stories out aloud, often to Daddy who was still in his cycling kit. As he had not seen him all day, bedtime was their special time together. On the nights I didn't read the story, I got into bed with him for a 'Big Mummy Hug', a term coined by Marcus.

He and I had a favourite video which we watched together when he was tired or overwhelmed. We called it 'Duck in the Winter'. We would snuggle together under a blanket. In the same way that his brothers had, he started to use his acquired language to describe things. One day he came home from gym club with his tutor and declared 'duck in the winter'.

He wasn't asking to watch the video. Luckily, I made the connection. He was trying to tell us that he had left his top behind.

It was his favourite long sleeve blue tee shirt with an appliquéd fuzzy goose on the front. He had never called it that before but it made total sense. From then onwards, it was known as the 'duck in the winter' top.

He labelled other things. 'Winnie the Pooh juice' meant blackcurrant squash in a blue cup. The cups had Winnie the Pooh printed on them. Over time, the printing faded and was barely visible. As the cups eventually became plain blue, I had to explain to people who came to help what he meant when he asked for it.

His language was improving rapidly. He was able to make most of his needs known. He could string words together into short sentences. At school, he was liked by the other children although I don't think he realised it. His best friend was still his brother, Thomas. He used to go to a 'Forest School' club weekly after school with his tutor. They carved sticks and made bonfires and shelters in the woods. He was happy in his wellington boots, wrapped up warmly in mittens and hats that I knitted for him in very soft wool. The striped hats became a trademark of his and even now, he still wears them in increasingly bigger sizes. He struggled to push his fingers into gloves, a not uncommon problem in autistic children, so I knitted mittens for many years as they are impossible to find in bigger sizes. For his birthday party, aged six, we invited children for a forest school party in the garden, cooking marshmallows on a fire pit. He was happy to go to the occasional birthday party when invited, but he didn't usually want his own birthday parties and always said he preferred to do something with us as a family. He turned down the offer of a birthday party every year until his thirteenth birthday, finally agreeing to an inflatable swimming party.

Trains had remained a constant in Benjamin's life. Wherever we went on holiday in England, we had to find a steam train to ride on. The other boys quite enjoyed train trips, but not like Benjamin did. He was in seventh heaven, chatting to the guards and often being allowed to look inside the driver's compartment.

One holiday in Yorkshire we drove miles, well over an hour away to a station. On arrival, he declared it was a diesel train and not steam. He didn't want to go on it. We drove another hour to find a steam train.

Star Wars was another of his passions, particularly Lego Star Wars. He loved building Lego and was really good at it as are all his brothers. One year, he won a prize for building a small Millennium Falcon model in the third fastest time of the day!

Thomas created his own Lego scenes. They were usually of his special interests. One was a fantastic 100m Olympic race complete with runners, spectators and camera men, another a football match and of course, he built models of the Titanic for his little brother, Marcus. He passed that passion on and Marcus too built Lego Titanics for years.

Marcus' nickname by now was Marky Parky and we often just called him Parky. Thomas was known as 'Mr T' or 'TT'. Hector was plain 'H'. Benjamin was still Mino, from Benjamino when he was tiny. We used these names for them but they also used them for each other for many years. The only ones that have stuck over time are TT and H.

We never shortened their real names. On holiday one year, I heard a guy calling 'Tom, Tom'. No response from Thomas. His name was Thomas. He didn't answer to Tom. Likewise Benjamin did not respond to Ben. When he started at the new primary school aged eight, his class teacher insisted on calling him Ben. We taught him to say, 'My name is not Ben, it is Benjamin'.

Chapter Fourteen

'May the fourth be with you!' - Benjamin

We thought life was fairly settled for the next year. We should have learned by now not to be complacent.

The benefit forms changed from DLA (Disability Living Allowance) into PIP (Personal Independence Payments) and were a nightmare to complete. Questions such as 'Does x need help with bathing?' with tick 'yes' or 'no' boxes which didn't cover it at all. I scribbled copious comments all over the form wherever I could squeeze them in. In one section explaining that yes, Benjamin can shower independently but last week he yelled at 10pm that there was water spurting out of the tap. He had snapped the tap head off and the water was like a fountain at full pressure. We had to turn the water to the house off, contact an emergency plumber and over the following days, arrange for a new bathroom sink and taps to be installed. It wasn't only the expense and bother, how would Benjamin have coped if we weren't there? He could wash independently, but not look after the things necessary for him to be able to wash.

It transpired that he had been trying to turn the taps off with his elbows, due to his OCD (obsessive compulsive disorder) which for him was a need for absolute hygiene. He always took longer than anyone else but we had no idea of his rituals. I was glad he had the language to tell us how he had broken the tap so we were able to replace the round head taps with lever ones and prevent it happening again.

You needed points to qualify for PIP and the assessors seemed to be on a mission to ensure you didn't get them. I was allowed to sit in with the boys and sometimes butted in to rephrase questions for them. It was quite challenging and there was no empathy like there might have been with a clinical assessment, just a person tapping away at a computer as they read out generic questions.

The worst part was that autism was categorised as a mental health disorder. When they asked Thomas if he had suicidal thoughts, he looked shocked. He didn't really understand the word suicide. They then expanded on it and asked:

'Do you ever feel like you want to kill yourself?' He looked horrified and very upset.

'Why would I want to do that? No, I don't want to do that!' and became quite distressed.

Another question was about mobility, obviously devised for people with physical impairments. My answer would always be that the boys could walk perfectly well but still needed an adult with them as their road safety was very poor.

Thomas would still dart across a road, in front of a car without looking. They needed constant supervision but she asked him the question directly:

'Can you walk without help?'

'I'm a runner,' he replied. 'I want to run in the Olympics.' The 'Yes' box was duly ticked and no points given.

It was always hard to explain the individual difficulties the boys had. Autism was an invisible disability to many.

I was looking after the boys full time and couldn't earn any money of my own so I was eligible to claim Carer's Allowance. You can only claim one allowance, regardless of how many disabled people you care for and it was the paltry sum of just over £60 a week. How did people who had given up work to look after their children, survive on that? I was grateful that we could afford for me not to work.

The LA turned up unannounced at the twins annual statement review just before they turned 16, to tell us needed to leave their school the next term. It was a blanket policy to move children back to local schools within borough. We kept our cool and argued that their current school could meet their needs and the sixth form colleges in our borough wouldn't be able to. The twins had high non verbal intelligence scores, without the levels of language needed to support them. They didn't fit into the severe learning disabilities courses but neither did they fit into mainstream classes. The local colleges could only offer either option but not the hybrid mix and most importantly, not the level of support that our boys needed.

We sat it out for six months. We never told the boys what was going on. It would have made them very anxious. I worried but Jonathan stayed calm. He thought it would work out fine. I wasn't as optimistic as he was.

Finally, at the last minute, at the very end of the summer term, we got a letter saying they could continue in their current placement. All of the colleges that the LA had consulted had declared that they couldn't meet their needs. We had known that all along. We had been put through completely unnecessary stress and the borough had probably wasted money too in a futile attempt to save it. Jonathan had been right not to worry.

We tried to always be one step ahead anticipating what might happen, but it's not always possible as we had just found out.

For Benjamin's 16th birthday, we gave him an adult Star Wars costume. Every year around May the 4th - 'May the Fourth be with you' Legoland had a Star Wars day, one of the highlights of Benjamin's calendar. The year of the new costume, no one knew or cared about his autism. He was a celebrity for the day. Small children stopped to have photos taken with him. He basked in the glory of being so wanted; a rare and lovely moment where he was the subject of so much positive attention.

Thomas was known as Mr Wikipedia at school as he read hundreds of facts and retained them all. He could tell you celebrities' birth dates and any detail you wanted or didn't want to know about. He could recite historical facts from a young age but as a teenager he widened his encyclopaedic knowledge to sports and film celebrities. But, he couldn't turn those facts into essays or use them to answer questions because he didn't have the English skills to do so, so he wasn't able to take GCSEs.

That summer, while their contemporaries sat GCSEs, Thomas did a single GCSE in art. Benjamin did art and maths.

Exam results day was bittersweet. By now I was fairly active on social media. On top of the national press front page pictures of glossy haired girls jumping in the air to celebrate their exam victories, I also had to read the proud declarations of other parents on social media.

It was hard at times to be pleased for others. Was I jealous? Yes, I was. I had accepted that my boys were never going to be able to do many of the things my friends' children would do, but on that day it hit me hard. My boys had passed one GCSE between them.

It was a reminder of how different they were and perhaps what they could have achieved if it weren't for their severe language disorder.

On that exam results day, a group of autism parents wrote on Facebook that we should celebrate what our children had achieved and have our own party. Our children's achievements are as hard won as any A* results but with little recognition for it. We always celebrated with the boys, usually by taking them out for dinner. We only went out to eat as a family for birthdays and special occasions so it was always a big treat when we did and they got to choose where we ate.

A year and a half later, on his third attempt, Benjamin finally got a pass in Maths GCSE. That was a huge day of celebration for us all.

There is no point in grieving for what they cannot do. We

always need to be positive about what they can do and what they have managed to achieve. We knew they would never be able to go to university with one GCSE each. We tried not to worry about the future and what possible jobs they might be capable of doing. We always tried to stay in the moment and only concentrate on the current year ahead. Focusing all our energy on the here and now was enough.

To a certain extent, the older boys were shielded by being at a special needs school. They didn't know what their peers from primary school were doing. They didn't really understand what GCSEs were and for that, I was grateful. They deserved to be proud of what they achieved without comparing themselves to anyone else. I needed to learn from them.

The boys returned to school as usual in September, Thomas and Benjamin feeling very grown up to be in the sixth form, which meant no longer wearing school uniform. They wore smart trousers, plain coloured shirts and ties with the addition of a suit jacket for Benjamin. Thomas felt the cold and insisted on wearing black running gloves in school, which didn't go down too well.

After years of Velcro fastening shoes and special tri athlete laces in their trainers, the boys were finally able to tie shoelaces which vastly increased their choice of shoes. They also progressed to tolerating wearing flip flops on the beach.

True to how they had always reacted to sensory stimuli, Thomas still chose long sleeves and long trousers with thick, almost padded socks. Benjamin chose short sleeves and shorts, even when it was cold and thin socks. He didn't seem to feel the cold, but Thomas did and needed reminding at 16 to wear a fleece or a jacket when he went out.

Benjamin's OCD meant he wanted everything washed after only wearing it a short time. I explained that his favourite clothes got faded and worn out from continual washing and we set up some rules for how often things should be washed if they weren't actually dirty.

Hector regularly lost clothing. He would go out with a carer and come back without his fleece or gloves. At school, despite me labelling everything, he continually lost his jumpers. He would abandon them wherever he was. It was a huge school, sometimes they would end up in lost property but very often, not. Luckily, there was a second hand uniform shop as the jumpers were embroidered with the school motto and in the first year alone, I think I bought nearly a dozen.

No clothing was in a fit state to be passed on from Hector, so Marcus was lucky to mostly get new clothes, except winter jackets and school uniform. He refused to wear anything with buttons on it or collars, so no rugby shirts for him. He wouldn't wear any of the large collection of traditional pyjamas I accrued over the years due to the buttons. His favourite clothes were t shirts with appliquéd material designs on them, mostly of animals, which he wore with stretchy striped velour leggings in the winter and cotton ones in the summer.

He often refused to wear certain tops and it was only many years later that he was able to explain that he didn't like pockets on the t shirts and he didn't like it if the design on the front wasn't placed centrally. It was a challenge to find nice tops that fitted his specifications. Jersey stretch long john style pyjamas were fortunately available in large sizes.

Earlier that year, Thomas had joined an athletic club at St Mary's University in Twickenham as he was keen to progress with his running. His running ability and his enormous enthusiasm was picked up by Paul, who we know as Peej, one of the voluntary coaches there, who took him under his very capable wing and has been a huge part of his life ever since.

We were part of the sandwich generation. The boys only grandparent, Jonathan's father, Michael, had Alzheimer's and was not managing at home on his own. We lived nearer to him than Jonathan's brother and I was expected to go to his flat every time he needed help or something went wrong. It could be a half hour drive minimum each way and longer in traffic and I wasn't always free to go. It was becoming increasingly obvious that he needed more supervision so I decided it would be easier to have him close by where we could be on hand.

We gave our tenant notice and moved Michael into the self contained flat within our house. It was a long, hard year. He was more demanding than any of the boys ever were in some ways, because he was lonely and had little awareness of what I was doing on the other side of the wall. He hadn't ever really understood their autism and the demands it placed on me.

He thought, like many do, that as the boys were at school most of the day, I was home alone doing very little. The fact that the boys had longer holidays than the state schools did, resulting in a minimum of 17 weeks a year, went unnoticed. I had acquired another person who wanted and needed my attention. I nearly went crazy that year. We had finally got the boys to a point where life within the house was manageable and now it no longer was.

He was able to cook and look after most of his own needs to begin with. On Sundays he would eat family supper with us. It was surreal. Five people talking on their own agenda about themselves. There could be five conversations going on at the same time. I might try to lead a conversation.

'Michael, the boys went to the zoo today.'

'There's a very good speaker at Putney Music tomorrow evening, would you like to come?' He might respond.

He could not engage with them. He needed to talk about himself. The boys also needed to talk about themselves.

It could be very confusing. Jonathan would stay silent with a half smile on his face. I would wade in, again and again, trying to redirect everyone's individual ramblings. We tried to use family mealtimes to practise proper conversations, but to anyone listening in, it would be hard to keep track of who was actually talking to who and about what.

Michael deteriorated after an accident where he crossed the

busy main road we live on without looking. He sustained a head injury and lost much of his independence following it although he still went out and about on his motorised buggy. He was forgetful and needed help to take his tablets twice a day and to get up and dress. At night Jonathan would have to wake him up to tell him it was time to go to bed.

We had a big celebratory dinner for him at home for his 90th birthday with friends and relatives travelling from Germany which he really appreciated, but after then, he became more confused. We tried to get carers to come in, but he wouldn't allow them to help him with the exception of a lovely man I found as a companion once a week. I couldn't look after him in the in the way that he wanted or needed, so finally I said it was too much for us and he moved into a residential care home the following spring.

I was hugely relieved. My four boys were more than a full time job.

In the holidays, we had young carer buddies for the boys. Some were university students and others were new graduates. They didn't do any formal therapy but they supported the boys to go out and about in central London, or to do various activities like swimming, minigolf in the park and watching films at the cinema. Often I would take a carer out with me when I had all four boys especially when we went to one of the theme parks. There was no way I was going on some of the nausea inducing rides at the theme park, and if one boy didn't want to go on a ride, they needed an adult to stay with them.

Many of them became close to the boys and stayed in touch after they left. It was quite hard to find the right people. Not as hard as finding the tutors had been but still hard.

I was only running one programme for Marcus but the boys were now at three different schools, two of which were quite a long distance away. It wasn't just the geographical logistics which complicated our lives but having three sets of teaching staff and various school events to attend. I couldn't do it without carers as Jonathan was working full time.

Life with three teenagers was easier than life with three barely verbal small boys had been. They could all bath or shower alone. They could all dress themselves, although I still had to sort out their school uniforms and leave them out ready, as they weren't able to find their own particular pair of grey school trousers from a pile or find their own swimming kit. Grey trousers were the common denominator. One morning Thomas appeared saying he couldn't do his trousers up. They were half way up his legs. He was confused. He just stood there, not knowing what to do, the trousers round his knees. They were Hector's and I must have accidentally put them in the wrong place in the cupboard, but he wasn't able to work that out, look at the size label or search for his own.

They still needed a great deal of looking after in so many ways.

It was not possible to put a functioning age on any of the boys. In many ways, it was like looking after much younger children.

Their self help skills were years behind. They could not take themselves out alone. They could not be left alone in the house but, at least, they no longer had to be constantly watched. Benjamin might get cross and stroppy but he no longer smashed or broke things deliberately. They only fought verbally with each other. At times, they were really quite nasty to each other. It was never physical though. It never had been. None of them have ever deliberately intended to harm anyone else. Even when Hector got picked on at school, he never retaliated physically although would give as good, if not better, than he got verbally.

None of the older boys ever read books. They could decode words and understand words one at a time. They couldn't read whole paragraphs and decipher the meaning but would skim over most written words and pick out perhaps a key word or two. Fiction was not something they ever experienced again after they grew out of me reading bedtime stories to them, but reading plain English in factual form like on Wikipedia was possible.

As a parent, it is hard to think your children cannot love what you loved. I spent my childhood reading. I would be lost without books. They are not. They are unaware of any loss. Hector cannot understand that I am not interested in technology and can hardly navigate my phone or use a computer when he is so proficient at it. He would be lost without all his gadgets and technology. I need to acknowledge that what would be my loss is not theirs. But sometimes, when watching an incredible play at the theatre, I am reminded that my boys will never appreciate books and plays in the way that I do, and it does feel like it is a loss for them albeit one that fortunately they are unaware of.

Benjamin decided he wanted to be a musician. He was showing some talent for the drums and had passed a few grades. He was now playing the piano and writing his own compositions. Because he didn't read music he had a system of numbers and annotations for the chords and wrote the lyrics alongside. He had the ability to listen to a song and then pick out the melody on the piano. His teacher Martin realised he had perfect pitch.

Their school Centre Academy decided to cancel Btec level three art after Thomas had already started sixth form, which was a huge blow to him. Art was all he ever wanted to do. It was too late to find another school and we knew the local colleges could not meet his needs, so he stayed and spent the two years in sixth form trying to pass foundation levels in English and Maths. Level two was accepted as equivalent to a basic pass at GCSE, so it would be worth the effort if he could manage it.

Fortunately, he was distracted by his running which was now able to take priority in the absence of art. He won a 5km race, which his primary school organised, to the delight of all his ex teachers and many of the parents who knew him. He took part in his final ever Canbury cross country race at age 17. On the second and final lap, I saw someone on his shoulder and panicked that they might overtake him. Ricky, the running shop manager, had come as always to support him and reassured me that in fact the other runner was on his first lap and Thomas was on route to glory. That was the biggest achievement of his running career until then. He had come 1st. I was the proudest mother ever. He was ecstatic as he posed for photos doing his trademark 'Tombot', a T symbol with his hands over his head in triumph. There were other schools competing that were not special needs. He had triumphed personally and for his school which had never had a pupil win before.

Hector hit the teenage years running. In fact, he had been behaving rather like a stroppy teenager since he was eight, so nothing much changed. He had an answer for everything. He was always determined to get his own way and it was hard to try and direct him at all. Balancing that though, was his natural enthusiasm and cheerful, cheeky nature, so the teachers handled him well even when he wasn't co operative. He started making short films which he posted on his own YouTube channel. My personal favourite was 'revenge of the pom bears' a cautionary tale of two bears, using two bear shaped crisps. They were witty little films, often recorded and edited up in his room, away from our sight.

Marcus was managing to keep up at school with the support of his tutors and was really happy there. I used to collect him most days and was always greeted with a big hug and a smile.

I had always cut his hair snipping little bits at a time while he watched TV. His hair became straighter over time and I could no longer cut indiscriminately, but had to cut it in a bob. Nearly everyone thought he was a girl. I left it a bit longer so he looked more surfer boy than girl, but he has a naturally pretty face and people still addressed him as a girl. He didn't care though. He didn't want his hair short.

One evening at suppertime, he propped a book up by his plate and proceeded to read. I resisted the temptation to celebrate, just taking a quick photo and writing a blog later that evening about it. I had a son who wanted to read, who liked to read. For me that was thrilling. He still liked me to read to him, it was our ritual and a chance for a cuddle. We devoured the whole of the

'Faraway Tree' series which had been a favourite of mine as a child and now I had a child to share it with.

My autism handbook, 'A Parent's Guide to Coping with Autism' was published that summer. The boys were all so proud of me. None of them could read it, but they knew it was about them in part. We had a launch party at home and Thomas insisted on wearing the same outfit as in the family photo on the back cover. I tracked down some ex tutors from many years before. One, Andy, hadn't seen Thomas since he was four or five. He confessed he had been wary of meeting Thomas again as he imagined him as an older version of how he had been then, rigid and unable to communicate. He was so surprised by the change in Thomas when he greeted him at the door and started chatting away to him. Thomas was so much more able than Andy had imagined he would ever be. We were so proud of the boys and how much they had achieved since those early years. There were a few tears that evening as Jonathan and I spoke a few words thanking some of the people who had supported us all.

When the book came out, we finally had to introduce the subject of autism to the boys. We were going to be featured in magazines and I had set up a Facebook page blogging about the boys and our life with autism. They would be able to see the posts and hear people talking about autism. They needed to know what it was.

When I asked Benjamin if he thought he was in any way different from other people, he thought hard:

'Yes, I am. I am better at drumming.'

He had no real awareness at all. He didn't know he was at a special school.

It was a challenge to tell the boys about their autism. How could we explain it to them? I didn't think it was fair to the boys to diminish their very real struggles by telling them that their autism was a gift or a superpower.

It was time they knew more. We talked it through a bit and

asked them about having their own tutors at primary school. Did they notice no one else had tutors? We explained autism was why they needed help to learn to speak.

Thomas took the information in his own, laid back way.

'I'm a bit disabled' he said.

He didn't mind. I think he has always known of his difference but he has never minded it. Now he had the word, autism, he could use it in his defence. A woman at a local college was very unkind to him during an interview.

'She didn't respect my autism' he said. He had buried his head in his usual stork like way, avoiding all eye contact with her. He was right; she certainly hadn't respected him.

He loves children but he said he didn't think he would be able to look after his own children, so he wouldn't have any. He also thought driving would be too hard so he didn't want to do that either. He had great self awareness of his own abilities and difficulties.

Most importantly, he had friends who accepted him for who he was.

Hector already knew he had autism. He had known since he first questioned having tutors at the age of eight. He is still unhappy about his diagnosis but we are trying to teach him to be proud of himself. We tell him often about how he was when he was very young, and how amazingly well he has done to be who he is today.

Marcus somehow knew too. He heard the word autism in our household so often. He had been born hearing it. He didn't feel different because he was the same as those he knew well and loved, his brothers.

Chapter Fifteen

'I got a 'destination'!' AKA a distinction at school.

Like much younger children do, our boys still made mistakes with the words they used. Many of them were endearing.

Some of Marcus' included 'flames on a stick' when he asked for sparklers on Bonfire night. Another was having 'sparkles' in his foot which is probably more accurate than 'pins and needles'. The cheese grater was called a 'sprinkler'.

The boys used their available language creatively. It showed their underlying intelligence, that they could use words so expressively.

Thomas talked of having 'pain inside my neck' when he had a sore throat.

Hector called a vineyard a 'grape farm'.

Thomas only recently talked about cutting onions and said, it 'melts my eyes'.

The boys were very literal and still believed whatever they were told. It is hard to teach sarcasm or irony to someone with autism. One regretful year, I finally had to tell them the truth about Father Christmas. I had managed to keep the magic going for many years. One year Hector had asked for a Nerf gun. I said no, I didn't believe in guns. He couldn't have one. So he said:

'I will ask Father Christmas for one then.'

He did, and Father Christmas brought him one, so he knew

it couldn't be me as he knew I would never have bought a gun. It was my yearly challenge to source whatever they asked Father Christmas for, usually something otherwise unavailable. Thomas requested a Roblox gaming card one year. They were only on sale in the USA. 'Father Christmas can collect them on his way round the world' he said. A local father, who also had an autistic son, was going on a business trip to the United States and very kindly bought me one, keeping the myth going.

We took the boys to see Father Christmas every year. People would eye us strangely as we joined the queue with large ten or eleven or twelve year old boys. As usual, we were catching up for lost time, as they hadn't understood who he was, or been able to visit him when they were tiny, but finally grasped the concept around the time other children their age no longer believed.

One Christmas Eve, Hector declared he wanted to set up CCTV cameras in his room to film Santa leaving the presents. He was old enough to think things like that through, but not mature enough to see through a fake white beard in a shopping centre.

We thought he had worked it out, until Christmas morning when he was adamant that he had 'seen' Father Christmas leaving his presents on his bed. In reality, it was me, creeping in after he had finally gone to sleep, much later than I would have liked.

They were too 'old' to still believe and Thomas had been teased at school about it, so by 15 it was, with great reluctance, time to tell them the truth. It was a difficult moment but they took it well, I think they must have had their suspicions by then. I told them they would still get stockings; nothing would change.

On a visit to a friend's farm one Easter, they watched a sheep give birth to twins. One was stillborn. They were intrigued rather than distressed. Thomas asked:

'Will it come back to life like Jesus did?'

In 2017, the twins turned 18. They were legally adults. It should supposedly have signified a big change, but for us, it just meant more paperwork with transfers to adult services. We celebrated with a party at home with a roving magician and fish and chips, inviting a mix of people.

We wanted them to continue in education to build on the talents they had. We invested in a private educational psychologist to assess them. We needed concrete evidence to prove how much support they would require. As always, we didn't trust the LA to provide what they needed.

From her report on Thomas at age 17 years and 11 months:

Thomas scored 7 percentile on verbal comprehension (borderline) but 84 percentile on perceptual reasoning (high average) which was consistent with the spiky profile he had showed at age ten. His language was still at a very low level. We could no longer call it delayed. He had a severe language disorder.

His reading comprehension was 1 percentile, graded as being 'very poor' and an age equivalent of 7 years and 0 months.

His profile also indicated 'a particularly high level of difficulty with emotional regulation'.

His independent skills were graded as being 'extremely low'.

From her report on Benjamin at age 17 and 11 months:

Benjamin scored 50 percentile on vocabulary and 91 percentile on non verbal reasoning skills. His language had improved vastly since his last comprehensive assessment at age ten.

He had devised his own method of learning language unbeknown to us. He loved to watch comedies on TV, particularly old comedy programmes like Dad's Army and would always put the subtitles on. I had knitted him a Private Pike scarf, undoing and redoing it four times until it was exactly to his liking. Not many people recognised it as Pike was from fifty years ago, but he loved it. We didn't realise why he put on the sub titles until one day we asked him and he told us that it helped his language.

He had become his own speech therapist and a very successful one!

His reading comprehension was 2 percentile, graded as being 'poor' with an age equivalent of 8 years 3 months. His perceptual reasoning was 2 percentile (extremely low).

Similar to his brother, his independence skills were graded as 'extremely low'.

'Benjamin experiences high levels of anxiety and has few strategies with which to manage this. For Benjamin to access education, his emotional needs must be supported, and these relate in particular to anxiety.'

Each report was over 20 pages long and included many detailed results and tests. I include some of them here to illustrate that the boys have long term deficits which hamper their ability to learn. So often people meet them and are beguiled by their charm and personalities, and don't realise the extent to which they are held back by their sometimes hidden but very real disabilities.

What placement would be able to meet their needs? The psychologist recommended a residential college. We didn't want this for Thomas and Benjamin for several reasons. Thomas was now established in many local running clubs including our local Richmond 'Parkrun' as well as continuing to run for St Mary's. For him, running had so many beneficial effects. It boosted his self confidence. It gave him a routine and some social life. Most importantly, it made him happy. Both the boys were well settled at home and how could we split Thomas up from Marcus when they were so attached to each other?

We researched various schools and further education colleges but couldn't find anywhere that could provide all the criteria the boys needed.

Finally, we found West Thames College, which offered the courses the boys wanted to do. Music performance and production at Btec level 2 (the equivalent of four GCSEs) for Benjamin and Art at level 2 for Thomas. But, they couldn't offer the level of support the boys needed. However, there was the Pears campus of Ambitious College, a special needs provision run by a charity, Ambitious about Autism (Ambitious), on the same site. Although most of the learners in Ambitious had more profound needs than our boys, Ambitious agreed to take them, enabling the boys to access the mainstream courses offered by West Thames College with the support of a dedicated one to one in class.

It was suggested Thomas took a level 1 Btec for a year as the class was much smaller and it would be a big change for him going from a tiny school of 50 children to a sprawling further education college.

Thanks to the detailed reports which the local authority could not argue with, having neglected to assess the boys themselves, it finally agreed to fund the placements. One of our arguments for Ambitious had been that if the LA refused, we might have to seek residential colleges which would be even more costly. Luckily, as always, the LA weighed up the financial costs of not agreeing with us and we got what the boys needed. Our only problem was that they agreed it too late for Ambitious to recruit the staff needed for them to commence in September. Fortunately the head of the college, Linda, being one of those rare flexible people in a position of authority, agreed to one of our current carers, a psychology graduate, accompanying the boys to their mainstream classes for the first half term.

At the same time as trying to sort out this big transition for the older boys, I realised that Marcus needed to move schools too.

He loved school. He was very happy to attend with his tutors. He was settled, but his tutors weren't. Having struggled for 16 years to find the right tutors, I hit a brick wall. Eventually, he had only one tutor three days a week who was adequate but not very effective. I had to educate him myself for part of the remaining two days, although there were some classes he could access at school without support. It really wasn't good enough. He wasn't getting the education and support he needed and deserved.

Having been let down three times in a row by potential new tutors, I finally came to my senses one morning at 6 am and realised that there was a clear message. It was time to end his programme and send him to the same school as Hector, More House. We had always intended to send him there but had been planning on a year later.

By now, it was after the summer half term break and too late to apply for September, but I did. More House (MH) assessed Marcus and offered him a place. They were rather shocked to read his current statement which had not been updated from when he was two and a half. It said:

'Marcus babbles constantly with some interspersed words. He enjoys scribbling. He wears nappies but will approach his mother if his nappy is dirty.'

Thank goodness they had believed me when I told them that I thought he was a suitable child for MH as his statement certainly didn't echo his current level of ability.

We applied to the LA for a change in his placement. It was a marginal situation as his current school were able to meet his needs with support. Once again, financial costs swung the deal. His programme was an expensive therapy and MH was a cheaper option. We obtained full assessments with the same educational psychologist for both Marcus and Hector later that year, our reasoning being that decent reports would support our application for Marcus to remain at MH for the next nine years or so. We did not want a scenario where the LA decided he needed to move back into our borough for secondary placement a few years later, when he was well settled. With Hector, we wanted to avoid the 16 plus trap we had encountered with his older brothers, that of the LA trying to move him back to a local sixth form thereby losing the specialist provision that the school could offer him.

From Marcus' report at age 9 yrs 3 months:

'Marcus's overall composite scores (IQ scores) indicate a sizeable difference between perceptual reasoning skills and verbal comprehension skills, with there being a difference of 42 percentile points. This indicates the continuing presence of a specific language difficulty.'

'Mrs Davenport (the very capable head of learning support at MH) confirmed the presence of significant language difficulties.

Apart from language processing difficulties she reports that sentence construction requires support, speech is unclear, understanding of abstract language is limited and Marcus often forgets what he was intending to say. Mrs Davenport highlights his difficulties to impact upon his social development and access to the curriculum.'

His processing speed index was 'below average'.

His reading skills fell in the 'average' range.

'Marcus has impaired social development, his social functioning is below average.'

Hector was the only one who would remain in his current placement and would not be changing schools in September. An added bonus would be he and Marcus both being at the same school for a few years. It would be so much easier, having only two different placements and only two sets of teaching staff to liaise with for the next few years.

From Hector's report at age 15 yrs 9 months:

'Hector's overall IQ scores indicate a sizeable difference between perceptual reasoning skills and verbal comprehension skills'.

His teachers had completed the index for his ability to regulate his behaviour. His scores showed as 'clinically significant'. She wrote 'Hector's elevated scores reflect problems with fundamental behavioural and emotional regulation and suggest these will influence cognitive functioning including application of working memory.'

His reading and comprehension was 2nd percentile.

'Hector's overall level of functioning falls at the low to extremely low range.'

'Hector has impaired social development.'

On the surface, Hector presented to most people as being more able than his brothers, but he still had severe deficits in many areas that needed specialist support. We were quite shocked reading through his results as even we had not understood the extent of his difficulties. We realised that he had been hiding or masking those difficulties with adverse behaviours and that life was in fact pretty challenging for him on a daily basis.

The cost of the assessments and reports were a very necessary investment in our boys' futures. They enabled us to successfully argue for the appropriate placements so all the boys would get the support they needed to succeed. Special needs education is an area of great inequality in this country, not just when comparing the resources and funding for special needs versus mainstream education, but there are also huge differences in the quality of provision between individual local authorities. Once again, we were fortunate to be able to afford the cost of these reports, but we knew many wouldn't be able to. How would they argue for the provision their children needed?

We had three teenagers in the house. Along with growing taller, the boys were growing their hair. Benjamin's had remained strawberry blonde and wavy, often curling into long loose ringlets. He thought his hair befitted a rising rock star. He would pull it back into a bunch at the base of his neck but leave it long and free when performing.

Thomas started to twist his up on top of his head into a topknot. Although straight, it was very thick and heavy. He had been fair when very young but was now a mousy brown but developed natural blonde streaks every summer and was amused when people thought he had dyed his hair. It was easiest for running if it was tied up.

Hector's cherubic blonde curls had turned dark brown. Some years he had corkscrew curls and some years not, depending on who cut it. While Benjamin looked very like his father, Thomas looked a bit more like me. The two of them would certainly never be picked out as being twins. Hector was his own person and didn't really resemble either of us. Marcus and I were the most alike and still are; he even has my straight brown hair.

None of them could be left in the house alone. If a stranger were to knock at the door and invite themselves in to perhaps 'fix' the television, the boys would happily let them in and walk out carrying our TV or worse. They would not know what to do if there was a fire or if a fuse tripped. They couldn't answer the phone and take messages.

By 18, other teenagers were independent. They had part time jobs. They went out alone or with friends. They stayed out all night. Some went on holidays with friends. They made many of their own decisions about their lives. Some could drive cars. They bought their own clothes. Some had sexual relationships if they wanted them.

Our older boys could do none of those things. They might never do them. Instead of them earning money babysitting, we had to pay babysitters to be with them. They should in theory have been able to look after their youngest brother. Thomas loves Marcus and would care for him as much as he was able, but he could not be left in charge of him.

We started teaching them some independence skills; how to cook dinner, how to put washing in the machine, how to change their sheets, how to choose and pack their own clothes for holidays. It all took time and had to be taught slowly. I would give them instructions but only a little at a time.

'Get seven pairs of socks and seven pairs of pants', they would place them on the bed, 'now, two pairs of pyjamas'. It was always so much quicker to do it all myself.

During the holidays, we usually took our own sandwiches with us. I can make packed lunches in minutes. Standing over the boys, instructing them to make sandwiches and supervising them collecting everything they needed for a day out took time and patience. I am short of time. I am also short of natural patience.

Teaching independence was a challenge and judging when they were ready for each new step, needed to be carefully managed. Failure could take us all backwards, so I didn't encourage them to do anything that was too scary, like travelling alone in the dark,

to. It was hard to explain to the older boys
ounger brother, had more independence than
had learned certain life skills before they did.
were very young and only had a few words,
I used to say that one of my goals for them, when they grew up,
was that they would be able to go to a pub and order their own
drinks at the bar.

Sometimes, dreams become reality.

Thomas and Benjamin were now old enough to go to the
pub. They could put their encyclopaedic knowledge to good use
in a pub quiz. They didn't win very often, the facts they knew
were often too obscure and their current general knowledge not
so good, but they enjoyed going out. We had a few regular carers
who were more than happy to accompany them.

In reality, turning 18 changed very little else for the twins
themselves. They were still a long way from independent living
and we didn't know if it would ever be possible for them to live
independently. We could only wait and see how they progressed
over the next few years.

September brought welcome changes. Marcus started going
to his new school in the taxi with Hector, leaving just after seven
a.m. every morning and not returning home until nearly six p.m.
It was a big adjustment to such a long day for him, but Marcus
appeared to take it in his stride.

The one hesitancy the school had had when offering him
a place, was that Marcus found it really hard to concentrate
surrounded by noisy and sometimes disruptive boys. He wasn't
the only one who needed specialist support to access education,
every other boy in the school needed it too. The school had been
concerned that he might not adjust to the sensory overload caused
by the others in the classroom. He actually settled much quicker
than we had hoped and within a term, he had learned to block
out the distractions and was able to get on with his work. For him,
changing schools meant a greater level of independent learning

as he no longer needed a one to one but was able to learn within a small group. He was now on an equal footing with his peers.

In total contrast, Thomas and Benjamin, who had been learning independently in very small classes, now reverted to needing one to one support again. They were back in mainstream again for the first time since primary school. They didn't object to the help they got, they were grateful for it as it meant they could get back to studying only the subjects they really enjoyed, music and art.

When they weren't in mainstream classes, they had speech therapy sessions, social skills groups and they both still needed to continue with English classes and pass Level 2 foundation English, the GCSE equivalent. Thomas additionally still needed to pass Level 2 maths. A few years later, we were so glad that they had persisted with getting those qualifications.

For the first time, they were able to travel independently, catching two buses to get to college which made them very proud. I sorted them out with mobile phones so that they could text or call me when travelling alone, which reassured them and us.

Thomas was delighted to be doing art again. As well as performing music, Benjamin was learning technical skills for recording which would definitely be of use to him on a personal level, but perhaps also in a future career of some sort in the future.

'The future' was a subject we tended to avoid. We didn't really want to go there mentally. We couldn't imagine the boys actually working in any independent way at that time. If they did find work, it would probably have to be with assistance alongside them. We had three years of further education ahead of them, so we were determined for us all to enjoy those years and not over stress by thinking too far ahead.

By the beginning of 2018, the boys were all settled and thriving in their new placements. We could breathe a little and turn our attention away from education.

Thomas was enjoying his running and was getting faster due

to his dedication and commitment. One problem was that, like his father, Thomas was very short sighted with a prescription of around plus four to five and he needed to wear glasses all the time. However, he refused to run while wearing them in case they fell off so, in essence, he was running with impaired vision. Much of his running was in Richmond Park with obstacles like branches and stones to trip over. He was also running at speed which further hampered his ability to watch the ground under his feet. I offered to buy him running glasses. He refused. I took him to the opticians, never believing he would actually manage to put in contact lenses, but wanted to give him the chance to try them. He succeeded with a great deal of determination, which is Thomas to a T.

On the next Parkrun he took part in, with his contact lenses in, he knocked a full minute off his PB (personal best), most likely because he could actually see properly to run. He then proceeded to win our local Parkrun for the first time in April.

Running at the level he did meant injuries were a strong possibility. We didn't realise that Thomas had torn a calf muscle for a few days. Although he has enough language to do so, he is unable to articulate pain or express it in a meaningful way that we can understand. He had four frustrating months, unable to run while it healed. How were we going to know next time he had an injury? Recently, after a cross country race I noticed him walking with a very stiff leg a day later. I joked with him that he looked like a pirate with a wooden leg. He thought that was funny, but still didn't express any pain. I persuaded him that it wasn't a good idea to run that evening. The next day, a physiotherapist confirmed he had a tear in his calf muscle. It healed quickly this time. Peej is very alert to checking him for possible injuries, but we have yet to devise a formula or language he can use to let us know he has pain.

At Easter, we drove to Disneyland in Paris. We had letters and proof of disability which allowed us to skip the queues. I don't think we would have managed the fantastic, but tiring two days we spent there without that essential concession. They were entranced by it all and found the energy to keep going for long days, despite, I am sure, being overwhelmed by the excitement and the whole atmosphere.

I hadn't considered the dates when I booked our annual summer activity holiday to Greece that summer. GCSE results came out while we were away. Nearly all the other teenagers getting their results on holiday were at independent school, academic kids who got high grades. Hector was so upset with his results, and I'm sure felt worse comparing his results against theirs, and not against his own school peers who, like him, had not passed everything. He failed English by one mark and would have to retake it to his annoyance, as he had hoped never to have to go to an English class ever again.

Hector would not listen when I tried to tell him that we were so proud of him being able to sit GCSEs, as we had never thought he would. He had done so well but he wouldn't hear of it.

There was no murmuring from the LA about changing schools, so in September, he remained at More House and moved into the sixth form to study creative media, photography and art. It narrowed his future options doing all creative subjects but those were the subjects he enjoyed, and the ones he was good at. He ended up having to retake English a further four times, failing by one or two marks each time. It was an awful undertaking for him that lowered his self esteem each time he failed, and it was very much an anti climax when he finally passed two years later. I was impressed that he stuck at it though and his tenacity paid off in the end.

Benjamin was at his happiest when playing music. By now, he had acquired his first guitar of many and was becoming a multi instrumentalist. He started to play in the occasional 'open mic' evenings in local pubs where anyone could turn up and play live. We were astonished at his confidence when playing. He suffered badly with anxiety but it didn't affect his playing. One evening, he spontaneously spoke to his small audience about his autism and how music meant so much to him, a brave and moving few words and I was so proud to hear him.

We decided to build Benjamin a soundproof music studio in our back garden.

It wasn't recording studio sound proof as that would have been a hideous expense but it was pretty good. He could play out there all evening and we could reclaim the front room which had been overtaken by all his equipment. Benjamin's greatest desire was to form a band and we hoped at some point, he would do so and they could rehearse out there. The old upright piano had to remain in the front room and it was a pleasure to hear Benjamin playing his beloved sixties ballads and often accompanying them vocally.

Thomas achieved a distinction at Btec Level 1 art and was due to skip Level 2 and go straight to Level 3, but the head of the art department who had suggested it, had unexpectedly left West Thames College. No one else could approve the step up, so it was agreed he needed to do Level 2 for a year. It did Thomas a favour in many ways as it meant he would have to stay at college for four years in total and not the original three that had been agreed.

Benjamin got a merit in Level 2 Btec (equivalent to four GCSEs) which was impressive as he had never studied music before. He moved on to Level 3 which meant he was now a year ahead of Thomas and at the same level as Hector.

Life felt quite stable for the first time in many years. We knew where all the boys would be for the next two years. Our house was finished and suited our needs. We had the annexe for rental income to service the additional mortgage payments from the building work. We now had the time, energy and spare money to book theatre tickets for ourselves and to take the boys sometimes. We took them to Regents Park open air theatre for the first time to see Peter Pan and parked on the other side of the park. On leaving, we realised the gates were locked but walked across the park anyway as it was late and would have taken ages to walk around. Our only way out was to climb over the park railings. Such a naughty adventure for the boys, but it was the highlight of their evening! Thomas having long legs and agility had no problem getting over and then proceeded to help me and the other females in distress who had the same idea as we had, offering his arms gallantly to get us safely over. The boys enjoyed going to the theatre and we ended up seeing every show in London featuring puppetry. We also managed to go to an open workspace and the boys were able to handle some of the puppets they had seen in those productions, Jiminy Cricket being their favourite.

The National Theatre offered relaxed performances. Similar to the cinema when they were younger, it meant people with disabilities could watch a show without recourse from others if their child made noises or was disruptive.

One of the nicest features of these performances was that the cast came out afterwards. You could meet and talk to them and pose for photos with them. The boys were delighted to talk to the real actors involved. Eventually, however, it all became too much for Hector in particular. The paradox of other autistic young people being able to make indiscriminate noises disturbed and irritated him hugely. He could not concentrate on the play so the whole concept of relaxed performances backfired on us. Luckily by then, repeated exposure to musicals and plays meant the boys were perfectly able to watch any show quietly without disturbing anyone around them. The relaxed performances had been instrumental in introducing the boys to theatre but from then on, we booked general performances.

Benjamin was really inspired by hearing the live music at some of the shows. He could see himself up on stage in some capacity, either as a musician or as an actor. He still hankered after doing some more acting having achieved a distinction a few years before at school in a drama Btec. Luckily, an opportunity arose.

Unusually, only a few of the music students at West Thames

College signed up for a second year. We could have tried to find a second year elsewhere but that would have meant a new further education college and losing the excellent support from Ambitious. In September, as I had predicted, the few who had said they would return failed to register for the new academic year. At the last minute, we asked to transfer Benjamin to performing arts at Level 3 while he waited out a year to start his second year of music at level 3. The LA had to agree to a further year's funding, as it was too late to find another option. As with Thomas, we had somehow swung another year in our favour. Benjamin was delighted to have a sandwich year to do some acting again.

By now, Thomas was just starting Level 3 and would be back in sync with Benjamin. His only issue was that, very late in the summer term, the college changed the pure art course to animation and games design as it was deemed to be more vocational. Thomas was a natural cartoonist, so the college thought the course would suit him. It didn't. It was terribly technical and mostly computer based. He missed drawing and painting but he stuck with it and persevered with a great deal of help from Chris, his one to one support at Ambitious. The new skills he acquired might have led to work opportunities but Thomas really didn't like it and vowed he would never use those skills. However, it did mean he would gain a valuable Level 3 qualification which is equivalent to three A levels.

Marcus moved up to the secondary stage of More House and coped well with the large intake of new students in year seven. It meant wearing a formal shirt and tie which fortunately he coped with, despite it having a collar and buttons. His hair was still long and Marcus didn't want to cut it despite being teased sometimes for looking like a girl.

'Would you like to have short hair like a boy or long hair like a girl?' I asked him when things got a bit rough on the teasing front.

'Long hair like a boy' was Marcus' perfect reply. He had to tie his hair back at school but Marcus was his own person and knew what he wanted. I was proud of him for asserting himself and not feeling the need to conform. He had started playing the trumpet a year before and now commenced piano lessons too. Marcus was keen and practised without any reminders, unlike Hector who had fiercely resisted music practice.

Hector was in his final year at More House School. He was wading through, finding it increasingly hard to concentrate in the seemingly less formal, more relaxed sixth form classes. In art, the teacher would play background music. He couldn't stand the distraction of it, or her choice in music. He couldn't work while other boys chatted. Hector would then end up distracting his class mates, as he was restless not being able to work. It was a vicious cycle which meant Hector did almost all of his work at home, sometimes leading to the suspicion that I was helping him to achieve the high standard of work he produced which confused his teachers who only observed him messing around in class. I sympathised as I am unable to work either with any background distraction. Unlike me though, Hector had no control over his working environment.

Hector was a talented photographer and excelled in documentary style street photos, taking photos of various demonstrations like 'Extinction Rebellion' and some wonderful images of the homeless for a project. He was also proving to have great skill in film making. He didn't enjoy the editing part so much as the filming, but he could do it quickly and efficiently. Often Hector used Thomas in his films, who readily complied with Hector's direction, but also made good use of our current part time carer buddies, many of whom were actors and were generous with their skills.

We visited some universities in London with the idea of his studying film, but they all had a high academic content which would mean researching and writing essays and not enough practical learning. It wouldn't suit him but what might? At one university, we fortuitously came across the art department and wondered if a year of an art foundation course might be a good 'gap' year for him while he decided what he might really want to do next.

That was always on our minds. What comes next?

Chapter Sixteen

'It was a brave play, to show the severe side of Autism. It is a play which everyone should see, just to get a glimpse of how life is for some families with all its stresses.' From a blog I wrote about a play, 'All in a Row'.

I wrote about the boys most days on my blog. They got used to me taking even more photos of them. Thomas and Benjamin were keen to be featured, Hector not so much, so I always checked in with him and explained what I was writing about and obtained his permission.

Trying to be an autism advocate wasn't easy. I am terrified of public speaking, all those eyes on me, so I always turned down those requests, but I agreed to speak on the radio or television where that was not the case. There was a play, a London fringe production, about a young boy with severe autism. I wrote a heartfelt blog in support of the play which many all over the world had tried to ban, due to its use of a puppet head as a device to remind us that the play was about a child and not the six foot young man portraying him. A Twitter war commenced, dubbed 'puppetgate'. I received death threats due to supporting the play. I had to retreat from Twitter as mentally, I couldn't take the abuse and the whole episode made me very anxious and unwell. I had my moment of unwelcome fame, being featured in the Washington Post and now have my name on a Wikipedia page. I went back to quietly blogging and have stayed under the radar since.

I could no longer call my boys' autism severe. I realise as I am writing it, what a profound statement that is.

They are now in a twilight area between those who are mostly non verbal and have severe challenges and those who are articulate and higher functioning. In this country we don't grade or classify autism anymore. It is a spectrum. It is easy to plot where my boys might fall language wise as there are definitive tests for that but how to categorise everything else?

Benjamin continues to suffer from significant anxiety which affects many aspects of his life. It rules him some days. We don't always know what is going on in his head but sometimes, when is very anxious, he will try to tell us. The very act of doing so causes him to stutter and fumble for words, when in fact he can be quite articulate at times.

Benjamin's anxiety is not fully understood even by us, his family, let alone others. When I mentioned to a social worker at a recent review that he was afraid of being out in the dark alone at night, she dismissed it saying:

'Well. No one likes the dark do they?'

I don't believe in forcing him to confront his fears like she obviously did. I would always send a taxi for him if one of us can't collect him. Independence needs to be kindly negotiated, in incremental steps, at his own pace.

A conversation many months later about why Benjamin was afraid of going out into his music studio in the garden at night revealed that he is scared of foxes. It was also one of the reasons he didn't like walking alone at night. It's not something I would ever have guessed and as ever, I am so grateful Benjamin now has language and can articulate fears such as this.

Benjamin's social anxiety hampers him from making friends. At college, in three years, he hardly ever had lunch with his class mates. Benjamin didn't know if he was welcome and he wouldn't dream of asking so he ate alone. Thomas in contrast, would always follow his classmates along to the canteen and chat to anyone who would chat back.

But give Benjamin a stage and his anxiety vanishes. He doesn't appear to have stage fright. He is confident and at ease performing in a pub or at college or at home if anyone will listen. He absolutely loves music. Benjamin now composes his own music, writing the lyrics too and playing any or all of the instruments. It really is very impressive that he now has such a range of skills and can pick up new, unknown instruments and learn to play them competently within a short period of time.

Drums is Benjamin's first instrument with the bass guitar a close second, but he has a growing collection of guitars, a saxophone, keyboards, a piano and I gave him an old accordion which is the one instrument he has yet to learn.

Benjamin can now fully occupy himself composing, researching, listening and playing various genres of music. He may be lonely for lack of friends but he is never alone when he has his music.

He is the most helpful of all our boys around the house and now has his own set jobs.

Thomas struggles the most with language and accepts that he does. We can no longer say he has a language delay. It is not delay. It is a severe language disorder and will remain so. Thomas may appear to be following a conversation, but will often just be picking up on key words and then chime in with his thoughts, which may not be relevant to the conversation at all. We have talked to him about being wary of discussing politics or controversial subjects as he often quotes verbatim from online statements he has read and is not fully aware of the facts or meanings behind them. The nuance of language is hard for Thomas who states facts in black and white.

Thomas recently said that he didn't understand why they tried to teach him Spanish at school as he finds learning English so hard and he feels that he is like the international students he knows for whom English is a second language. It is an analogy I have always used and illustrates Thomas' acceptance of who he is.

When people take the boys at face value and make assumptions about their abilities, I try to explain their language disorder as being akin to trying to cope in another country in which people speak a different language and you have only the basics of it. If any of us were to go and live abroad without being able to speak the local language, we would be floored by simple things like answering a phone, watching the TV, reading a book, ordering dinner in a restaurant. We would certainly find it almost impossible to find paid work that wasn't at a very basic level. We would struggle to talk to others who didn't speak our language. But, and this is a very big but, it would not diminish our intelligence and how we view the world and what we think and wouldn't change who we fundamentally are.

It must be so frustrating for the boys not to be able to easily verbalise or to write what they feel. They are starting to communicate some of their internal thoughts much better as they have got older but it doesn't roll off the tongue for them. It is an effort for them to find the words and use them appropriately.

Thomas recently told us why he hadn't eaten mashed potato when he was younger. I had presumed the texture of it was a sensory thing. Not so. He told us that at primary school, he had been given mashed potato served with an ice cream scoop and had expected it to be ice cream and to be cold and sweet. He said it was disgusting and that was why he had never eaten it since. Once we reintroduced it to him and persuaded him to try it again, he decided he liked it.

There must be so much we do not know or understand because they weren't able to tell us. It is only now that these glimpses into their lives as children are starting to be revealed.

His difficulty with language doesn't stop Thomas socially. He will talk happily to anyone who is willing to be talked to. He is very amiable and charming. He has professional athletes who follow his social media accounts. He has photos taken of himself posing with Olympians. Through Peej, he is well known in the running fraternity, counting people like the founder of Parkrun among his friends. Thomas thrives on running and competing in races, not just to win, but to catch up with all his mates. He is busy training six days a week and doesn't really have time for much of a social life outside of his running but it is enough for now. Thomas says he is too busy for a girlfriend at the moment but I know that is one of his wishes for the future.

Thomas also finds sequencing and following instructions challenging. Each task needs to be broken down into small steps. Peej has been a huge support to him when running, teaching him when to warm up, how much warming up to do, when to change his shoes or remove layers of clothing, how to attach his timing label to his shoelaces or his paper race number to his top. These are all basics but then he also needs to learn strategy. For a long while, it was just about Thomas running his fastest but as he improved, he needed to learn more about technique and tactics. He now has his sights set on competing in the Paralympics, a realistic goal for him.

His other passion in life is art. We are so thankful that each of the boys has a very definite creative talent. Not a savant talent like people would like to think they have, but a skill which they can work on and progress with and enjoy doing. Thomas showed an early talent for art in various forms as a child. He now chooses mainly to focus on illustration and drawing, but is skilled in other areas too like photography, water colours and animation (which he dislikes despite his ability). He creates wonderful birthday and other cards, sometimes taken from photographs of people, but rendered in his own style. When he is not running and has down time, Thomas will spend many happy hours absorbed in drawing, often of places we have visited on trips around England.

People often remark on how handsome he is. Thomas could perhaps become a sports model at some stage if he has the time and we have the time to execute it for him. It's hard to watch him on holiday, trying his hardest to be included. Thomas will dance alongside beautiful girls. He is an attractive, fit young man so they are more than happy to dance with him, but when the dancing stops and he attempts to chat them up, it all falls apart. Then my heart breaks for him.

Benjamin too would dearly love a partner and at some stage we may have to look into online dating agencies for the boys, as I don't know how else we will find others they are compatible with.

Ah, Hector. What can I say about Hector that he will be happy to hear? Hector's self esteem is the lowest of them all. He doubts himself, he is hard on himself. He thinks people think he is 'thick' because at times his processing speed and his ability to find exactly the words he needs to express himself are just not there instantly. He doesn't want to be defined by his autism diagnosis which he wishes he didn't have. He doesn't consider his remarkable ability to edit his films in detail and at speed should give any credit to autism. Hector is very self aware which is so hard for him. His brothers in contrast were unaware of any differences or difficulties they had until very recently. He has been acutely aware of his autism since a very young age. He wants to be able to read fluently. Hector can't bear to read emails, because the level of concentration and processing required exhausts and infuriates him. No matter how often Jonathan and I tell him how amazingly well he has done so far, to achieve what he has, he dismisses us.

Hector's boredom threshold is low. He needs occupying and not by playing computer games either. He wants stimulation. He needs direction. If he is given a project that interests him, all is well. Hector will create a brilliant short film or take a skilful set of photographs and can draw very well, but he lacks focus and ideas of his own. He is also developing into an entrepreneur, painting and designing his own range of shoes, taking professional head shots, buying and reselling vintage clothing.

Hector is more independent than his brothers. He goes out alone to meet with friends, he can manage his bank account and his finances. He has quite firm ideas of his own likes and dislikes and strong opinions like most young men his age. He also has a high tolerance for alcohol and is partial to a cocktail or two, but detests beer. He likes to cook and is quite interested in food but not in clearing up. His bedroom is strewn with clothes and possessions, again typical of most his age, whereas Benjamin's bedroom is neat and orderly with everything in its place.

Hector doesn't have much empathy for his brothers and is often irritated by them.

When we are out together, the boys bicker with each other, loudly. We have yet to successfully teach any of them to moderate and lower their voices. They don't always know what is appropriate to say in public, and can shock those who overhear them.

Sometimes, we get funny looks from people observing us all. The boys can all go into sensory overload if they are jostled in crowds. Places like airports and busy shopping centres can be overwhelming and they react by getting louder and more short tempered with each other.

I don't think Marcus will become a moody teenager. He is gentle and loving and content. He works really hard at school. When we had to choose subject options, every teacher suggested their subject would be good for Marcus as he is so enthusiastic. We still don't know where his true strengths lie as he tries so hard in every class. Unlike Hector who was always getting conduct points for arguing back, Marcus never gets anything but house points for doing well. They are like chalk and cheese in that respect.

Marcus plays the trumpet and piano and practises them both without fail every night. He really enjoys playing music and is progressing well on both instruments. He is on target to take several GCSEs. Who knows what other talents Marcus may or may not possess. What he does have is kindness and some understanding of others feelings.

Marcus' best friend is his big brother Thomas. His language is already at a higher level than Thomas' and he will probably overtake all his brothers academically. He is very accepting and tolerant of them all which is hardly surprising as he was born into a family where autism is the norm and not the exception. When they argue, he just ignores them and gets on with whatever he is doing. If Thomas gets upset, he comforts him with:

'It's alright TT' and may even put his arm around him, a mature head at times on an otherwise young for his age boy.

Marcus is totally acceptant of who he is and what he can do which is always to try to do his best. I wish I had known when he was diagnosed how he would grow up and that I needn't have worried at all about him. We have never taken it for granted that Marcus would acquire language, enough to be able to read books independently and research online and to follow the dialogue in TV programmes and films. It has been wonderful for us to watch him progress.

Having all four boys with high needs has meant that we have never been able to offer any of them prolonged individual attention. We have had to spread ourselves thinly amongst them. But they have learned valuable social skills from being part of a larger family; patience to wait their turn, the importance of sharing, the ability to negotiate, interaction with others and flexibility. I hope those wider skills outweigh them not having had 100 percent attention from us at all times.

By the end of 2019, life was ticking along fairly smoothly. Benjamin had wavered about making a decision to complete either the second year of performing arts or returning to the second year of music. He just loved to perform. We knew that Benjamin's true talent was music and not acting but we didn't want to squash his self esteem. We succeeded in steering him gently back towards music. There was a real possibility of him finding work in the music industry but not in the acting world where only the exceptionally talented find work.

We celebrated the boys' 21st birthday on March 1st 2020 with a party for all the young and not so young people who cared for and supported them. They performed a double act in true twin style, Benjamin on guitar and vocals and Thomas strutting his stuff, flossing (a dance move which involved co ordination and snake hips) and making up for his lack of musical ability with his enthusiasm. 'Sweet Caroline' was one of his absolute favourites even before it became a popular football anthem. Benjamin played a version of a Beatles song 'When I'm 21'.

Then the world changed. There was a world pandemic and we were in lockdown.

Everywhere shut. We were ordered to stay at home.

Hector was the only one who was, dare I say, pleased to be home. He was struggling at school. Marcus was happy either way; he liked school but equally he was a boy who loved to be home with us and his brothers. Thomas' main worry was whether he was allowed to keep running as well as going on the permitted daily walk. Benjamin had his music room and all his instruments to keep him occupied, but Covid 19 added to his already high level of anxiety.

For the first weeks, we tried to establish a daily routine. We knew the boys needed structure in their day, so it was course work in the morning, lunch which we all ate together and then activities and music practice in the afternoons. The daily walk was saved as the highlight of the day and something to look forward to late afternoon.

Marcus and Benjamin had online live music lessons but otherwise work was sent by school and college for them to complete on a daily basis.

The dining table was the only place where our limited internet coverage reached, so Jonathan had to conduct work calls and work at one end, while the boys variously grouped around the table. While the boys struggled to concentrate and filter out the background conversations around them, for Jonathan, who was used to being in an open plan office surrounded by others talking, it felt less isolating to be in a work like situation.

Their general anxiety was high about everything but especially about this frightening new disease. We had to stop Thomas watching news programmes as they were scaring him and we tried hard to reassure the boys that we were safe and we wouldn't get sick.

I had a busy few months devising art and craft sessions on the dining table for the boys which they all enthusiastically joined in with. The table became the family hub. Despite us having a large house, no one wanted to go off into their own spaces anymore, but felt more secure huddled together.

We walked daily in Richmond Park, passing families walking with their adult children who had evidently returned home from university or flat shares for lockdown. For them it was a novelty to be walking together; for us it was what we had always done, every weekend, since our boys were born. Covid 19 was a leveller in some ways.

We ate every meal together. Previously I had fed the boys when they returned hungry from school at six and Jonathan and I would eat later together at eight when he returned from work. Now every night we all sat down to family dinner together which, as a bonus, was good for their conversation skills.

Thursdays at eight was when we emerged for five minutes to clap for carers and wave at our neighbours. Benjamin counted the days down until it was Thursday again, we never missed a night. It started with the boys bringing out pots and pans to bang but week by week, Benjamin added another snare drum until he played his full drum kit out in the street, entertaining the neighbours and passing cars.

We finally got to grips with Marcus' 'headaches'. Sometimes he had complained of a headache at school and had been sent to the medical room to rest. It transpired that what he was trying to say was that he had thoughts in his head which made his head hurt. He was a sensitive child and easily upset. In music class, they had talked about different singing tones. He had his piano lesson straight afterwards and his teacher wrote to tell me how distressed he was, as he couldn't get the thought of the castratos' 'surgery' out of his mind. It had caused him a 'headache'.

We shielded him and his brothers from most of the talk about Covid. Jonathan and I feigned a relaxed attitude to it, trying to keep the boys from being scared. Benjamin carried hand sanitiser everywhere with him, using it liberally. His brothers all refused to use it as it made their hands red and sore and a loud, annoyed 'oh Benjamin' would erupt in the car when the over powering smell of his sanitiser suddenly hit them.

Easter holidays meant long days to fill with none of the activities that we usually did with them. The boys did a fundraiser for Ambitious about Autism in the back garden, doing 27 activities 27 times each. Thomas continued to train and ran daily in the park. Peej, his saviour, did online exercise classes for him and a few other young runners he knew which gave him some much needed social contact. Our only other social times were talking at a distance to people we met in the street or standing on the pavement outside Sally's house saying hello. The boys adjusted remarkably well considering the abrupt changes to their lives.

When school started again in a very limited way and only for those with strict criteria for needing to attend in person, we didn't apply. Although we could have pressed for them going in due to their autism, it was far safer for everyone if they didn't.

We made a decision based on risk. The boys were increasingly anxious about not keeping up and completing their studies. They were used to one to one support and I couldn't be there for each of them. We employed three of our young very able carers to come on various days to assist them with their work and with occupying them. The only people we were really putting at any risk were ourselves as were the only old ones. We didn't shout too loudly about it as there were strict rules about anyone meeting indoors but as the boys all had EHCPs (Education and Health Care Plans - which had replaced the statements of special educational needs) they were in fact eligible for support. The impact on their mental health was a serious consideration by this point. Jonathan was designated a key worker and was kept very busy with government work, often dealing with issues created by Covid. His being at home full time did not mean he had more time to spend with the boys as he was working harder than ever. Having young people in hugely bolstered the boys' moods; they played cards with them and took them out for walks, talking to them individually.

Our other 'friends' were our five cats. A year earlier, I had decided to breed our beautiful, gentle cat Megan, as the boys adored her and one of her was not enough to go around. She ended up having a C-section and rejected her four kittens from birth. I had to hand rear them day and night which made me quite ill with sleep deprivation.

The boys and I of course fell in love with them all and we had ended up keeping three, Merlin, Mowgli and Maisie. They each adopted one and made it their own special cat. They had been indoor cats, being Persian Ragdolls but the weather in lockdown was unseasonably warm and meant we had the back doors open all day, so the cats gained their freedom while we lost ours.

The day lockdown lifted, we were in the car heading to Yorkshire on our Barnard Castle tour! Yorkshire always meant walks so it really didn't feel much different to our usual trips despite the restrictions. We hardly ever ate out on holiday, mostly self catering so it was business as usual for us in many ways. Thomas and Benjamin took part in the Ambitious College end of year ceremony for learners online sitting at a table outside with the magnificent backdrop of Whitby Abbey.

Hector passed his subjects with really good grades. We were seriously impressed even if he appeared not to be. We enrolled him locally in an art foundation course hoping to reignite some of his passion for art which had sadly waned.

There was no activity holiday that summer, so we bought inflatable paddle boards for the boys with the money we hadn't spent. They could use them locally on the Thames and even in the sea when we went to the Isle of Wight in August. They were competent enough not to fall in, but we always sent them accompanied by a carer as neither of us was capable of even standing up on one.

It was a relief for us all when they returned to school and college in September. Hector found his course easy and was enjoying making art again. He hoped to make some new friends as he knew very few people locally.

We got used to the restrictions and the boys adjusted well to wearing masks whenever we went out. I bought them a selection with their own themes, music ones for Benjamin, graphic designs for Thomas, art and photography ones for Hector and various animals for Marcus. They hung on a rack by the front door. The boys could have used their autism as exemption from wearing them, but they wanted to keep other people safe when they travelled on the bus. It also avoided any possible abuse which people not wearing masks were sometimes subjected to.

We were back in lockdown before Christmas but Christmas Day for us wasn't much different to any other year. We had learned many years before that it was so much nicer for the boys when it was only us all day and there were no expectations or time constraints put upon them by anyone else. The days either side of Christmas were much harder though. All the shows I had booked were cancelled but we watched one live stream performance of A Christmas Carol with candles and mulled cider and tried to kindle some atmosphere. The boys missed our usual activities and of course there was no carers' Christmas party night, no carol concerts and no Christmas fairs, but we did take them into London to see the lights.

This second long lockdown, we weren't able to make the best of things as we had previously. The boys were fed up. It was cold and they were locked in again and no one knew how long for. The novelty factor of being at home full time had well and truly worn off. Other people were finding it hard to be cut off socially. For us, it was nothing new. We had always been restricted from the social life that others were able to have. Sitting at home, watching TV on a Saturday night had mostly been our normal since the boys were born.

The boys needed a social life more than we did. They were unable to join groups on Zoom as interaction via a screen was so much harder than face to face interaction for them. They didn't read. The television they watched was limited as they had long outgrown children's programmes but most of the adult programmes required a higher level of verbal understanding which they didn't necessarily have. They missed not going out and about to college where the interaction wasn't so much with their peer group but with all the adult members of staff who knew them well. One of Hector's aims in going to a local college for a year was to gain new friends so he was thwarted by the online classes and hardly any chances to mix socially.

Hector was the most fed up. He didn't know what to do with himself. For the best part of a year, his daily entertainment became food shopping with me. He needed that time to download and to talk. He found it frustrating, living with three brothers who he could not hold a decent conversation with. They could talk, but talk and reciprocal conversation are two very different things. His year at college had been more than disappointing.

By the time, college reopened, the boys' courses were finished. They had gained qualifications, but no friends.

Then, the unbelievable happened.

We had applied for Benjamin to study music at degree level and we did the rounds of music colleges earlier in the year. His auditions were all held online and he was offered a choice of places. We were disappointed with what they offered socially for him but then visited the one university he had applied for and realised it would suit him perfectly. It was local so he could continue to live at home where we could support him. His results came out and he was offered a place by the University of West London (UWL).

Benjamin was going to university! It was an incredible achievement. Our little boy, who at three could only hum a single note, was going to study music at university.

We thought we would aim for one more year of education for Thomas and that the same art foundation course that Hector had just finished might suit him as a transitional year. It didn't happen, due to the total incompetence and disregard from the college we had applied to. Finally in May, I was so exasperated that he still didn't have a confirmed place and that he was getting so stressed by it that I had to change tack.

On the spur of the moment, I phoned UWL where Benjamin was heading and asked if there were still spaces on the graphics and illustration course. There were, so despite not having applied through UCAS, we put in a late application and Thomas sent in his very proficient and talented portfolio and was offered a place. Although having only achieved one GCSE originally, he had gained valuable UCAS points from his Btecs and thank goodness he had stuck with and passed his English and Maths foundation levels which were now needed.

Both of the twins were heading to University!

Hector had entered his first film making competition the previous summer with a documentary about coming out of lockdown and astounded us all by winning. I persuaded him to apply again to do a film degree. It so happened that UWL had tied up with a local film school and was offering a degree which was quite practical and wouldn't require long essays and film analysis, but would be more industry based. He was accepted on his previous year's grades.

We would never ever have dared to dream that any of the boys might go to university. We only ever hoped for things in small phases, never daring to look too far into the future. If you had asked us only a few years ago what the boys would be doing by now, we would have told you we didn't know.

Even three years ago, the possibility of university would not have been a consideration. We weren't even sure that they would succeed at Level 3 but they did, all three of them.

They would continue to need a great deal of scaffolding behind the scenes to keep moving forwards and to achieve their dreams but their sheer tenacity and determination got them to this point. We must surely be the proudest parents ever.

Our fabulous boys are going to University!

Acknowledgements

Where to start? Who to thank? There have been so many people over the years who have journeyed alongside us at different stages of the boys' lives. I would like to name you all, but daren't for fear I leave someone out. If you aren't mentioned in the book, it's not because I left you out deliberately but because I made a point of only naming people when it fitted in with what I had written.

I think I'll stick to protocol and just thank those who have been involved with this book which started life many years ago. From blogging I learned that what people needed most from me is hope. I hope that this book provides that in abundance.

Firstly, a huge thank you to Jane Louis-Wood who initially helped me transform an account into a story using an old fashioned method of paper, red pen and our own system of pigeon post! Alas, some of the funnier bits had to be removed and you will have to bribe us with gin to tell you more.

I acquired an agent, Robert Gwyn Palmer and together we rejigged the story a little further. He found me a publisher but sadly, the deal fell through. I'd like to thank him for seeing the potential in this book and his belief in it which bolstered my resolve to get it out there in print.

Kizzy Thompson took over trying to place my book but not for long as Lockdown stopped play. I am grateful to her too for her faith in my book.

When some semblance of normal life resumed, the book was

out of date in more ways than one. I embarked on a serious re write and re edit with the help of two fantastic, fabulous friends, my chief cheerleader Sharon La Ronde and Jane McCready, a fellow mum of an autistic boy and tireless campaigner for early intervention therapy. They read each chapter as I worked on it, managing to read copious tracked changes on top of the original manuscript and offering their wisdom at every stage. Charlie Bate was a really helpful reader as someone who doesn't know the autism world and could read it from a neutral point of view. It would be nice to think that a few people who don't know much about autism will read this book so I didn't want to use exclusive language.

Jonathan deserves thanks for listening to years of my woes and vacillations about whether I should seek a traditional publisher or self publish this book. He also assisted with the final edit, the real final that is, not counting all the 'final' edits that have gone before. He and I both agreed that re reading the book each time brought back memories, often difficult ones, which didn't diminish with subsequent readings.

And finally a big thanks to all my Facebook followers who inspired me to write this book with their many questions about the boys which I have tried to answer. Thank you for all your encouragement that this book needed to be written.

If you have enjoyed reading this book I would be very grateful for any positive reviews on Amazon or elsewhere which help to get the book noticed.

About the Author

Sarah Ziegel is a former nurse and has been a full time mother and carer to her four autistic boys for the past twenty-three years.

Her first book: **A Parent's Guide to Coping with Autism** was published by Hale/Crowood in 2016. It is an essential guide for parents and carers and is the result of Sarah's experiences of autism. It covers the emotional side of looking after children with autism alongside practical advice and personal anecdotes.

You can follow Sarah's Facebook page: A Family's Journey with Autism where she blogs regularly.

She also writes not so regularly on www.sarahjziegelwordpress.com where you can read an archive of past blogs.

Sarah lives in Richmond, Surrey with her husband, Jonathan, all four boys and their four cats.

Illustration by Hector Ziegel.

Printed in Great Britain
by Amazon

46839613R00148